DEMOCRATIC EDUCATION
STRETCHED THIN

DEMOCRATIC EDUCATION STRETCHED THIN

How Complexity Challenges a Liberal Ideal

David J. Blacker

STATE UNIVERSITY OF NEW YORK PRESS

Published by
STATE UNIVERSITY OF NEW YORK PRESS
Albany

© 2007 State University of New York

For information, address
State University of New York Press
194 Washington Avenue, Suite 305, Albany, NY 12210-2384

Production, Michael Haggett
Marketing, Anne M. Valentine

Library of Congress Cataloging-in-Publication Data

Blacker, David, J.
    Democratic education stretched thin: how complexity challenges a liberal ideal / David J. Blacker
    p. cm. -- (SUNY series, philosophy of education)
    Includes bibliographical references and index.
    ISBN-13: 978-0-7914-6965-1 (alk. paper)
    ISBN-13: 978-0-7914-6966-8 (pbk : alk. paper)   1. Education--Philosophy. 2. Education--United
States--Philosophy. 3. Democracy 4. Contextualism (Philosophy) I. Title   II. Series: SUNY series in
philosophy of education
    LB14.7.B56   2007
    370.1--dc22   2006004611

10 9 8 7 6 5 4 3 2 1

To Jessica, Abby and Josh

Contents

Acknowledgments

I'm especially grateful to those who provided comments on part or all of this manuscript at various stages along its way. They are: René Arcilla, Jan Blits, Walter Feinberg, Jessica George, Robert Hampel, Chris Higgins, Meira Levinson, and Kevin McDonough. I also owe a large debt to the anonymous reviewers for SUNY Press and the anonymous reviewers and editors of the below-listed publications in which earlier bits and pieces appeared. I am also very happy to recognize Lisa Chesnel and Llewellyn Somers, at SUNY Press, for their copious assistance and editorial acumen.

Portions of this book are drawn from earlier published material of mine: "Proceduralism and the Orthodox Backlash Against Students' Rights," *American Journal of Education* 108 (2001): 318–355, by permission of the University of Chicago Press; "Complex Equality and Democratic Education: The Challenge of Walzer's Spherical Pluralism" and "More than Test Scores: A Liberal Contextualist Picture of Educational Accountability," in *Educational Theory* 49 (1999): 181–206 and 53 (2003): 1–18, by permission of the Board of Trustees of the University of Illinois; "The Institutional Autonomy of Education." *Journal of Philosophy of Education* 34 (2000): 229–246, by permission of the Philosophy of Education Society of Great Britain and Blackwell Publishing; "Civic Friendship and Democratic Education," in Walter Feinberg and Kevin McDonough, eds., *Education and Citizenship in Liberal-Democratic Societies: Teaching for Cosmopolitan Values and Collective Identities* (2003): 248–272, by permission of Oxford University Press. I am grateful for these permissions.

I am highly indebted to the following scholarly organizations for allowing me to present papers that became parts of this book: The Philosophy of Education Society (North America), The Philosophy of Education Society of Great Britain (PESGB), The Middle Atlantic States Philosophy of Education Society and the Ohio Valley Philosophy of Education Society. I also benefited greatly from the following venues where I was invited to present my work: the 2001 Gregynog Conference at Gregynog Hall, Wales, hosted by the PESGB and the University of Wales; St. Edmund's College and the Faculty of Education at the University of Cambridge

(UK); the conference on "Collective Values and Cosmopolitan Rights" in Montreal, Canada (June 2000) ably organized by Walter Feinberg and Kevin McDonough and sponsored by the Spencer Foundation and the Social Sciences and Research Council of Canada; and, at the University of Delaware, colloquia hosted by, in turn, the School of Education and the Legal Studies Program. Across these occasions, scores of individuals commented on my work, saving me, I'm sure, from at least some of my many errors. In this same vein, I am enduringly grateful to students in my graduate seminars on democratic theory and education at the University of Delaware and at Teachers College, Columbia University. I greatly benefited from these students' many insights concerning central aspects of this book's main points, especially those of Bill Lewis at Delaware, and Greg Bynum, Darryl De Marzio, Laura De Sisto, Seth Halvorsen, and James Stillwaggon at Teachers College. I am also grateful to the University of Delaware for the sabbatical leave in Spring 2005 that allowed me to complete much of the manuscript.

Generous help in preparing the final manuscript was provided by Marcia Blacker, whose copyediting skills are deeply appreciated. I would recommend that every author have a loving mother who happens also to be a professional editor. I also offer a very sincere thanks to Michael Haggett and Laura Glenn at SUNY Press. Their diligence and professional attention to my manuscript are greatly appreciated. At the University of Delaware School of Education, with great competence and a dry sense of humor, Maryanne Bowers performed many small and large tasks through the years of this book's production.

Finally I thank Josh, Abby and Jessica, for their steadfast and loving support, including their general ability to put up with me. I hope I can be as understanding of what their projects require of them as they have always been of what mine do. I doubt, however, that I could ever inspire them as much as they inspire me.

Introduction

An uneasy conglomeration of ideals and institutions, democratic education faces challenges from friend and foe alike. Many of its most powerful friends are of the type who do not like to be refused. Nation, culture, religion, and globalized business—to name a few—each strongly make their demands. In doing so, they ensnare our school system in an intricate web whose strands consist of stronger and weaker obligations. Everyone wants something. But satisfying everyone is notoriously difficult and unlikely to be sustainable. One can bend over backward only so many times before one breaks. Democratic education's foes pose another sort of problem. In a way that once again grows bold, they question the very terms in which democratic education has been understood for generations, at least in the United States, namely, as a system of state-owned and -operated schools that as such abides by judicially elaborated constitutional restrictions on religion. These foes question whether the state has managed its educational obligations in a way that is compatible with what they themselves hold closest to their hearts, their religion in most cases. The public school system thereby comes to be seen an unwelcome interference, even a menace, to intense and durable pre-existing convictions. This, then, is the core of the challenge of complexity to democratic education: being asked to deliver more than it is able at the same time as it is asked to deliver less.

That is not all, however. Still more complexity is added with the thought that even if, *per impossibile*, all the interested and mutually contradictory parties could be satisfied, the sum of those satisfactions might not add up to anything coherent, where coherence is understood to mean democratic education's standing for anything on its own terms, terms that are not wholly reducible to the external demands of those who have pressed around it. For while it has its short-term attractions, a mentality of simple service can grow excessively servile, in the sense that abjectness may diminish autonomous identity and motive force. The challenge of complexity in this way challenges democratic education itself. This book attempts a conceptual response to that challenge. In short, it offers (1) an apposite description of the challenge of complexity and (2) a normative argument for how the response to it ought

1

to proceed. I claim that significant conceptual changes are in order. I aim to show why this is so and what some of these changes should be.

More specifically, I contend that an intensification of conditions of social and ideological heterogeneity—"pluralism," in short—requires us now to stretch our conception of democratic education beyond its often understandable obsession with the inclusion of cultural and other forms of diversity. Though schooling for all is and remains a primary imperative for any meaningful conception of democratic education, the challenge of complexity is much more than a question of accommodation. It is not reducible to the distributive question of who gets what and how much, but is rather a question of the very meaning of the "who" and the "what." This is a sensitive point, so let me be clear. It would be an understatement to say that education inclusion movements, widely understood, from racial desegregation to the education of children with disabilities, to many others, have and continue to possess the greatest moral urgency; they represent central elements of democratic education's historic promise of universal education. To these past and ongoing struggles no words on this page could do proper homage. All the same, liberalism's generations-long focus on educational inclusion has left it ill-equipped to respond to those who question not the inclusion—as would, say, the racial segregationist—but rather the worthwhileness of the object of the inclusion—as would, say, the arch-fundamentalist who rejects the very idea of public schooling.

Although necessary as a treatment, the medicine of inclusion has had some poor side effects on democratic education's philosophical health. Most prominently, it has wearied its imagination, fatigued democratic education's ability to see itself in any other than the quantitative terms of who gets what and how much. Contemporary battles over school finance equity supply important cases in point. Morally and practically essential, they can at the same time be imaginatively limiting. Though often subtle, this limiting can be powerful. For an overfocus on inclusion can function as a false philosophical comfort: not in the sense that the actualities of inclusion are easy, but in the sense that strategizing toward inclusion into something is not the same thing as examining the value of that something itself. It is understandably practically difficult to worry about effectively distributing something while at the same time worrying over the value of what it is that one is distributing. Doing so could even hamper one's effectiveness. Still, basic rationality requires us, at some point, to attend to the object of the inclusion as well. It would be a sad outcome indeed to labor to distribute a thing that, upon reflection, turned out to be undesirable.

Hence my central claim that complementing educational inclusion in its many forms must be an equal concern with the terms through which people—liberal political theorists included—make overall sense of their lives. The human yearning for meaning and satisfaction in life—moral, religious, aesthetic—must not only be tolerated by liberal policies but positively embraced as the basis for building any world worth living in. A vision of democratic education commensurate with this insight not only accommodates the human yearning for meaning, but also recognizes how it itself is built out of those yearnings. It is this recognition that keeps nihilism and instability at bay.

To see better how this is so, it is first necessary to overcome a historical-discursive trap that has been laid for democratic education by what I call in chapter 1 "religious orthodoxy" and "liberal proceduralism." These two antagonists have unintentionally colluded in the banishment of richer ways of expressing our hopes for our education system. Clearing the way of their ideological detritus will allow a salutary attention to be paid to a politically neglected kind of pluralism having to do with the diverse arenas of human activity, as I shall call them, "spheres of involvement," where individuals experience their lives' deepest meanings. These spheres consist of political attention-getters such as law, religion, and cultural identity, but also such as friendship, art, scientific inquiry, even sports and romantic love. Education is one of the most important of these spheres, as it cuts so widely across the others. Applying a modified version of political philosopher Michael Walzer's theory of complex equality that I name "liberal contextualism," the central argument of chapter 2 is that social justice requires duly accommodating these spheres, maintaining and even fostering them in the service of the overall richness of our lives. Liberal contextualism helps articulate what has gone wrong when one powerful sphere, such as business, attempts to bully others by inserting its own internal values into places where they do not belong (as would be the case, e.g., if a pupil purchased a grade). At the institutional level, education continues to be the object of excessive bullying. But our complex world makes it important, though it is often difficult, to distinguish illegitimate bullying from legitimate demands on the system.

That this need is now critical is seen in the intensity of today's politics of educational accountability, such as that surrounding the U.S. *No Child Left Behind Act* (2002) and other regulatory measures. In the face of augmenting accountability pressures, educators are unsure in what terms they ought to take their stands—or if they should be taking stands at all. My initial argument entails that it is important for the sake of both education and democracy that educators do in fact stand somewhere and speak resonantly as partisans of education itself and not just as foot soldiers for business, politics, and so on. But what might this kind of self-assertion look like? Is it always justifiable? Even though there are abuses, the need for an independent judiciary is widely understood. So is the analogous need for professional autonomy in fields as diverse as medicine and military intelligence. Education also needs a kind of autonomy, perhaps to be thought of as a K–12 update of the old German-imported "freedom to learn, freedom to teach" ideal of higher education. Chapter 3 shows how liberal contextualism can provide a defensible normative basis for this needed educational autonomy, one that is both true to the historic ideals of democratic education and responsive to what citizens want from their schools. It does not require abandoning traditional liberal ideals of liberty and equality so much as enriching them and seeing them anew alongside other things we care about. Chapter 4 sketches how this might be conceived in the pressing arena of educational accountability.

But policies aimed at the level of institutions will only get us so far. Let's say educational institutions obtained the above-recommended educational autonomy. What to do with it? What might it mean for the individuals actually inhabiting those institutions? I suggest that, properly understood, democratic education crucially requires cultivating both a certain inwardness directed toward oneself but also a certain outwardness directed toward others. Chapter 5 presents the case that this inwardness involves a moderately demanding introspective moment akin to Cartesian hyperbolic doubt, whereby one may be said to have won autonomy by effecting a volitional stamp on one's most fundamental projects. A needed companion to the inwardness, chapter 6 describes the abovementioned outwardness as requiring a sociable directing of one's personal passions such that one is appropriately reasonable toward others. This account is inspired by David Hume's moral psychology. Though canonical, Descartes and Hume are still fresh and vibrant in this context. Chapter 6 further develops the Humean themes through a policy-relevant notion of "civic friendship," inspired by both Hume and John Rawls, that for illustrative purposes is applied to selected U.S. church-state controversies. My concluding considerations in chapter 7, meant to be taken as suggestive rather than summative, consider and then embrace a couple of key hidden prejudices that lie within widely embraced elements of liberal contextualism. These shed surprising light on how democracy and education must be conceived as aspects of the same moral enterprise. Not a neutralist doctrine, liberal contextualism unapologetically wears its bias toward education on its sleeve.

Part One

Politics and Policies

Chapter One

The Impasse

Proceduralism Versus Orthodoxy

PROCEDURALISM AND ORTHODOXY

Democratic education has been developed but also diminished by two interested and mutually hostile camps with very different basic pedagogical outlooks and agendas. I'll designate these camps with the imperfect labels "religious orthodoxy" and "liberal proceduralism." Each outlook continues forcefully to influence U.S. public schools, in obvious as well as not-so-obvious ways. Of overwhelming importance on the contemporary scene is a steadily growing orthodox disenchantment with the very idea of public schooling that is manifest in phenomena such as support for vouchers, home schooling, and other withdrawal initiatives. All this must be understood in large part as a rebellion against liberal proceduralism, perceived by orthodoxy as, in a way paradoxically, simultaneously aggressive and nihilistic. A good place to examine this dynamic is in one of proceduralism's key triumphs in education: the ascendancy, especially since the late 1960s, of an expansive conception of students' rights. Orthodoxy wants none of this development; these liberal "victories" are from its point of view indictable failures. Though often portrayed as such, this is not merely a blind and reactive lashing out on the part of orthodoxy. It may be drastically wrongheaded from a liberal proceduralist point of view, but the religious orthodox backlash against students' rights is nonetheless surprisingly coherent.

On my analysis, taking religious orthodoxy's critique seriously is key toward revealing how current school policy debate has been artificially narrowed, straitjacketed into overly tight parameters by these win-at-all-costs ideological antagonists. The problem is that neither can win; they are locked almost necessarily into a no exit sort of stalemate, where their very

7

definitions of themselves require the existence of one another; they cannot do without their antagonistic "others." So it is that they lock into one another's gaze, a mutually myopic obsession that debilitatingly restricts our collective educational vision. Our basic conception of democratic education has in this way suffered by becoming artificially thinned, as if starved of sustenance by the very forces that created it, neglected and abused by its own parents, as it were. Democratic education is victimized by a kind of ideological child abuse perpetrated by some very bad parents. We may love them still, but we must also get beyond them.

My illustration of this imperative proceeds in the following manner: First, I'll explain and defend my chosen terminology, and in the process describe how religious orthodoxy and liberal proceduralism tend to translate themselves into antagonistic education policy prescriptions. Second, I'll use this simple yet cogent set of ideas to examine the under-theorized yet crucial area of students' rights and the concomitant demise of the traditional doctrine of in loco parentis. Third, as distinct from the fortunes of what I'm calling its liberal proceduralist variant, I'll assess the limits of liberalism's general ability to mount a principled response to the challenges presented by the religious orthodox withdrawal from public schooling. In my view, contemporary liberalism, like any victorious ideology, must avoid succumbing to a hubris that will, if unchecked, tend to push itself self-defeatingly too far. Liberalism needs to better recognize its limitations, dependencies and debts. Through its history and current tensions, U.S. schooling provides a very good lens for seeing these.

THE LABELS "LIBERAL PROCEDURALISM" AND "RELIGIOUS ORTHODOXY"

A note about why I've favored the phrases "liberal proceduralism" and "religious orthodoxy" (which, for convenience's sake, I'll often shorten to "proceduralism" and "orthodoxy"). I do not mean this pair of labels in a strict philosophically technical sense, but rather as loose and convenient shorthand for describing what I take to be the main *actually existing* moral-cum-political positions across a range of education policy controversies. Roughly, though, by "orthodoxy" I mean something close to what John Rawls and other liberal theorists mean by "comprehensive doctrine": a worldview or outlook that supplies answers to final questions about human existence and the cosmos, orders the virtues, and otherwise supplies to adherents something substantive and determinate toward ultimate meaning and purpose. Among the United States's actually existing orthodoxies is what I'm calling "religious orthodoxy," by which I mean to encompass an assortment of Bible-based religions and, most notably, various Christian fundamentalist and evangelical orientations. This latter supplies the most widespread and politically salient examples. There are of course as many different types of orthodoxy as there are religions, sects, cults, philosophies, and so forth, and the potential number of them is infinite. But in most areas of the United States, only the Bible-based orthodoxies are large and organized enough to count significantly in the politics of education at local, state, and national levels. For these reasons, along with its connotations of a certain doctrinal strictness, "religious orthodoxy" seems to me the best label for present purposes.

Arrayed at most points against religious orthodoxy is what I'm calling "liberal proceduralism." Here my meaning is akin to what political philosophers call modus vivendi liberalism, whose core commitment is to a liberal but above all efficacious strategy for "going along to get along," that is, to widely recognized rules of fair play, organized around notions such as due process and the like. As is true in terms of its historical development, there may be substantive moral commitments to such ideals as equality and freedom (or, at the thinnest, some ideal such as Hobbesian self-preservation) underlying liberal proceduralism. But, as I'll elaborate below, as it actually exists as an effective political force in education, liberal proceduralism rarely gets around to substantively linking its commitment to process with the championing of particular positive ideals. As it has actually developed, liberal proceduralism is epitomized by the mass of constitutional, case, and statutory law that more and more, particularly since the 1960s, directs and even micromanages school operations. In fact, this nearly all-encompassing process of juridification—in schools and elsewhere—represents a triumph of liberal proceduralism.[1] Against what is often portrayed, it is a mistake, I think, to view the primary antagonism as that between God-fearing orthodoxy and an equally militant "secular humanism" that is advancing its own conception of human flourishing. Though there are secular humanists who advance human perfectibility as their highest ideal, in education policy religious orthodoxy's primary antagonists are better described as animated by a deliberately content and substance-eschewing liberal proceduralism that forcefully asserts human rights and kindred notions, but has almost no propensity and/or ability to justify such commitments in terms of anything larger than the commitments themselves.

As is the case with orthodoxy, proceduralism can come in infinite varieties, each of which typically emerges from some more substantive outlook. Almost any such outlook may become—please forgive the ugly word—"proceduralized." There is a Roman Catholic proceduralism, a proceduralism arising from Bolshevism, a proceduralism appropriate to an ancient Persian satrapy, and so on ad infinitum. Proceduralism exists as a sort of exoskeleton that may come to encase and ultimately replace its generative substantive core doctrine, whatever that doctrine may be. Some may experience this replacement as tantamount to a Hegelian master-slave reversal, where the procedures that were originally meant to advance "the cause" or help "fight the good fight" become ends in themselves, such that the original core doctrines have been all but forgotten. Alert idealists will often see this process as a betrayal.

In accord with this picture, where more philosophical precision is necessary, I'll distinguish the liberal kind of proceduralism from the kind of liberalism that confidently advances its comprehensive core commitments and as such is, in fact, a kind of liberal orthodoxy.[2] To make the distinction stand out as much as possible, and to continue following Rawls, I'll call this kind of liberalism "Enlightenment liberalism," which would include such philosophical exotica as Kantians, utilitarians, certain natural law theorists, "strong" or "participatory" democrats, and others.[3] In these Enlightenment liberalisms, there is an articulated moral, even metaphysical core—a conception of the Good—that underwrites whatever attendant prescriptions may be on offer. There is some larger story concerning the role liberal virtues such as reason and autonomy play, perhaps a teleological story of human progress, some kind of theism or pantheism, or some more elaborate narrative explaining why, in the end, we should prefer liberal virtues to others. So my terminology is largely consistent with Rawls's and allied accounts, but I intend the labels "religious orthodoxy" and "liberal proceduralism" in their more historical and sociological senses rather than in the subtler senses that are possible.[4] Additionally, as I explain below, I intend them mainly to express educational outlooks, and as such they have no essential affinity with political distinctions such as "left-right," "liberal-conservative," "religious right-secular left," though there may be strong affiliative tendencies. Thus my qualifying phrase "actually existing," meant to indicate a concern with the policy disputes as they have in fact presented themselves. Though philosophers and others can dream of a thousand variations and alternatives, "religious orthodoxy" and "liberal proceduralism," when properly specified, will provide appropriate labels for my analysis.

RELIGIOUS ORTHODOXY AND
LIBERAL PROCEDURALISM AS EDUCATIONAL OUTLOOKS

In the United States, liberal proceduralism and religious orthodoxy have had inextricably interwoven careers. Since the arrival of the first European settlers, the two orientations have both united and divided Americans, sometimes as distinctive allegiances pertaining to identifiable groups, yet just as often within the hearts and minds of individuals themselves. The frequently intolerant orthodoxy of early New England, for example, John Winthrop's quasi-theocratic "City on a Hill," was simultaneously intermixed with nascent liberal concerns with basic freedoms, as would befit a group of erstwhile religious dissidents. Middle colonies like Pennsylvania and New York, while eventually more liberally tolerant of religious diversity than their New England neighbors, could scarcely be said to be lacking substantive, even state-sanctioned religious visions of the true commonwealth. From the start, educational policy represented a confluence of these powerful riverlike forces where, as a product of them both, the City on a Hill envisaged and enacted schools for itself. Colonial Massachusetts's touchstone Old Deluder Satan Act (1647) required every settlement with greater than fifty families to maintain a school in order to teach children basic literacy to combat the ignorance upon which Satan (and also Catholics) could allegedly prey. "It being one chief project of that old deluder, Satan, to keep men from the knowledge of the Scriptures . . . It is therefore ordered, that every township in this jurisdiction, after the Lord hath increased them to the number of fifty householders, shall then forthwith appoint one within their town to teach all such children as shall resort to him to write and read."[5] Schools exist to further both the liberal goal of universal enlightenment via the individual's ability to think and reason for him- or herself, right alongside the orthodox agenda of promoting a particular version of Christianity. With a Calvinist twist, this brand of energetic Protestantism saw these two goals as inseparable: since salvation results from our own individual effort, we must first be able to identify it on our own, extracting ourselves *by our own efforts* from confusion and sin. Literature scholar Andrew Delbanco describes the psychological intensity of this peculiar vision of salvation through learning: "In the course of this instruction, laypeople had to learn how to distinguish between true and false grace—between the real thing and the counterfeit version that taunts you by lifting you up only to drop you down lower than where you began." And to banish the thought of any intergenerational resting on laurels, preachers like John Cotton would warn, "Do not think that you shall be saved because you are the children of Christian parents." Every individual needed to acquire these salvific powers of discernment, the ability to "go home and consider whether the things that have been taught were true or no."[6]

This urgent need to enable everyone to see things for themselves, while originally the provincial product of Puritanism, had its own powerful expansive momentum; the Enlightenment cat of discerning by one's own lights is let out of its bag. But it is released into a world of less and less consensus over religious and other matters—a dissensus partly of internal provenance and partly from an increasing immigrant influx of ever more different others with ideas of their own, including internal immigrants such as Native American Indians and ex-slaves. There is simply no guarantee, once all these heterogeneous individuals "go home and consider," that the conclusions they each reach will accord with any orthodoxy, even the one that set them to considering in the first place. It is a safe bet that John Cotton did not anticipate this. Yet religious orthodoxy persists in that it keeps supplying the yearning, the questions that only it is designed to answer; the God-shaped hole in our hearts persists. The problem is that the questions can no longer reliably be stilled by the traditional metaphysical comforts, and a fortiori by any that are collectively shared. This leaves simply more and greater "going home and considering," this time minus Cotton's or anyone else's bedrock verities on which each of us is foreordained to land. We are, in a way, turned out of our own houses in a sort of self-imposed exile of the mind and heart. We search and continue to search; we become "seekers" for whom any landing or settlement becomes necessarily provisional, temporary, or both. In this way the original religious impetus for learning to see by one's own lights becomes fused with the Enlightenment drive for the same. It is a perpetual attempt at orthodox fulfillment through adherence to liberal process, a notably robust yet combustible fuel mixture for ideals.

This peculiar incongruity is one way of understanding the marked American tendency to see the road to collective self-improvement—even (perhaps especially) where we are deeply conflicted about what exactly counts as improvement—as running through education, where we transmit orthodoxies or their remnants while we simultaneously cultivate the competencies needed by searchers on the open road. This creates the unstable situation of religious orthodoxy having to rely on inherently unreliable liberal processes of inquiry, unreliable in the sense that those processes will not guarantee to orthodoxy any outcome. This instability becomes quite visible as a series of ambivalences in U.S. education policy where, across a range of controversies, religious orthodoxy and liberal proceduralism have encamped across from one another, rising to battle from time to time.

As basic "philosophies of education," liberal proceduralism and religious orthodoxy may be distinguished by their differing understandings of their own relationship (or lack thereof) to an encompassing and supervising conception of the Good and, more specifically, by the patterns that those understandings tend to follow. For liberal proceduralism, education is most accurately described as a search for the Good, whereas orthodoxy of whatever type is more at home conceiving of education as initiation into some more or less determinate and settled conception of the Good. Well-known binaries for parsing this distinction rise to mind: proceduralism focuses on means and orthodoxy on ends, process and product, negative freedom and positive, journey and goal, instrument and project, procedure and substance, and so on.

The education of liberal proceduralism emphasizes the need to give students tools that will be useful and/or necessary in their individual search for the Good. This is to be distinguished from the phrase "liberal education" which, insofar as it arises from an agreed-on curriculum, canon, or both presupposes a strong association with some substantive vision of the Good and, through that often-covert dependency, actually shares a deeper kinship with orthodoxy.[7] The education of proceduralism tends to emphasize equipping and enabling the learner for the search, stressing such academic and social skills and dispositions as critical thinking, dialogical competence, techniques for conflict resolution, and where relevant to the pursuit of extracurricular goals, various basic and more subject-specialized literacies (reading, science, art, history, etc.). It rests on a certain democratic faith, a kind of pluralist Jeffersonian-Peircean conviction that in the long run a heterogeneity of competent voices—the more the better—is more conducive to truth-seeking in whatever field of endeavor than is a homogeneity maintained by exclusions of various sorts; at its purest it is suspicious of the move to keep out the riff-raff, Platonic and Heideggerian assumptions that "the many" or "the they" necessarily lead one into the perdition of inauthenticity. Though proceduralism can sometimes use the language of virtue to describe the requisite democratic competencies, it is generally unable to give a full account of the grounding of those virtues, other than the circular one that they are to be cultivated because they are necessary for democracy.[8] Conversely, to the extent that a fuller account is provided, liberal proceduralism thereby shades into its own kind of secular orthodoxy, which is to say it becomes once again its parent, the more comprehensively committed Enlightenment liberalism that requires a substantive conception of the Good. The true liberal proceduralist, though, always stops just short of such self-confirming certainties. An apt motto for the education of proceduralism would be André Gide's aphorism that advises us to follow those who seek the truth but beware those who have found it.[9]

In the most general terms, if it is to remain itself, proceduralism must beware any tendency, including its own, to metamorphose into its pedagogical opposite, orthodoxy. If proceduralism is the verb that wants to control the action, orthodoxy aspires to be the subject of the sentence. For by definition, the orthodox—particularly the religious orthodox—understand themselves to have found the truth or at least its proper vicinity. Orthodox education in its many variants presupposes this: it is typically conceived as initiation into a relatively settled conception of the Good, a means by which to inculcate into students a love and understanding of a determinate conception of the Good that itself remains more or less unquestioned. The motto here is "The Lord is my shepherd; I shall not want" (Psalm 23). In contrast to liberalism, orthodoxy may in this sense more legitimately call its virtues "virtues" because their necessity is accounted for by the comprehensive conception of the Good on offer. As a strict function of this conception, most actually existing orthodoxies tend to stress in their pedagogical programs virtues reflecting the augmentation of the ruling conception, those that would increase its nearness, accessibility, scope, and intensity of adherence, and the comprehensiveness of its application. Orthodoxy accordingly typically fosters the cultivation of a package of virtues containing such as integrity, consistency, loyalty, community solidarity (particularly vis-à-vis those with alien beliefs), steadfastness of faith, proselytizing zeal, and/or piety. As Alasdair MacIntyre has convincingly argued, one might even say that orthodoxy is a precondition for such character traits or virtues in that without some substantive basis they are arbitrary and ultimately meaningless. MacIntyre writes: "unless there is a *telos* which transcends the limited goods of practices by constituting the good of a whole of a human life, the good of a human life conceived as a unity, it will *both* be the case that a certain subversive arbitrariness will invade moral life *and* that we shall be unable to specify the context of certain virtues adequately."[10] Without the bedrock of some telos-supplying orthodoxy, any durable ideals of character or virtue are, literally, lost. With no ultimate raison d'être, they simply crumble. Orthodoxy avoids this specter of nihilism by fashioning the individual as a vehicle, literally, for the greater Good; a person's ultimate satisfaction should consist in realizing and accepting one's place in the universe so ordered. Outside this Good-ordered (often God-ordered) network of purposes, life is cold, lonely, chaotic, and ultimately meaningless. So understood, orthodoxy, particularly in its eschatological, biblical manifestations, further carries with it the assumption that society and politics are, even at their best, ultimately instrumental to the Good, and so are to be judged finally by the extent to which they facilitate the flowering of the favored orthodox conception.

As I elaborate below with reference to the case of contemporary religious fundamentalism, this is one reason why politicized orthodoxy can be surprisingly protean strategically: one moment the orthodox Christian or Muslim is a libertarian defender of basic constitutional freedoms and the next moment, often on seizing control, an archenemy of the same. From the orthodox point of view, this is actually not hypocrisy but rather the sublimest integrity: using political rights for the sake of the ultimate Good, the Good-identified ends most obviously justifying the political means, a kind of rule-utilitarianism of the holy.

These considerations are key for appreciating how orthodoxy and proceduralism each have their own kinds of heterogeneity and homogeneity, in sharp contrast to the typical picture that tries to make natural allies between, on the one hand, liberal proceduralism and diversity and, on the other, religious orthodoxy with that which is monolithic. For proceduralism and orthodoxy both foster their own kinds of heterogeneity as well as homogeneity. When examined more closely from this angle, there is a surprising degree of both internal diversity and internal uniformity allowed in both orientations. In orthodoxy, for example, there is generally wide latitude given concerning the paths by which one might come to the Good. One might, say, come to faith by an absurdist leap, aesthetic catharsis, or via some kind of emotional or moral revelation. One might always have had it, come gradually to it, or come to it from out of the blue all at once, on the road to Damascus, as it were. One might even be argued into it, or otherwise convinced by intellectual means, for example, a cosmological proof or the like. Especially for religious conceptions of the Good, the permissible motives and means for entrance seem nearly inexhaustible. Even self-interest and heteronomous desires to achieve rewards and avoid punishments (e.g., heaven, hell, excommunication, etc.) are typically deemed acceptable, and, in fact, often are regarded as pedagogically necessary for getting children habituated reliably: stories and simulations of the joys of heaven and torments of hell are particularly effective. All sorts and manner of routes to the Good—even those associated with somewhat baser, self-interested motives—are usually possible. In this sense, there exists a very big tent for the faithful, often capacious enough to permit a much richer diversity than is commonly recognized. High-minded, low-minded, rational, fanatical, long timer, newcomer, sinner, saint, and so on—there may be as many routes to salvation via the Good as there are individuals. As means to its relatively fixed ends, orthodoxy is capable of admitting the wildest diversity.[11]

Similarly, and in this case true to its reputation, liberal proceduralism perpetrates its own wild diversity, a value pluralism about ends that is limned only procedurally. Aside from cases where certain ends such as slavery or genocide would seem inherently to violate the relatively thin norms of basic fairness on which liberal procedures are based, liberal proceduralism recognizes that many different systems of value may simultaneously be reasonable, that is, not violative of basic liberal procedural constraints, such as due process rights. Moreover, underlying liberal proceduralism more generally is the assumption that, despite the expected convergences around practical matters, rationality will in a larger sense produce not a convergence of value-outcomes but rather a divergence. When it is given free play, rationality writ large necessarily leads to disagreement and differences about what in life matters most; truth seeking will and should lead individuals on different paths (including, potentially, into orthodoxy). Even John Dewey and other liberals who look to scientific procedure as a model for democratic political process do not admire science so much for any alleged political implications of its substantive conclusions (as in the case of social Darwinism, most conscientious liberals would recognize the naturalistic fallacy in normative prescriptions purporting to be derived from science alone) as for the fairness and openness of its procedures, the Protestant-derived, quasi-democratic presumption that in principle anyone could repeat the experiment and so verify or refute it on his or her own. In this way science liberates our minds, though the substantive propositions those minds are supposed to embrace once they have been liberated cannot be decided a priori. There is, then, a socially ameliorative effect to be anticipated from scientific method as a frame of mind—if, that is, it is inculcated as widely as possible via education—in the indirect sense that because of it our collective intelligence and aptitude at solving social problems will be heightened. Wherever it might ultimately lead, this kind of Deweyan faith in the ameliorative effects of scientific method writ large is as far as it is possible to be from any ipse dixit orthodoxy. The Deweyan emphasis on "growth," like its Lockean forbear "liberty," reveals less an allegiance to anything standing static and a priori than to a certain kind of socially dispersible activity, a restlessness that expands, chooses, grows, and the like, but not in any predetermined direction.

Despite the types of heterogeneity they permit, however, proceduralism and orthodoxy form mirror images of one another's characteristic forms of intolerance. For orthodoxy, revealed Truth stands as an a priori standard by which worthiness in all its most significant senses is measured. Whatever diversity among routes to getting there, there *is* a "there" there, a "there" that supplies a unifying and direction-providing telos, combing out all snags of divergence in proportion to their nearness to the gathering point provided by the One True Good. Whatever may have been our starting point and journey, we are all to end up in the same place, illuminated in the light of the Good. (One often finds here an accompanying license to intervene "for their own good" in the practices of those who seem consistently to land in outer darkness.) By contrast, liberal proceduralism's rational seekers, while they are not required to end up in the same place, are expected to travel in roughly the same agreed-upon manner; they have to follow the rules. In the final analysis, the liberal proceduralist's performance is evaluated according to the soundness of the reasons for her chosen route, her arguments and justifications, the fairness and openness characterizing the course of her life, defined most relevantly by her decisions, the defensibility of the moral choices she has made by her own lights.

These are the two orientations' most basic priorities. For proceduralism, the soundness of one's reasons and justifications has moral and intellectual primacy, whereas the precise answers one finds as a result of adhering to the procedures thus sanctioned are of secondary importance. For orthodoxy, however, proximity to the Good/God is of primary and overwhelming importance, far more significant than the antecedents and arguments that have caused and characterized one's movement into that nearness.

By way of illustration, consider briefly two hotly contested school policy controversies and how the primary antagonists tend to draw their battle lines. (Again: not how they *could* be drawn by suppler and subtler minds, but how they tend actually to be drawn.) First is evolution versus creationism, a conflict enduring across a range of historical permutations, from the star-studded *Scopes* "Monkey Trial" of the 1920s (Clarence Darrow and William Jennings Bryan were the two sides' advocates), to the defining U.S. Supreme Court cases of recent decades, most notably *Epperson v. Arkansas* (1968) (a state may not ban the teaching of evolution) and *Edwards v. Aguillard* (1986) (so-called "equal time" for creationism laws have no secular purpose and therefore violate the Establishment Clause), to recent controversies surrounding the Board of Education of the State of Kansas rescinding and then restoring a state requirement that local school districts be able to opt out of evolution as part of their science curricula and the Dover, Pennsylvania school district's utilization of a neo-creationist "intelligent design" textbook in the context of its biology classes.[12] Whatever the complexities of current and proposed statutory remedies, I would suggest that the larger logic of this disagreement is fairly clear and simple. The liberal side champions largely proceduralist goals such as critical thinking, unfettered inquiry and scientific literacy, on the argument that our schools simply cannot produce scientific literates if they ignore for no good reason an entire area of scientific inquiry. To do so would, in fact, compromise the very idea of science and scientific method by voiding a priori an entire area of research, in effect asking students to base their beliefs about the world on something other than empirical evidence. It would also undermine the ability to coherently teach biology and biologically-based fields because evolutionary theory constitutes these areas' very organizing principle. As the paleontologist Stephen Jay Gould pithily summarizes, teaching biology without evolution would be "like teaching English but making grammar optional."[13] At its most consistent, the proceduralist defense of evolution in the science curriculum does not rest upon any particular affinity (or lack thereof) for any larger *conclusions* about the world implied by evolutionary biology, but rather on the conviction that one must pursue the truth of the matter—whatever matter—wherever honest and competent inquiry leads. One might ultimately be right or wrong, but any deviation from procedural purity would properly be considered illiberal. Science and evolution are from this point of view inextricable; to abandon one would necessarily be to abandon the other.

By contrast, and notwithstanding the weak legitimating gestures toward a "creation science" or an "intelligent design" (that allegedly just happens to accord with Genesis), the actually existing orthodox view of the matter, when presented honestly, stands quite clearly and straightforwardly opposed to the liberal-allied proceduralist view. An explanation of so fundamental a matter as our origin as human beings and, before that, life forms of whatever type, must cohere in some demonstrable fashion with the biblical account. Since all ultimate meaning and what one might call symbolic sustenance must derive from that account, then that account's status and sway over the lives of adherents must never be compromised. In this sense, the Church contra Galileo had it quite right: to the naive enthusiast, talk of a nongeocentric universe might seem to be a discovery bounded within the realm of astronomy and not religion or morality. As has been the historical drift, even within the Church, one is made to accept the reasonability of such a fighting retreat, the "progressive" distinction between matters of science and faith. But earlier Church leaders knew that once the Bible's authority is rendered contingent in one area, there is little to stop it being questioned in other areas as well, a slippery slope, literally, to Hell.

Even allowing for the hermeneutical complexities of ascertaining any text's meaning, those who would pick and choose among Scriptural passages offer precisely a liberalized version of religious orthodoxy that is, in short, no orthodoxy at all (particularly when this "editing" takes place ever further outside the established and official canons of commentary and interpretation). The very sorting, of, presumably, the "reasonable" passages from the "unreasonable" ones, presupposes liberal procedural norms of critical thinking, evidentiary sustainability, and, even worse, so many expedient adjustments to social convention. But as a matter of psychology and common sense, it is difficult to control these procedural dispositions and to circumscribe what one might think of as their authorized jurisdiction. The Biblical account must remain supreme, whatever its implausibility to secularized ears. Far too much is at stake. An important contemporary example of what is at stake is fundamentalist Christian alarm over what it sees as the morally nihilistic implications of evolutionary theory, particularly in the area of evolutionary psychology, where evolution allegedly causally explains behaviors such as rape and murder. Even where fundamentalists are willing to embrace such subtleties as the distinction between "explaining" and "explaining away," they are wont to deny emphatically that these distinctions can be sustained pedagogically in the actual teaching of children. As Michael Farris, President of the Home School Legal Defense Association, in a newspaper editorial entitled "Study Indirectly Shows the Evils of Evolution," writes, "[I]f, however, you want your kids to believe that rape, racism, and murder are always wrong—even when committed on a high school campus—better keep them away from schools that teach evolution, lest they follow this theory to its logical anti-social conclusion."[14]

One simply cannot understand the orthodox opposition to the teaching of evolution without understanding this characteristic fear of an unholy slippery slope. Admittedly, there are confusingly mixed signals arising from the political debate, especially from those in the orthodox camp who have convinced themselves that they are advancing liberal procedural norms such as equal treatment (of the two views) or critical thinking (e.g., the alleged pedagogical benefits to students of comparing the two "theories") when they fight to assure a place for creationism/intelligent design in the science curriculum. In the heat of the battle to sway public opinion, orthodox advocates very often try to claim *all* arguments, including the liberal ones, for their side. (In doing so they often also betray their deep lack of affinity with what science would require of them, as when they claim that any time there are disputed points within a scientific field, as there always are, the whole field is therefore simply a matter of opinion.) For true religious orthodoxy, however, these are just strategic moves, whatever the ideological casualties the orthodox camp suffers as a result of the liberalizing political process. What motivates orthodox activism to take sides on matters of policy is by definition directly rooted in the perceived relationship of a policy to the orthodox conception of the Good. All else is merely tactical.

Another symptom of this ideological opposition can be found in debates over sex education in public schools, from lessons about sexuality and pressing topics such as venereal disease and AIDS prevention to headline grabbing instances of condom distribution and the like. The reigning orthodox position is that premarital, and certainly adolescent sexuality is wrong, period: "Just say no." (Again: there is of course any number of possible orthodox positions regarding sexuality, including actual and imagined religions and cults where, say, teenage sexuality is encouraged. But these kinds of exotica have little political relevance.) This absolutist position most obviously stems from the biblical prohibition against extramarital sex. Here, sexuality is first a moral issue, not one of psychology or health. It is an arena within which free will and soul-worthiness is tested; failing here is tantamount to failing as a person. Further, the orthodox see giving information about sexuality—no matter how noncommittal is the mode of this information's transmission—as implying an official acceptance of sin, a wholesale giving up that says, "since we cannot stop it, we might as well make sure the kids do it safely." It is a matter of good hygiene and rational prediction concerning what is known to psychologists and health professionals about adolescent sexual behavior.

While this sounds like the very soul of reasonability to liberal proceduralist ears, the orthodox mind can only see this reality-accepting gesture as an outright condoning of what it views as a damningly sinful promiscuity. Utilitarian predictions about the likely consequences of sexual behavior are beside the point (except perhaps as evidence of God's displeasure). By contrast, the proceduralist view—which happens to be the official view in most school districts, with the common but small qualification that abstinence should enjoy priority as a "preferred" method—is that more neutral goals such as health, safety, and the prevention of unwanted teen pregnancy trump the substantive concerns of orthodox groups. Proceduralists in administrative roles are typically happy to "agree to disagree" with their more determined constituents, usually offering offended parents the ability to opt their own children out of the sex education as a path of least resistance. In this way, the proceduralist panacea of more choice (at least *parental* choice) is viewed as a way to resolve such problems. Of paramount importance to the liberal proceduralist school official is ensuring the health, safety and future life chances of the children in his or her care, not for any particular purpose, but to make sure everyone maintains his or her life options in as full a way as possible.

When the condoms are distributed and rhetorical war ensues, we then have a dispute that is stronger and deeper than is typically evoked by the term "disagreement." It is conflict over what even *counts* as morally significant. For religious orthodoxy, something counts to the extent that it is relevant to the accepted or revealed conception of the Good. For liberal proceduralists, something counts (qua public morality) insofar as it is instrumental to or considered a component part of the shared procedural norms of fair play. The educational ramifications of each view are stark in an area like sex education. While the orthodox seek to integrate sexual behavior and belief into their substantive, Good-ordered system of values and virtues, the proceduralist champions the creation of individuals who are equipped and disposed to make sexual choices (according to the rules of "good," i.e., efficacious, choosing) by the light of *their own* beliefs, whatever those may be. Proceduralism can certainly identify as problematic a sexually active teen on a doomed quest for peer acceptance pursuant to a sense of self-worth. Such a client should be counseled toward a change. Yet proceduralism would also be bound to recognize as a problem a teen who is abstinent for the wrong reasons (e.g., "I'm fat, so fear of humiliation keeps me a virgin"), who therefore ought also be counseled to change, even though that change might lead away from abstinence. Absent subtler forms of motives-scrutinizing Kantianism, though, for the orthodox, staying away from sin is staying away from sin *simpliciter;* many methods may be permitted for keeping one on the right path toward the Good; the struggles and tribulations, the "lust in one's heart," as it were, can be forgiven. Again, the only "evidence" necessary is proximity to the Good and the symptoms thereof (e.g., the prosperousness of God's elect in Calvinism). Liberal proceduralism scrutinizes the choosing process, orthodoxy the choices themselves. Characteristically, neither allows much of a basis for mutual recognition.

STUDENTS' RIGHTS AND THE DEMISE OF IN LOCO PARENTIS

An additional and more significant lens through which to view this divide is the postwar rise of students' rights, along with the concomitant demise of the older doctrine of in loco parentis (Lat. "in place of the parent"). Traditionally relatively unquestioned, in loco parentis held that, when children are in its care (during the school day, on school grounds, including bus transportation), the school has the same level of authority and responsibility for its students as have parents for their own children at other times; school and parent in effect pass back and forth the legal baton of guardianship. In this setting, the protections of the Bill of Rights, qua protections against government, do not really apply; for students' rights purposes, because its application defines school officials as temporary parents, in loco parentis effectively removes schools from the constitutional realm. If the child sent to her room for talking back or for having cigarettes in her purse has neither First Amendment "freedom of speech" nor Fourth Amendment "unreasonable search and seizure" claims against her parents, then neither would she have such claims against her teachers or principals. But in loco parentis no longer obtains in this way, largely as a result of key U.S. Supreme Court decisions. This is particularly true regarding the "authority" part of the old arrangement. (The "responsibility" part remains and even grows, mostly via tort claims involving educator negligence, often in the form of legal duties and standards of care and the like.)[15] This demise of in loco parentis underlines the extent to which liberal procedural goals have, for better or worse, crowded out the more forthrightly morally based "school rules" characteristic of previous eras.

The *Tinker* case (1969) is the signal liberal proceduralist victory in this area.[16] Writing for the *Tinker* majority, Justice Fortas famously asserted that, along with their teachers, students do not "shed their constitutional rights to freedom of speech or expression at the schoolhouse gate," thereby inaugurating the present era of students' rights.[17] During this period, students have won progressively greater constitutional protections across an impressive range: freedom of speech and assembly, rights of due process in discipline, particularly regarding suspensions and expulsions, in the Fourth Amendment area of protections against unreasonable searches and seizures, as well as more recently in other areas of emergent national concern such as sexual harassment perpetrated by school personnel or other students (where the school has turned a blind eye).[18] In addition, although court-mandated desegregation and related compliance efforts are clearly waning, statutory due process protections continue to expand quite powerfully concerning the formal rights and related services owed to disabled students by federal statute (viz., the *Individuals with Disabilities Education Act* [IDEA]) and its reauthorizations, including a newer, larger and more controversial group of the "learning disabled."[19]

In each of these areas, procedural norms reign more or less supreme as the official modes of justification. It is important to concede, however, that the above constitutionally based students' rights gains are rooted in ideals of equity and fair play that do, admittedly, form the spare substantive core underlying the liberal proceduralism of the U.S. Constitution. (Again: I am not dealing with ideal philosophical types, but merely with strong tendencies as they actually exhibit themselves politically.) Yet, however substantivelybased in the genealogical sense, this actually existing liberal proceduralism must continually distance itself from its own, more substantive, Enlightenment liberalism progenitor. This occurs in at least two major ways that help ensure its merely procedural nature and disallow it from devolving into Enlightenment liberalism. First, the constitutional settlements—the great liberal legal victories—are almost always couched in neutralist terms that require governmental actors de jure to bracket out substantive content from decision-making processes. The zone of discretion for educational authorities, where they may exercise relatively autonomous moral action (as opposed to mere rule following), has correspondingly shrunk. Second, even though these victories, qua constitutional settlements, have by definition a traceable lineage to substantive moral ideals of liberty, equality, and so on, they are not typically experienced that way. Owing, among other things, to a scarcity of official commitment to public legal education (a kind of civic education deficit that is under appreciated), "privacy," "equality," various "freedoms-*of*," and so forth, are usually experienced as *mere* procedures. As such, they so often degenerate into matters of blind rule following or irrational- and/or capricious-seeming bureaucratic dictates that help produce debilitatingly widespread frustration and cynicism. The great ideals of the day are proceduralized into mountains of paperwork, elaborate rules and bylaws of forgotten provenance, and increasingly, a timid, though, in many cases, bottom-line rational, reluctance to stand up to lawyers' demands on behalf of their clients' rights, usually in the form of some official's procedural violation. Both of these processes form what one might describe as liberalism's new pathos of distance from its own core ideals. This is a defining aspect of what I've specified as the victory of liberal proceduralism, over not only religious orthodoxy but also over more substantive secular understandings of liberalism itself (e.g., what I've been calling Enlightenment liberalism, which is comparatively forthright about its deepest normative commitments and how those matter to its vision of the human Good). This victory is quite apparent in today's public schools.

Tinker itself is emblematic. The student-plaintiffs wore black armbands to protest the Vietnam War. When their Des Moines, Iowa high school disciplined them for doing so they erred, largely because, as the Supreme Court reasoned, it was clear that school officials were singling out for sanction *this* particular expression (viz., opposition to the War) rather than simply prohibiting for some pedagogical reason certain kinds of behaviors or expression in general. A telling point in the students' favor, for example, was the fact that the school had previously allowed other expressions, including on one occasion a German military insignia. It was clear that the students were punished because of a disagreement with the *content* of their belief, rather than a more "innocent" desire by school officials to carry on their responsibilities as educators. Hence the *Tinker* test: student freedom of speech may be curtailed only where the expression would constitute a "material and substantial disruption" of the educational process.[20] (Though modified in subsequent years, most notably to exclude "school sponsored" activities such as school newspapers,[21] along with instances of obscenity or vulgarity by students,[22] *Tinker* and its test remain good law.) As stated in the decision, quoting Justice William Brennan's use of the Holmesian metaphor, the "marketplace of ideas" on which democracy depends is to be valued such that a certain level of turbulence arising from students' exercise of free speech rights must be tolerated.[23]

What the public school must never do is engage in "viewpoint discrimination"; it must officially maintain a principled, content-neutral indifference (with only a few highly specified exceptions) to the particular views being expressed. This same prohibition against viewpoint discrimination applies to the selection and/or removal of library material,[24] school decisions about the existence of noncurricular-related student groups,[25] and the use of school facilities by outside community groups.[26] Each of these laws is, on my view, eminently reasonable when taken on its own individual merits, and so my argument does not take issue with any of them per se. I'm trying instead to underscore how the mandatory priority of ideological neutrality in school administrative decisions represents a victory for liberal proceduralism, rather than for any particular substantive vision of the Good. As such, Enlightenment liberals should not take too much heart from this pattern of case law, remembering that all that glitters is not gold. For, as is true in so many other areas of life, the de jure has a way of becoming de facto in terms of how people actually conduct their lives. This means that the rule that must be followed—in this case a content-bracketing neutrality—becomes internalized as a habit of thinking, an impulse, even a *vis à tergo* "conviction" that does not always stop at viewpoint *discrimination* but also often proceeds in practice to prohibit *viewpoint* altogether. As a school administrator or board member in these litigious times, one is usually better safe than sorry; having an identifiable viewpoint on any potentially disputable matter can become extremely costly, and it is rarely worth the risk. No school administrative decision is likely to be momentous enough to become, as they say, the hill on which one is willing to die, to end one's career. With this further prudential reinforcement, the proceduralist momentum is all-but irresistible, as no public school can afford to maintain any real and sustained connection with any substantive conception of the Good, a state of affairs one might term "whateverism."[27] As a result, to quote from Gerald Grant's classic study *The World We Created at Hamilton High*, "a school tends to be reduced to a set of procedures for guaranteeing individual rights and setting forth what is legally proscribed.[28]"

Consider some further proceduralist victories in the public schools. Far from the courtrooms where they are propounded, the great substantive due process protections are typically experienced in a highly formalistic way, as a gamut to be run of rules and procedures usually inexplicable to those affected by them, where those most intimately involved are "not to wonder why . . ." Examples are easy to find. Take the often Byzantine procedural requirements regarding long-term suspensions and expulsions. Rooted in the substantive ideals of the Fourteenth Amendment (both the Due Process and Equal Protection Clauses), substantial due process protections obtain for punishments involving long-term suspensions and expulsions (defined as over ten days) because public school attendance is considered to be a "property" interest. And so, as in the case of any attempt by the state to deprive citizens of property (e.g., fines, garnishments, seizures, etc.), augmented procedures must be followed in deciding and implementing such a penalty. With regard to suspensions and expulsions, the Court has drawn the line at ten days: students are considered to be deprived of their state-created property interest in public schooling if their punishment requires their removal from school for over ten days.[29] (Though there is no "right" to education mentioned anywhere in the U.S. Constitution,[30] all fifty state constitutions have language guaranteeing free public schooling, thereby authorizing the application of the Fourteenth Amendment to this state-established "property interest.") This of course does not mean there is any prohibition against such punishments—any more than there is a prohibition against the state depriving a citizen of whatever it seeks to take away, up to and including life itself in capital cases—but only that the proper procedures must be followed in order to convict.

As in many areas of law, though, adherence to the substantive constitutional core (those all-important clauses) is so often experienced as a thick forest of red tape and assorted hoop jumping that it rapidly diminishes in its appearance of rationality. In large part because of these procedural protections, school discipline, and in particular suspensions and expulsions, have become incredibly expensive and complicated maneuvers for which even medium-size school districts must retain full-time legal counsel. And, as is generally true concerning the relationship between law and human, and in particular, bureaucratic behavior, the actual litigation is of much less overall consequence than is its subsequent chilling effect (sometimes desired, sometimes not). When contemplating a suspension or expulsion, say, in a school district with a "zero tolerance" policy for drugs and/or weapons possession, school officials typically must *first* decide on the punishment's procedural feasibility, *then* on its justice (qua dessert) and overall effects on the welfare of the school community. As a result, there has developed a widespread sense among school administrators (a patently obvious matter among those with whom I have worked) that there exists too wide a gulf between what "real" justice would require and what the procedural encumbrances will in fact allow, precipitating a sort of legitimation crisis in contemporary school discipline. Such irresolution is typical of what Powell, Farrar, and Cohen famously call "the shopping mall high school." The juridified moral climate of such schools is summarized by one of Powell et al.'s administrator-subjects, who observes that "the law seemed to teach that students had many rights no matter what they did and few responsibilities. It was often too much trouble and too great an expense to suspend or expel the unruly."[31] As James Davison Hunter suggests, the larger worry is that such conditions render traditional approaches to moral education—and perhaps moral education of any kind—as "little more than vacuous platitudes, lacking any morally compelling logic and emptied of binding moral authority."[32]

Likewise, substantive victories for students' rights in other important areas have predictably become proceduralized in ways that are difficult at times even for experts to follow. Take the Fourth Amendment prohibition against unreasonable search and seizure. In the landmark school search and seizure case *New Jersey v. T.L.O.* (1985), the Supreme Court sought to define a standard for school officials who wish to search students. The resulting "reasonable cause" standard, a middle ground between the "probable cause" required of police and the absence of a standard for parents (parents do not need a warrant to search their own child), certainly makes a great deal of common sense. Yet from reasonable cause quickly emerges a laundry list of do's and don'ts. In the actual conduct of their duties, school officials are made to worry over such matters as whether they can search the inside pocket of a jacket as well as the outside pocket, whether school lockers are technically the property of school or student (or joint property), pursuant to resolving the question of whether students have a reasonable expectation of privacy there, whether or not students' luggage on a band trip is searchable, and so on. There are many examples from which to choose to illustrate this frustrating procedural ambiguity. Here is a fairly recent federal court case from Chicago.[33] One morning at an inner city school, a sixteen-year-old student entered his school building without going through the metal detectors like everyone else. (Invited by school officials, Chicago city police offers sometimes conduct random "suspicionless" metal detector searches of students.) Spotted by a police officer and told he had to go through the metal detector, the student refused to go through, and then revealed a semiautomatic pistol tucked beneath his shirt, claiming, "someone put this gun on me." The court reasoned that the mere fact that he had not wanted to go through the metal detector was insufficient "reasonable cause" for searching him, on the grounds that the student "could have just turned around and gone home for any number of reasons, being sick, forgot something, forgot his lunch, forgot his books, forgot his homework or what have you."[34] On this basis, the student's weapons charge was then thrown out because it was secured by an illegal search (violative of the Fourth Amendment). I think it is safe to say, particularly in the wake of well-publicized shooting incidents of late, that this kind of application of the reasonable cause standard strikes most everyone involved with schools as perverse, perhaps, as something like proceduralism run amok. Whether this judgment is accurate or not, though, the above example epitomizes a trend whereby in loco parentis is being decisively replaced in public schools by a juridified proceduralism, even in areas where children's very lives are quite materially at stake. Perhaps in a kind of reaction to such situations, the Supreme Court has recently diminished students' Fourth Amendment rights in the area of suspicionless searches, specifically with regard to randomized drug testing for students involved in competitive extracurricular activities.[35]

Prudently following the advice of the well-paid attorneys that every school district of any size must now retain, this proceduralism becomes an

ever-thickening forest of fine-print legal notices, waivers, footnoted com-
pilations of bylaws, and so forth—an endless ritualistic stream of signings-
of-things-with-fine-print-that-nobody-reads. Further, it is clear that such
proceduralist requirements are understood more often as self-protection
(from lawsuit) by the institution itself rather than as a matter of substantive protection for the student-citizen. The ideal of protecting citizens
from government thus gives way decisively to a strategy of protecting government from citizens. Picking up the cue, many parents have themselves
internalized this understanding, and often come to school with a significant chip on their shoulders, a chip whose existence is due to their own
not inaccurate belief that the school is really looking out for itself first, the
welfare of their own child rating an ever more distant second. Avoiding
costly litigation is the school's real goal. This is the sort of thing that gives
liberalism a bad name, as the sponsor for an alienating process of juridification across just about every imaginable area of the schooling process.

Yet my point is not that the legal protections are unnecessary or to
make rhetorical hay out of abuses and anomalies that may occur. In many
cases the protections are undoubtedly necessary; undeserved punishments
from time to time are indeed identified by the augmented due process
protections. Operationalizing substantive values such as those presented in
the Bill of Rights necessarily involves making rules out of them. I'm only
suggesting that, instead of being the glorious victory for substantive ideals
of equity, freedom, fair play, and so on. that it often announces itself to
be, this juridification of schooling is so pervasively experienced as *mere* red
tape procedure that it is really a victory only for the barest liberal proceduralism. For most individuals involved, the connection between the procedural details and the substantive ideals is so obscure as to be nonexistent,
perhaps taken on faith or, more likely, accepted with cynicism as realities
of "the system." Most people continue to experience these rules as mere
procedures without any real rhyme or reason, an experience of government hard to square with the democratic ideal of self-governance.[36] From
this point of view, students' rights are depressingly hollow victories.

The orthodox response to this proceduralist hegemony in the area of
students' rights follows a fairly simple logic that is made complex only by
the shifting sands of political context. Almost by definition, orthodoxy
must defend in principle in loco parentis as a guide for how school officials should deal with students who are children. Since it is hard-entailed
by the relevant substantive conception of the Good, the orthodox educational program does not contain any inherent respect for "parents' rights"
or any such notion.[37] What is above all necessary is to position children

properly vis-à-vis the Good, and schools no less than family life itself are properly understood as subservient to this goal. Understood in this light, and contrary to ostensible appearances, the fact that many parents choose a strictly orthodox upbringing and education for their children does not represent a victory for those parents' right to choose, or any inherent authority they may have over their own children. Such authority is biblically based, not as a political right (which would of course be anachronistic) but as a divinely instituted command that is in and of itself worthy of respect and allegiance. The fact that many orthodox proponents of religious schooling rhetorically champion parental rights in contemporary policy debates (e.g., school vouchers) is usually an example merely of strategic expediency over and against the liberal proceduralist hegemony. For what they are actually asserting is their right to choose *for their children* a situation in which choice is to be restricted, the straight and narrow path that leads to the Good. This libertarianism of convenience possesses no built-in commitment to any *other* parent's rights, but seeks rather to maintain and carve out an extrajudicial and self-enclosed island of homogeneity, wherein rights may be "safely" given up.

The history of Protestantism and public schooling in the United States bears this out: the first public schools from colonial times on were usually unashamedly Protestant, regarding such practices as reading from the King James Bible as effectively neutral, either from willful ignorance or from an intentionally assimilationist agenda (e.g., the concern over Americanizing turn-of-the-nineteenth-century immigrants). When Catholics sought understandable refuge from what they saw as so many agents of Protestantization by creating their own system of parochial schools, such a move is understandably seen as a victory for parents' rights.[38] This reaction against forced Protestantization was strongly vindicated in the *Pierce* case (1925),[39] which struck down an Oregon law, backed by the Ku Klux Klan among others, that sought to require universal public school attendance, thereby effectively outlawing religious (read: "non-Protestant") and other nonpublic schools. Ruling for the two private school plaintiffs (a military academy as well as a Catholic school) the majority opinion held that parental rights were sacrosanct: "The child is not the mere creature of the State; those who nurture him and direct his destiny have the right, coupled with the high duty, to recognize and prepare him for additional obligations." *Pierce* thus represents a dramatic validation of parental rights in education (even while in the same breath it recognizes the right of the state to enact reasonable regulation of nonpublic schools). Yet, as widely as today's orthodox cherish these protections, they are for them only instrumentally valuable, insofar as they allow individual parents to make the *correct* choices. A commitment to parental rights is not at all built in to orthodoxy's guiding philosophy of education. Indeed, far from embracing anyone's rights—students' *or* parents'—as core commitments, orthodoxy most naturally (though, in the present context, ironically) embraces something much more akin to in loco parentis, that is, the transference of those parental rights and responsibilities en bloc to educational authorities, usually of the clerical variety. And this transference of authority well describes the situation that obtains today in any private school, absent any particular contractual provisions to the contrary. Private schools do not have to recognize students' rights at *their* schoolhouse gates in any of the aforementioned areas constituting the students' rights revolution in the public schools. The situation is contingent purely on the private contract between the parents and the private school: if parents do not like the situation (i.e., if they decide that in loco parentis should no longer obtain), they may remove their child to another private school or to the public school serving that area. Liberalized private schools may offer provisions in their own school rules that resemble due process rights and the like (e.g., Quaker/Friends Schools), but their doing so is entirely at their own discretion and not constitutionally mandatory. In other words, such practices are not true rights at all but their contractually contingent shadows.

This suggests that, much contemporary political rhetoric aside, the raison d'être for orthodox schools has no essential affinity with either parents' or students' rights. Most orthodox schooling, in fact, is more naturally hospitable to an unapologetic authoritarianism consistent with the legal doctrine of in loco parentis and preserved by *Pierce*. When the orthodox champion vouchers for religious schools or the further deregulation of home schooling, they are actually arguing for an increased dominion of in loco parentis and, consequently, for a diminishment of student *and* parental rights in education. Orthodox parents are really fighting for the right to be able to *cede* their parental rights, via the installation of a particular regime of in loco parentis with which they happen to agree. Some parents may, of course, feel that their parental authority has been augmented by, say, a voucher regime, but this would be entirely contingent on their good fortune at being able to find—and afford, even with whatever sum the voucher would bring—a private school sufficiently congruent with their desires. For a large percentage of parents, this would present them the merely illusory freedom of the vegetarian who may choose between McDonald's and Burger King. Many Protestants, for example, feeling, in most cases rightly, that the public schools were once *theirs,* and so there was "in the good old days" no legitimacy problem from their perspective for in loco parentis as a guiding principle for the school system as a whole, now wish to reestablish those good old days by retreating from the now-fallen public schools (ruined by proceduralism) into islands of in loco parentis where they can transfer their own authority to a school they like in peace, unencumbered by the permissive legalism of the liberals. What was once ideological control of the entire system (historically, U.S. religious orthodoxy's preferred option) is no longer feasible, so the second best option is to encourage a serial orthodoxy of so many little kingdoms where every orthodoxy reigns supreme, unchallenged by an obtrusive and ultimately empty proceduralism. The apotheosis of this retreat is, of course, the home school, where educational and parental authority are "restored" into one seamless and unquestionable whole.

In a bold gambit to escape the orbit of proceduralism in education, the orthodox now envision a sort of pluralism of orthodoxy—consistent with what Kent Greenawalt calls a society of "Diverse 'Fervent Believers,' " an aggregation of orthodox groups with a modus vivendi—where every parent "chooses" the private authority under which their children will be schooled, subject either to only the most nonintrusive regulatory parameters (e.g., reporting attendance figures, ensuring fire safety, and the like), or to none at all.[40] Parents who do not agree with a given school's mission or practices can be shown the door, and they themselves can seek the door pursuant to another educational "contract" if need be. Whether they settle or however much they roam within this system of choice, though, they will now be freed from students' rights and placed back into a more comforting, extra-constitutional world where liberal procedures are of decreasing relevance. As orthodoxy would intend, children in such situations would understand any rights they have in the school setting to be entirely contingent on whatever the adults around them recognize as sanctioned by their reigning conception of the Good, rather than as features of their standing as rights-bearing citizens in whatever social context. For the orthodox children-students, such a situation allows the wider, public world to be shrunken considerably in favor of a world that has been ordered by their parents. From the orthodox perspective, this would have the additional happy consequence of vastly augmenting the power of adult authority to monitor and constrain the consumer-driven youth culture that is often so off-putting to them as traditionalists. Indeed, it is this wild and threatening cultural face of students' rights as a diminishment of adult authority that arguably provides the initial and most visceral impetus for the orthodox recoil. The orthodox see proceduralism as ultimately leading to an accommodationist stance by school officialdom, where a relativistic "do-your-own-thing attitude prevails."[41] The clothes, the music, the language, the piercings and tattoos, the attitude, and so forth, are all interpreted as evidence of a fallenness made possible by the wholesale abdication of parental and educational authority.[42]

In historical terms, the new system of choice offers orthodox parents a bargain where they must give up a bit of their missionary selves, their proselytizing ambitions vis-à-vis the larger society (e.g., efforts akin to the attempts to assimilate non-Protestant children into the public, i.e., Protestant, schools of yesteryear). But what they gain is an intensified, internal homogeneity, where the scope of their moral action narrows from a large-scale national crusade to a small-scale, more familial kind of symbolic coherence. They exchange width for depth, quantity for quality, an exit strategy offering many advantages to the orthodox. As I hope to have made clear, the desirability of this exchange is entirely consistent with the nature of Bible-based orthodoxy itself.

LIBERAL WORRIES: REACTIONS AND OVERREACTIONS

The resultant potential for the violation of fundamental rights troubles all forms of liberalism, including proceduralism, recognizing as they all do the more-than-occasional tension between the liberty of the parent and that of the child (this is one of the distinctions between any form of liberalism and the libertarianism of the contemporary U.S. right).[43] In extreme cases along these lines, as legal scholar James Dwyer fears, it may well even be that "[c]hildren of religious objectors arguably have less political power than any other group in this country."[44] Furthermore, enabling orthodox parents the *absolute* power to structure the *entire* ecology of their children's upbringing also gives rise to the potentially serious developmental concern for civic education that if children do not obtain an experience of their own emergent political freedoms and responsibilities, it is unclear just when—if ever—they will do so as adults. One might suppose that authoritarian schools will generate personalities structured by the experience, individuals who are themselves authoritarian or who are excessively craven or otherwise dependent: bullies or sheep. In this way, a thoroughgoing orthodox hegemony throughout childhood might lead to alarming levels of civic incompetence, bringing to mind the Jeffersonian anathema of human beings "born with saddles on their backs, [and] a favored few booted and spurred, ready to ride them legitimately."[45]

If it is indeed true that an authoritarian upbringing is more likely to create a politically incompetent adult, then the civic education worry has great weight. But it seems to me that this is too large and empirical an "if" on which to build much of an argument. First, although it has the ring of plausibility, the causal connection between an authoritarian upbringing and civic incompetence would actually have to be proven; it does not enjoy patency. Indeed, one might question any simple understanding of this connection. Hannah Arendt, for one, premises her critique of progressive, "child-centered" education on precisely the conviction that an authoritarian, "teacher-centered" classroom may actually be superior in its ability to liberate and forge solidaristic bonds among students.[46] Some Catholic schools may indeed promote civic virtue as effectively as their secular counterparts or, equally easy to imagine, there may be public schools that fail to produce much civic virtue or virtue of any other kind.[47] At the very least, it seems difficult to say. Orthodox schools could surprise us by the level of civic competence they generate, and a regime of such schools might possibly be able to remain democratic, again, perhaps in the manner of Greenawalt's "Diverse Fervent Believers," wherein each group maintains its own strong beliefs while simultaneously operating with the attitude of securing with one another a mutually beneficial modus vivendi (as Greenawalt argues, not the optimal outcome from a liberal perspective, but nonetheless recognizably and workably democratic).[48] Rather than warning us away from any orthodox role in the schooling process, then, the conceivability of such a scenario illustrates a great strength of democracy: it can tolerate many different pedagogies and does not need to seek a uniformity of belief (much less of practice) among those who would help perpetuate it through teaching. Democracy is able to contain a diversity of ways of being successful at civic education. While it may be counterintuitive to some, there is no good reason for government owned and operated schools to enjoy an automatic monopoly here.

But does this mean that liberalism has no response to the orthodox withdrawal from public schools? There is something of an impasse, it seems. Liberal proceduralism is hamstrung by its commitment to individual rights, particularly those of parents as embodied in the *Pierce* compromise, where non-public schooling is permissible but is subject to reasonable state regulation. Anything more than "reasonable," though, would seem to go beyond what contemporary liberal proceduralism could stomach, because it would involve a powerful challenge to parental rights, historically one of the most sacrosanct of all liberal rights. The proceduralist, very much like the drift of today's status quo, seems doomed to the long-run frustration of strengthening students' rights and associated protections on the inside of the school system while, inversely, becoming decreasingly able to intervene with those who have chosen to exercise their right of exit. From a regulatory standpoint, as the public school system becomes increasingly rigid internally due to accountability and other pressures (not just students' rights, but also tort liability, the regimes of standardized testing, layer upon layer of health and safety measures, and so on), it fosters a decreasingly regulated and unaccountable twin who stalks about on the outside. Like a return of the repressed, an ever-more disciplined and "safe" school system creates ever-wilder possibilities outside of itself. Proceduralism is thus rendered somewhat schizophrenic due to its own timidity vis-à-vis parents.

But not all liberals are so worried about parental rights. Enlightenment liberalism would arguably have much less difficulty overturning the *Pierce* settlement in favor of greater state regulation. Enlightenment liberalism by definition seeks to universalize its core conception of authentic personhood, even if this means a radical curtailment of parental rights regarding the upbringing of their own children; if parents stand in the way of the creation of autonomous individuals, so much the worse for parents. Enlightenment liberalism concedes nothing to Bible-based orthodoxy. As a forthright champion of the universality of children's rights and allied notions, it would justify maintaining and expanding not only current constitutional protections for public school students, but also the extension—by police power where necessary—of these protections into private schools and even families. Private schools and, a fortiori, religious orthodox schools would therefore have to be made to adhere closely to liberal ideals, putting great pressure on *Pierce*'s notion of "reasonable regulation," and rendering questionable the extent to which there could then be any nonliberal orthodox schools at all.

I take this to be the position of Dwyer, who argues forcefully that the best interests of children require us to regard them as persons of equal status to whom equal consideration should be extended. It is uncontroversial for liberals that children enjoy moral equality with adults (if not superiority, as in certain utilitarian formulae). Things get complicated, though, when we try to imagine just how this general idea is to apply. For Dwyer, it should be applied as a rights claim that children may exercise against those of their parents, necessitating a change in the status quo in family law, where there is a high degree of deference to parental judgments about their children's welfare (itself based on very old Lockean and common law assumptions about parents naturally knowing their children best and caring for them most). On the grounds that a child's educational interests, as a subset of her temporal interests (the only ones that should rightfully count), always trump whatever spiritual interests parents may think obtain, Dwyer wishes to remove the current legal presumption in favor of parents. This is necessary owing to cases where a child's putative liberation would require extrication from a stunting traditionalist school of which the parents approve. (For Dwyer, such settings would include most all religious orthodox schools of whatever affiliation, fundamentalist Christian, Catholic, Jewish, Muslim, etc.) Acting on behalf of their best interests, the state should, in effect, help these educationally at-risk children escape from what one unsympathetic reviewer of Dwyer's book characterizes as Dwyer's vision of "a vast Gulag peopled by children unfortunate enough to be born into traditionalist religious families."[49] Marshaling the theoretical resources of Enlightenment liberalism, Dwyer seeks to bestow upon children a new voice for resistance against their parental oppressors.

Behind the veil of ignorance in Rawls's "original position," Dwyer argues, we should consider which principles we would endorse were we children growing up in X, Y, or Z contexts. Ignorant of determinate features of one's situatedness (e.g., race, class, gender, religion, whether or not one is parent or child, etc.), behind the veil one nonetheless retains widely enough shared normative commitments that do not obviously depend on any particular comprehensive conception of the Good, which Dwyer rightly says would be the "'fixed points' in our normative culture" against which we should test our proposals.[50] So, as he is constrained to do in employing the theoretical device of the original position, Dwyer commits himself to rely "only on substantive secular values that [he believes] are broadly accepted." (Consistent with this restriction, he also claims to eschew reliance on comprehensive liberal commitments such as moral autonomy as being good noninstrumentally.) Allegedly among these "fixed points" is the principle that "no one is entitled to control the life of another person and that rights protect only self-determination and individual integrity."[51] Something like this principle must premise the near-universal revulsion toward the idea of chattel slavery. It would also expose the inconsistency recognizable in the argument that my freedom is abridged if I am not allowed to restrict the freedom of someone else.

So Dwyer is probably right that something *close* to the above principle is as much a fixed point as we could actually find. Yet close is not enough to support the grand ambitions Dwyer has for the idea, particularly his correlative notion that all "other-determining" rights are in a fundamentally different category, facially inconsistent with self-determination as he and, he supposes, most of us would understand it upon proper reflection. What Dwyer somehow ignores is the patent reality of situations where self-determination is simply not an option, both regarding certain individuals (e.g., those suffering form certain severe disabilities) and all of us for certain portions of our lives, most importantly during our childhoods. This qualification to the principle of self-determination would be at least as much of a "fixed point" as the principle itself, one that most any sane person would recognize. Parents, of course, often exercise their other-directing in the service of a child's long-term ability to exercise self-determining rights (e.g., sending a reluctant child to school, making a child do chores to teach responsibility, self-discipline, etc.). Like everyone else, Dwyer must certainly know this, but for some reason he steadfastly refuses to recognize it theoretically, which leads him in turn to place too much weight on the self-determining/other-determining distinction. Such is his zeal to conclude that one species of other-determining rights, parent's rights, are "illegitimate."[52]

Whatever warrantability this distinction might have, though, it certainly does not hold in the areas most relevant to childhood; the chain is only as strong as its weakest link. Yet Dwyer wants to apply the self-determination other-determination distinction at precisely that weakest point, in the context where it is least plausible. What, really, makes widely recognized special cases of other-determining rights, such as those possessed by parents (for their children's own good), so banishable from the original position? As widely recognized qualifications to self-determination, why do they not also qualify as fixed points of our normative culture? It seems to me that they fairly obviously do, and that Dwyer is simply mistaken to think otherwise, perhaps blinded by his understandable horror at some of the awful educations to which some parents doom their children. *Pace* Dwyer, there seem to be at least two relevant ideas that are part of our fixed normative culture: (1) people should control their own lives and (2), the qualification of (1), that parents normally must exercise other-directing rights over their own children for those children's own good. That *both* ideas are parts of our fixed normative culture obviously and severely undercuts Dwyer's argument.

From the liberal perspective I think I basically share with Dwyer, the menagerie of disturbing orthodox pedagogical exotica (mostly Christian fundamentalist and Catholic) that Dwyer describes presents liberals with cases where we must swallow our bile in favor of a judicious balance with the other weighty concerns also in play. Absent child abuse or neglect in the criminal sense and also, as I have argued at length elsewhere (see note

#11), excepting very rare cases where parents might try to exert *total* control over a child's educational experience via alternative schooling according to an out-and-out fanatical doctrine, the default position should be a parentalist one. Unless there is compelling evidence to the contrary, parents should indeed enjoy the traditional presumption of privileged insight into their own children, what is best for them, and that they are motivated by bonds of love and duty to work toward what is best as they see it.

Following the persuasive critique of Stephen Gilles, the main reason for this "parentalist presumption"—one that Dwyer seems altogether to miss—is not that it guarantees success (by any definition) but that, as a matter of fact, it beats the other alternatives hands down.[53] For it is not the case that we are presented with a choice between those championing parents' interests and those with privileged insight into children's true interests or, to use Dwyer's own terminology, the other-directing rights of parents who wish to control their children versus the self-determination of the children themselves. This is a misleading way to put it. The real choice is between *competing* other-directing rights and claims, *adults versus other adults* who are fighting over what is in a child's best interests. Dwyer's vision seems to dream of some kind of escape from this situation on the wings of omniscient and always-benevolent state agencies, courts, and attendant experts who will know better than parents, particularly ones that have been deemed irrational by that same officialdom (e.g., to paraphrase a point Dwyer makes throughout his book, included in this category would be parents who are observed to place undue weight on a child's "spiritual" rather than "temporal" interests). But, as Gilles rightly points out, "Children's upbringing will be determined by adults whether child rearing authority belongs to the government or to individual parents. Thus, the question is not whether our childbearing regime will entail other-determining governance of children by adults; it is which adults will enjoy the freedom to engage in this other-determining behavior."[54] The point is not that the state and its agencies *never* know best, but rather that, since neither it nor anyone else can claim an a priori privileged position from which to discern those best interests, the parentalist presumption should remain as the default. Absent an unwarranted faith, bordering on naïveté, in the ability of state bureaucracies to assess and care for flesh and blood children, parents should remain the preferred choice among the competing other-directing claimants.[55]

Yet there is a deeper problem even closer to my present concerns. Dwyer seems to think—and in this he is not alone among contemporary liberals—that civic education and education in general are best served by working hard to sever them from the larger comprehensive commitments within which they must be rooted if they are to make any ultimate sense to the actual individuals who are supposed to conduct them. The problematic assumption seems to be that one ought to purify political morality by purging it of the almost necessarily irrational comprehensive commitments of the various actually existing orthodoxies, a sort of secularizing crusade that wants many of the fruits of traditional religion (e.g., honesty, self-sacrifice, community) without wanting to recognize the roots, trunk, and branches that make those fruits possible. This desire is, I'd submit, characteristic of contemporary baby-boomers and others who, particularly as parents, find that they want all of the "small g" goods one receives from traditional religion without having to accept the "large G" Good that has made the former possible. They want committed people to care for their children (saints, in fact, who are highly competent, responsible, and caring, yet are eager to work for almost no money); volunteers to staff community enterprises (e.g., emergency services, hospice and eldercare); military personnel who would die for them or their "national interests"; a place somewhere other than work, school, or both where they and their family might experience a sense of belonging (often in place of eroding extended family ties); an intersubjective arena wherein the inevitable yearning to face up to final questions about life and existence is recognized as central, even determinative for the other aspects of one's life; and so on. All this they want, but without the older authority structures and the theology, and, one might add, the sacrifice, discipline, or guilt. We want so much that has traditionally been animated by orthodox commitments to the Good, but wish to minimize if not discard the animating orthodox principles themselves.[56]

This textured ambivalence is reflected in proposals such as Dwyer's, which would enforce a certain secularism with an almost religious fervor, even into the most intimate areas of human life, while simultaneously relocating questions concerning the ultimate Good as much within the formal-governmental realm as possible, exquisitely rational regulations that distrustfully direct the movements of all-too irrational actual individuals. It is a crusade smacking of a certain moral fanaticism akin to that of a Nietzsche or a Lenin, figures whose love for humanity in the abstract is matched only by their contempt for the actual human beings who always fall short by comparison. While I share a great deal of Dwyer's concern about the bullying that can be perpetrated by religious zealots, it is vitally important for liberals to remember that the deep and difficult-to-control passions that lead some to widely condemned pedagogical practices arise from the very same wellspring of passion without which any worthwhile civic life would itself be impossible to maintain; it cannot just float alone in the air without any external supports. This means that liberalism must, among other things, cultivate and even be defined by a proper humility toward religious or secular orthodoxies that, aside from blind habit and inertia, are the only replenishable suppliers of such supports. For it is not at all clear upon what else any meaningful civic or moral education could be based.

In the sociopolitical world we actually inhabit here and now, what, really, are the alternatives? Gilles rightly cautions against any easy assumption "that a robust secular morality will take the place of the traditionalist religious faith," pointing out that the "default way of life in our mass culture is not moral philosophy (Kantian, Millian, Rawlsian, or whatever) as preached by secular intellectuals—it is materialistic hedonism as practiced by ordinary people. Many thoughtful observers, of all persuasions, see such lives as selfish, slavish and superficial."[57] Liberalism simply cannot drive itself too far, for then it begins to move like a scythe through the preconditions of its own existence: the deeper yearnings to which orthodoxy responds and forges into an uncircumscribable range of commitments, among which is a very large range of ways of committing to democracy itself. Though it must energetically control any pollutants they might emit, liberalism must—for democracy's sake if for no other reason—keep open these workshops of human ideals. For reasons such as these, the Enlightenment liberal approach I am identifying with Dwyer is implausible in education even on its own terms. For if it is pursued too single-mindedly, Dwyer's brand of Enlightenment liberalism undermines itself, in effect, clear-cutting and rooting out too many possible sources of deep commitment to the democratic politics that it itself needs in order to flourish.

What democratic education requires instead is less an insurance policy against human irrationality than an augmented imperative toward sincere and sustained attempts at mutual understanding among citizens, part of what Rawls, in the course of articulating his middle-ground alternative of political liberalism, calls "civic friendship" (a phrase that will be made highly explicit in later chapters). This kind of move represents the best impulses of the liberal tradition: away, where possible, from coercive state regulation and toward mutual understanding through moral suasion. Thus I see an optimistic scenario wherein the orthodox backlash against liberal proceduralism's regime of students' rights improves liberalism by requiring it to find its best self in response, the one that is creative, respectful and fittingly humble in the face of the final questions about our existence to which we will never have certain answers. Yet if liberalism cannot overcome its manic oscillation between proceduralist and Enlightenment extremes a kind of pessimism is more warranted. At present, a supine, proceduralist acceptance of the orthodox withdrawal seems to be the order of the day, where a wholesale lack of confidence in the public mission of public schools stands in danger of ceding the moral argument to a diverse but blinkered and balkanizing collection of orthodoxies.

As has been its genius, though, liberalism must once again in school policy find a new regulatory settlement and reimagine democratic education in a way that will advance universalistic ideals of equality and freedom simultaneously with the particular senses of well-being and visions of human flourishing that make life worthwhile for the actual individuals who are the ultimate locus of concern for liberalism and democracy. It won't be easy, however, and there is no guarantee of success; it is very possible that, with great historical irony, at the very height of its global military and commercial dominion, the United States will lose the ability coherently to reproduce itself via its own public schools. However, as the rest of this book means to show, there are much more interesting possibilities.

Chapter Two

Complex Equality and the Educational Sphere

THE OTHER KIND OF PLURALISM

A first step beyond the proceduralism-orthodoxy false dilemma is to realize that the pluralism that the former allegedly welcomes and the latter allegedly eschews is itself plural. Nowhere is this more apparent than in the educational context, where schooling in a democracy attempts an elaborate moral juggling act: keeping in the air what I'll argue are the three main forms of pluralism along with key universalistic norms grounded in liberty and equality. Can democratic education juggle all of these balls simultaneously?

The pluralisms being balanced are related to one another, but they are also importantly distinct as well. How we conceive of them as connected to liberty and equality has significant ramifications for determining what hopes are appropriate for our educational institutions. No one said it was theoretically pretty. As always, those seeking theoretical elegance had best look elsewhere than to education. Yet this is probably as it should be. In the same vein as Michael Walzer's caution that "a world that theory could fully grasp and neatly explain would not, I suspect, be a pleasant place,"[1] I think we would have more to fear from a squeakily clean system of education whose place in the scheme of things and prospects for reform could be reliably gauged and calculated. As I will elaborate in this and later chapters, complexity can sometimes be a saving grace.

Of the three relevant types of pluralism, only two are widely discussed in the educational literature: psychological and cultural. The former represents an important and morally indispensable artifact of modernity's bedrock concern for individuality and its varieties. Its most famous theoretical formulation in education is probably in Dewey's notion of growth as an educational ideal. For Dewey, education's foremost aim is to conduce to an experience of individual growth within the context of a socially responsive and continually evolving lifeworld. The ultimate justification for education lies in its contribution to this individual-social-natural mutualism within which each person develops. That which frustrates individual growth in this sense is ex hypothesi apart from education, whereas that which facilitates it is coextensive with education itself.[2] On the contemporary scene, one of the most influential exponents of this kind of growth-oriented psychological pluralism is Howard Gardner and his theory of multiple intelligences. Driven by the idea that traditional social assumptions about intelligence arbitrarily exclude the actualities of individual human diversity, Gardner argues that we should adopt a more expansive conception because there exist many more legitimate avenues for growth than we have historically honored.[3] Democratically disposed educators have warmed to this idea, as it provides scholarly legitimacy and elaboration for one of progressive teaching's deepest moral impulses to serve the child in all of his or her uniqueness. In this way, just as in the quasi-organic Deweyan dialectic, the theory of multiple intelligences advances the idea that the individual and society are deeply interrelated and their prospects for mutual growth inextricably intertwined. Education in its best and most democratic sense both mediates and fosters the plurality of human types, which in turn fosters the most livable, equitable, and most deeply rewarding society of which we are capable.

If psychological pluralism is the microtheory, cultural pluralism supplies the macrotheory. In its educational articulation and like its psychological counterpart, education's normative appropriation of cultural pluralism attempts to widen out the circle of respect for human diversity. It tends, however, to operate from a different base of assumptions about human subjectivity. Foremost among these is that whatever individuality in the simple unencumbered sense we may possess, human beings are necessarily the creatures of the cultures within which they are always formed, wherever and however those cultures may exist (e.g., as geographically-tethered traditional cultures or diasporic cultural communities resulting from emigration or made possible by new forms of technological mediation)[4]. This underlying assumption of intersubjectivity premises the cultural pluralist's policy prescriptions. Under conditions of cultural heterogeneity, such as those obtaining in our own and most any contemporary nation-state, the logic of this major premise leads to the conclusion that if any of the particular identity-forming matrices are disadvantaged vis-à-vis material or nonmaterial resources (e.g., respect) then ipso facto so are the individuals within those matrices. As an extension of this idea, a more communitarian cultural pluralism holds that a healthy diversity of cultures is itelf an intrinsic good, whereas the more classically liberal approach holds that, given the cultured nature of subjective identity, cultural pluralism is integral to individual flourishing.[5] In either its individualist or culturalist formulations, though, and analogous to education's normative appropriation of psychological pluralism, democratic education has largely committed itself to the enterprise of expanding its ideas and assumptions about culture from, in the case of the United States, a relatively narrow middle-class Anglo ideal to a more encompassing "multicultural" approach that "celebrates" or at least acknowledges diversity. Debates rage on, of course, over what precisely this commitment involves, how exactly to implement it and, often, the level of sincerity with which it is advanced. For given its wholesale bureaucratization, the rhetorical drapery of multiculturalism may hide disingenuous motives, for example, as Marxists have long argued, when an emphasis on multiculturalism obscures class antagonisms.[6] Even so, since neither ethnic chauvinism nor secessionism are widely considered morally or politically viable (at least in the U.S.), educators have largely devoted themselves—again, at least rhetorically—to the expansive normative agenda that the fact of cultural pluralism seems to entail. In the words of Nathan Glazer, "we are all multiculturalists now."[7]

This leaves what I am calling spherical pluralism which, in contrast to the other two, has not been an object of sustained discussion in educational theory, despite the interest it has generated in parent fields such as sociology, political theory, and philosophy.[8] Without meaning to diminish the importance of either psychological or cultural pluralism, I argue that the exclusive focus on these two has blinded educational theory to the great richness and moral power that lies within this intermediary realm. Spherical pluralism focuses on the plurality of values or goods around which evolve the dazzling variety of human practices, traditions, customs, institutions, and ways of life that structure and shape so much of our experience. The relevant goods are found in spheres such as religion, parenting, status, kinship, law, politics, economics, aesthetics, and indeed, education. These spheres may cut across, run through, or represent aggregations of both cultural and individual identities; and so, however obviously related to them, the realm of spherical pluralism seems significantly distinct from that of both the individuals who "inhabit" the spheres and the cultures that order those spheres. As I'll argue, an allegiance to spherical pluralism prohibits educators from unreflectively reproducing a narrow range of goods and instead enjoins them to preserve and proliferate a heterogeneity of spheres in the service of an expansive vision of the possibilities for the good life overall. Educators should become more consciously aware of their role in the life, breath, and breadth of spherical pluralism: a material, aesthetic, and moral sine qua non for any individual life worth living and any culture worth living in.

In what follows, I'll further describe this other kind of pluralism by drawing on the work of Walzer and others, and raise some critical questions that suggest modifications of the theory of distributive justice—complex equality—to which spherical pluralism gives rise. Attention to Walzerian complex equality, I'll argue, shows education theory's need for what one might call a certain theoretical bilingualism, that is, more specifically, the need to develop two relatively distinct justificatory languages that must underlie any critique or prescription for reform: one inescapably universalizing, the other irreducibly particularistic. Before imagining yet another totalizing harmony of them, educational theorists must first learn to speak both of these normative languages. Doing so gives rise to what this book terms "liberal contextualism."

SPHERICAL PLURALISM AND COMPLEX EQUALITY

The basic idea of spherical pluralism is found at many points in the Western intellectual tradition, and a cursory global glance reveals it to be found in equally ancient (if not more so) non-Western traditions of spherical separation, such as those generated within the framework of Hinduism in India or the Chinese genius for integrating traditions that tend to operate on different experiential planes like Confucianism, Taoism, and Buddhism. Probably with some Eastern influences of its own, the architectonic of Plato's *Republic* is emblematic. Plato famously constructs an elitist (though peculiarly so) caste-like society in which the division of labor and also the morality proper to each of the three social groups he identifies is legitimized by a semimythic narrative of a natural or divinely sanctioned distinction among human types: bronze, silver, or gold.[9] Most interesting for present purposes is how Plato constructs his utopia by segmenting its individuals into assigned areas and then establishing different values and concomitantly different distributive arrangements within each of those areas. The ruling philosopher class (the cream of the secondary class's crop of warrior-guardians), for example, while possessing a monopoly on political power must in exchange forego all claim to wealth. The philosopher kings live a spartan barracks-like existence and hold no significant individual possessions.

Neither are they to have familial ties to a particular kinship group, as the circumstances of their paternity are to remain unknown (where after they are to be educated in common along with other proto-guardian youths). By contrast, the bronze group of ordinary citizens may engage in commerce and personal enrichment to their heart's content and they may also live in ordinary families. (The text is unclear as to how, given that Plato explicitly rules out heredity as the basis for the caste assignments, the infant guardians-to-be are selected and removed from their bronze families.)

However unacceptable are its details to modern egalitarian ears, among those things of enduring interest in Plato's proposal is his insight that the life and vitality of a community as a whole can sometimes depend on a certain kind of separation and even segmentation. Though the Guardians have political power, they are not subject to what Plato regarded as the most common forms of individualizing corruption, namely, the temptations of wealth and the personal favoritism (for a family member or, perhaps, a lover). Conversely, while those of the bronze merchant and artisan class may enrich themselves from the till of the market, owing to the caste differentiation they are prohibited from parlaying that wealth into political power; in short, those who have cannot rule, whereas those who rule cannot have. Unlike the reality of our own (and Plato's own) actual society, the walls between wealth and political power are to be kept as high and otherwise unbreachable as possible.

Despite his absolutism's uses for it, Plato's founding insight about sociopolitical separation—a sort of ancient version of Robert Frost's aphorism "Good fences make good neighbors"[10]—is indispensable for understanding the school-state relationship. For it makes explicit the internal social heterogeneity that necessarily underlies systems of formal education by positioning schooling pivotally both to erect and mend the fences among the spheres in order to maintain those spheres' internal distinctiveness. To the extent that a society is stratified by economic class (which was certainly true of Plato's world[11]), that mechanism of education-cum-schooling will function, to use Joel Spring's pessimistic phrase, as a "sorting machine."[12] To the extent that it is not stratified (or at least not surreptitiously or coercively so), it may operate as a good shepherd, channeling the individual talents and aspirations of each into the needs of society as a whole—the utopian Platonic ideal of social harmony [idiopragein].[13]

This "art of separation"[14] and the conflicts and resolutions it has engendered serves as a major and maybe even defining theme in Western history from late antiquity onward. The political history of medieval Christendom is structured in large part by the grand-scale jockeying between Pope and secular authority, where political power is to be divided in some fashion between God's realm and that which is rendered unto Caesar, Emperor, or King.[15] Later, the rise of capitalism itself in the northern Italian city-states of the late Middle Ages and early Renaissance might be described as the assertion of a new sphere of bourgeois trade motored by its own impera-tives, challenging along a variety of fronts the privileges of both the landed aristocracy and the clerical elites who together constituted the traditional order.[16] At around this same time, the settlement of *Magna Carta* (1215) might also be described as a spherical separation, one effected through the establishment of limitations to the authority of the English monarchy by subjecting even it to the law (at least in its dealings with the nobility). This separation is the source of the modern notion of due process: "No free-man shall be captured or imprisoned or disseised or outlawed or exiled or in any way destroyed, nor will we go against him or send against him, except by lawful judgment of his peers or by the law of the land."[17] In the present context *Magna Carta* is rightly venerated as the inchoate but fateful assertion of a legal sphere no longer *in principle* merely a tool of political or ecclesiastical authority. More recently in this same historical vein, one of the chief characteristics of American constitutionalism is precisely this penchant for spherical separation: from the brachiation of the powers of government into executive, judicial, and legislative spheres to the disestablishmentarianism of the First Amendment to the more recent legal enshrinement of a separate sphere of privacy in *Griswold v. Connecticut* (1965), where the separateness was not only affirmed but claimed to be long antecedent to other spheres: "We deal with a right of privacy older than the Bill of Rights—older than our political parties, older than our school system."[18] To the frequent consternation of cul-tural conservatives and postmodern partisans of identity politics alike, contemporary liberalism has generally found itself defending separations such as these, an unsurprising tendency given liberalism's birth in the titanic separation between public and private that in large part defines political modernity itself.

Despite its centrality, the full normative force of spherical pluralism has been only recently appreciated and given a sophisticated theoretical articulation, most notably in the radically pluralist and antireductionist notion of "complex equality" first developed by Walzer in his landmark book *Spheres of Justice* (1983) and then modified by sympathetic critics and Walzer himself in subsequent publications. Walzer's key insight is that if we are to adumbrate an account of the "just" or "good society" in the largest sense, we must do so with an abiding sensitivity and respect for the wide and not-so-easily mutually translatable range of socially valued goods that are to be found, in varying degrees of health, in any human society. A direct progenitor of Walzer's view is Daniel Bell's notion of a "disjunction of the realms": a division among the "techno-economic structure, the polity, and the culture." These realms "are not congruent with one another and have different rhythms of change; they follow different norms which legitimate different, and even contrasting types of behavior. It is the discordances between these realms which are responsible for the various contradictions within society."[19] Even more so than for Bell, however, for Walzer the social sources of value are innumerably and indeterminately plural, and although he is more or less agnostic regarding the ultimate ontology of these sources (unlike, say, the more forthrightly realist pluralism of Isaiah Berlin[20]), he takes it as axiomatic, as I shall, that it is impossible and undesirable for the blooming and buzzing diversity of human experience to be evaluated under the aspect of a single discrete good. By contrast, regimes under the sway of what Charles Larmore terms "a cult of wholeness"[21] are almost by definition totalitarian: one thinks of the picture of the Heroic Man under communism or fascism, the Good Christian, Jew, or Muslim under theocracy, or, in extremis, the economic maximizer of laissez-faire capitalism, or even the autonomous chooser of traditional liberalism. Such regimes seek to order everything—and by whatever means, including, often, violence—under the aspect of One Single Good. Complex equality's general commitment to a plurality of social goods stands against this kind of reductionism by attending to the constituent internal norms, assumptions, practices, traditions, and so on, that make those social goods what they are. For these are the spheres of justice: morally, epistemologically, and sociologically disaggregatable (sub)forms of life that have a distinctive telos—historicists arguing that they are to be understood developmentally, those of a more realist bent arguing for a (to them) solider metaphysical-theological foundation.

In *Spheres of Justice*, Walzer describes eleven spheres: membership, security and welfare, money and commodities, office, hard work, free time, education, kinship and love, divine grace, recognition, and political power—though he is at pains to emphasize, especially in responses to critics, that his list is a loose one and not in any way complete: "I can't provide a diagram nor decide upon a definitive number (my own list was never meant to be exhaustive). There isn't one social good to each sphere, or one sphere for each good. Efforts to construct a systematic account along these lines quickly produce nonsense . . ."[22] Against a vulgarly structuralist attempt at decisively schematizing the spheres and their interrelationships, the Walzerian account preserves a kind of looseness, in my view appropriate, as its categories aspire to capture phenomena that are necessarily diachronic, interactively transmogrifying (e.g., in the right settings, money can become charity, education a credential, work a citizenship right), and otherwise irreducibly local and complex, and so are resistant to an overly zealous systems logic. What is "in" or "out" of a given sphere simply is not a matter that admits of precise codification. It has more to do with the kind of social understanding often identified by neo-Aristotelians as *phronesis* (Gk. "practical wisdom"), a kind of contextual knowing characteristic of experts in a particular social practice, one that is irreducible to explicit rules and algorithms. Social theories, unlike those of the natural sciences, must take into account the "inside" perspective and points of view of those actually inhabiting the social context in question; what a social setting *appears* to be to those involved in it is inescapably relevant to what it *actually* is. Bird's-eye view analytical descriptions of social life will only go so far.[23]

Further, one of the main elements of this complexity—as well as one of the core and most controversial of Walzer's ideas—is that the spheres maintain a relative autonomy among them, primarily in the sense that within each of them there can be identified a distinctive distributive pattern following from the nature of the social good or goods around which the sphere is constituted. For example, Walzer argues that the realm of "office," which has to do with institutional hierarchy and professional competence, is constructed around a principle of merit, where authority and power are justified and then distributed as a function of an ability effectively to carry out one's proper task or to innovate appropriately and accountably within institutionally assigned ends. By contrast, in the sphere of health care, to use one of Walzer's more controversial examples, resources are to be distributed by need. Not that need is *in fact* the sole—or even the primary—distributive criterion most operative in the contemporary U.S. health care system. Hardly. But Walzer suggests that need is in some socially recognized sense the *deepest* criterion in that, whatever the ugly realities generated by inequitable access to health care resources, it remains the criterion truest to the social meaning of health care. At her best, a health care practitioner (who to a large degree, qua an earnest practitioner of the good in question, occupies a relatively privileged interpretive position) does not let someone bleed to death outside the ambulance bay of the emergency room—even if the injured person lacks citizenship papers or, more commonly, proof of insurance. In this light, much of the resistance to the ascendancy of managed care HMOs by physicians is not simply the American Medical Association's occupational realpolitik (though there certainly exists much of this), but, more comprehensively, it is also a sphere-specific moral response to a perceived excessive sacrificing of patient care on the altar of profit. The person of practical wisdom within the sphere—the Aristotelian *phronemos*—is the one most likely to sense these violations in concrete situations. Others of course may sense them, too (particularly the victims), but the practitioner in her own element must be given her due, for not everyone is on an equal-status footing within each sphere. Nor should they be: when it comes to medical decisions, why should the views of the competent person of serious purpose who has devoted her life to medicine not be weighed more heavily than those of the casual observer? So long as that medical authority is not transported into areas in which it is irrelevant, including the over-extension of a particular judgment (e.g., the physician who not only warns me that smoking is bad for my health but then also seeks to coerce me into quitting), the relative autonomy that underlies the differential distribution of authority within the sphere not only is not a problem but is to be welcomed.

The idea that authority ought always to be divided equally rests on an oversimplification of justice that complex equality means to correct. Some types of authority distribution are just and some are not, and one determines which is which only ad hoc, by attention to the nature of the goods over which the authority is presumed (remembering that with regard to political power in a democracy the ideal distribution of authority is simply egalitarian rather than hierarchical). Walzer offers this particularistic (or contextualist) understanding of distributive justice as an alternative to a traditional liberal reliance on a kind of "simple equality," where equal justice is a matter of securing equal access to, opportunity for, or in the strongest case, possession and effective disposition of some determinate quantity of what is decided in advance as the all-important social good. At its crudest, an effort at simple equality would attempt to guarantee a quantitatively equal amount of some specified social good to every individual. Usually, this transforms the pursuit of social justice into an effort to secure monetary equality among individuals via some form of income redistribution. The central intuition here is that there is at bottom only one thing that really counts (again, usually de facto this means money), and thus social justice is realized as a function of the equal distribution of that thing.

Responding to the same concerns, a more sophisticated version of simple equality holds that justice demands a certain minimum income or command-of-resources threshold to be achieved for all persons. Depending on the level of the threshold, this could justify, at one end of the interventionist spectrum, a form of socialism or strong welfare state to, at the milder end of the spectrum, some degree of progressive redistributive taxation. A well-known version of this understanding of simple equality is the Rawlsian difference principle, where any income differentials must be justified as ultimately benefiting the least well off.[24] In educational policy, one often hears a form of this as a justification for so-called gifted education: it is fair to expend a disproportionate amount of resources on the gifted because of the presumed high rate of return on the original social investment in them, as their future medical breakthroughs, scientific discoveries, contributions to culture, and so forth, will ultimately benefit all of us including, most relevantly, the most disadvantaged. Whatever its intricacies, the Rawlsian approach assumes what one might call a procedural simple equality because it holds that justice involves finding a single trans-spherical distributive formula (in this case one derived from deontological principles that are by definition categorical). For Walzer, this sort of procedural or threshold thinking is properly construed as a parameter or bounding side-constraint applicable within the distributive spheres of many vital resources such as housing, food, and medicine. But it cannot apply to all of them as a metaspherical principle according to which all social goods should be distributed.

Walzer's view is not that simple equality is intrinsically undesirable but that the larger quest for social justice is misconstrued if it is conceived exclusively in such terms. In my view, Walzer is best thought of as a species of social eudaimonist bent on elaborating in an inclusive and pluralist manner the contours of "the good society" overall. He strongly presumes, it seems to me, a vision of human flourishing—or at least of one of its necessary conditions—that is threatened by the bogeyman of reductionism; the autonomy of the spheres ought to be recognized because what is truly worthwhile in individual human lives and human societies is generated from within the genius of those spheres. Consistent with this insight, Walzer concludes one of his essays with: "It is when we reflect on distributive justice in its largest sense, and on the values that we would like to see realized in all the spheres, that complex equality comes into its own."[25] Ultimately, then, the autonomy prized by traditional liberalism is instrumental to the development and flowering of human goods that express not just our political terms of cooperation but our deepest and most comprehensive attachments. Ironically, given his egalitarian commitments, Walzer's appeal is therefore to "justice" in an ancient sense consistent on one level with Plato's *Republic* and its conception of justice as propriety: to each his own—where "each" now means a separate sphere, rather than a mythically legitimized social caste system within which individuals are to be assigned. For the sake of its own internal richness and its ability to promote human flourishing by cultivating deep attachments to human goods, a society must look to preserve the integrity of its spheres.

Complex Equality Modified

Complex equality must, however, account as much for the equality as it does for the complexity. As several trenchant critics have observed, Walzer's original formulation is open to much criticism along these lines.[26] For the commitment to equality itself would seem to depend on universalistic (i.e., metaspherical) considerations that would have to stand alone over and against the particular spheres. Any number of caste-like complex inequalities are, after all, very easy to envision, a fact that casts suspicion on what appears to be an overreliance on whatever convention and tradition happens to generate. Securing social heterogeneity for Walzer's eudaimonism seems to come at the high cost of inattention to the many forms of social inequality that may thereby be sanctioned. What if convention dictates that Indian untouchables do not really "need" health care? Or African-Americans education? Or Saudi Arabian women political rights? Put as a general question, how can Walzer's theory square its spherical pluralism and spherical autonomy with its simpler yet universalizing allegiance to social equality as an overarching ideal?

A key element in constructing an answer to such questions has been David Miller's sympathetic critique and refinement of Walzer's original view, a revision Walzer himself seems to endorse. Miller argues that although proponents of simple equality err in trying to locate a single determinate social good as the object of social justice (e.g., money or political power), there does seem to exist a more amorphous kind of distribution that is in fact metaspherical. Miller describes this as a simpler equality of "status" or "recognition" that functions as a grounding moral criterion for assessing the overall societal pattern created by the various spherical distributions. In addition to the eudaimonism outlined above, what is ultimately worthwhile about complex equality is that it provides the best mechanism for fostering "an egalitarian society in which people's behavior towards one another is not conditioned by differences in rank, in which specific inequalities—in income, say—do not crystallize into judgments of overall personal worth, and in which barriers of class do not stand in the way of mutual understanding and sympathy."[27] This meta-spherical claim tempers Walzer's eudaimonism and indeed modifies it in a more universalistic direction—one, however, that does not quite collapse back into an advocacy of what might be termed a *strong* notion of simple equality because of the centrality Miller's scheme still accords to spherical pluralism. The minimal conception of simple equality thus allowed is always to a high degree dependent upon the spherical contexts that supply its preconditions.

Miller summarizes his argument as "distributive pluralism plus equal citizenship leads to equality of status," where it is the latter that really counts so far as justice is concerned.[28] It is thus more than simply that preeminence in one sphere ought not be translated into benefits or status in another, but also that our experience of recognition and status toward one another *in general* ought not be exclusively related to our position in any single sphere. Though the proverbial starving artist may live modestly, she can nonetheless carry with her a certain status equality relative to the very rich. Though they may live in palaces and fly Learjets and so are patently her superiors in the realm of money, she might feel superior to them in the realm of learning or aesthetic sensibility. Or the small town office manager's prowess and clout with City Hall combined with his position as a leader in the world of local politics may more than compensate for the fact that he lives in a modest house, drives a cheap car, and the like. Instances of this kind of thing are legion, most of them having to do with alternate venues for status recognition within our wealth-worshiping (and in this way antipluralist) society: the proverbial starving artist's sense of superiority of taste over and against her fat cat patrons, the teacher's gratifying sense of durably influencing the lives of multitudes of children relative to what she perceives as the relative emptiness of her sister's investment banking job,[29] the nurse who puts patients first coming into conflict with a bottom-line hospital bureaucracy, the thrill of discovery to which the scientist clings despite her funding being controlled by image-obsessed politicians, the religious believer's sense of "witnessing" among her blindly godless compatriots, the teenager with a sense of style, the perfectionist athlete, carpenter, or salesperson, the beat cop who barely makes a living wage but knows he is indispensably relied on, the stay-at-home mother of five whose cumulative parenting wisdom leaves her new-parent friends awestruck—and on and on, and in the best case ad infinitum. In an ideal society of complex equality there are as many of these respect-garnering spheres as there are individual talents and proclivities.

As in the Aristotelian conception, each of these different spheres constructs its own *arete* [excellence] which defines the contours of the sphere both positively and negatively by identifying its exemplars and failures, veterans and neophytes, devotees and dilettantes, insiders and outsiders, and even friends and enemies.[30] Miller argues that we have the best approximation of a just society—that is, we will maximize the chances for achieving an inclusive equality of status—to the extent that we foster the growth and development of these plural realms (autonomous distribution) while also maintaining the basic political rights of the Enlightenment individual (equal citizenship). In other words, the more expansive our conception of the variety of worthwhile human practices, the more likely it is that each individual will be able to find some arena in which to excel and be recognized. This is not unlike the way in which the expansion in our conception of intelligence advocated in Gardner's theory of multiple intelligences allows us to locate, respect, and develop forms of human excellence that we did not "officially" recognize and reward previously. With Gardner there are now seven or eight ways one can be smart, whereas before there were only one or two, a development that increases the potential for individuals to garner Miller's basic kind of status.

A relevant example is offered by Patricia White in her discussion of the school's mission toward what she calls "democratic self-respect."[31] For White, democratic schooling must aim at a certain expansiveness regarding the bases of self-respect available for students in order to foster their identification with the values of the school and also in the long run to render them efficacious politically as well as in their lives generally. This, for example, is one of the main moral justifications for extracurricular activities of various kinds, as they provide so many plug-in points for students who might not gain recognition and self-respect through the traditional avenues of mathematical, verbal, or interpersonal performance. The school, however, should not promote just *any* basis for self-respect since these might be trivial, self-absorbed, or even hurtful to others.[32] Rather, schools should encourage a pedagogy of reflection on the bases of self-esteem itself, thereby offering a continual challenge to morally inappropriate types of self-esteem while at the same time opening up and exploring the great variety of possibilities for it to which our limited horizons and prejudices would otherwise blind us. White elaborates:

> The teacher is always concerned with the necessary destabilizing job of weaning children away from morally unacceptable forms of self-esteem. But also, in a more positive way, schools should be having what might

be called a revisionary effect on the bases of self-esteem, by offering the broadest possibilities for children to find worthy bases for favorable opinions of themselves that at earlier stages could not have entered their consciousness. A typical recognition of this is the comment, "I would never have thought I would be playing in chess tournaments, thinking of doing math at college . . ."[33]

Not only, then, should schools provide the self-esteem plug-in points, but they should pedagogically interrogate that self-esteem and, most important, transform and multiply the bases of appropriate types of self-esteem for individual students. Hardly a mere "feel good" curriculum (though one can imagine inattentive educators corrupting the ideal in this way), it is not a matter of "lowering standards" but rather of continually expanding our limited sense of what human excellence can mean. In microcosm, this pedagogical commitment to a kind of structured expansiveness pursuant to individual transformation exemplifies Miller's broader suggestion that "the more spheres a society contains, the better from the point of view of complex equality," because "the more social goods there are, the less likely it is that individuals can be ranked socially on the basis of their performance in one sphere alone."[34] Thus is provided a morally inclusive momentum to spherical pluralism's ancient sense of propriety concerned with what is proper or "does justice" to X, Y, or Z.

At the same time, however, Miller's health-preserving injection of equality necessitates a judicious bounding of the range of permissible status generating arenas by metapluralistic constraints that would block the development of immoral or otherwise socially undesirable spherical activities—the inappropriate bases of self-esteem intimated above. Most obviously, fascinated though we are with the Mafia and despite whatever may be their interesting history and internal "virtues," criminal enterprises would need to be banned in all of the spheres, and racial discrimination purged from many and perhaps most of them. Regulatory boundaries are thus generally necessary to help control the straining centrifugal force that some spheres may develop were their autonomy completely unchecked (e.g., organized religion's collapse into persecution or an overly independent military's coup against a civilian government). In practice, this bounding, parameter-setting function is that of national and subnational constitutions, which in the United States means common, case, and statutory law and all manner of derivative state regulation.

Understood in these terms, to redraw the borderlines between the relatively autonomous spheres and their regulatory parameters is to redefine society itself. In the United States, the systematic persecution of African-Americans has arguably been the most significant catalyst for such redefinition: the gradual post–Civil War process of incorporating the Fourteenth Amendment and the civil rights movement being two powerful cases in point. These legal-constitutional examples are especially appropriate, given the careful balancing act for which Miller's equation (i.e., distributive pluralism plus equal citizenship equals equality of status) seems to call, an act analogous to—and in fact, manifest in—the careful balancing of interests so characteristic of jurisprudence itself. The grand balance for Walzer, Miller, et al., is thus between the centrifugal force of the autonomous spheres on the one hand and on the other the necessarily universalistic regulatory mechanisms that must bound those spheres. A close analogy is with a similar balance at the level of cultural pluralism: a nation-state made up of rival nationalities without common regulatory boundaries is not properly speaking pluralistic but rather serially monistic. Spherical pluralism depends upon its regulatory boundaries in a similar fashion. It does not take a Derridian deconstructionist to see that for the institutional life of the modern democratic state the ostensibly antagonistic pluralism-monism binary masks a deeper coagulating interdependence.

But from the normative point of view, how should this interdependence be conceived? Or, to ask the same question, how might we resolve what seems to be a looming legitimation crisis[35] between the spheres of justice and their regulatory boundaries? If, as Richard Arneson points out, to "preserve whatever degree of integrity of the separate spheres is deemed desirable, state action is required,"[36] how then are these sphere-state negotiations to be worked out? This problem is only compounded by the frequent persistence of intraspherical conflict where there exists no internal consensus within the sphere concerning the nature of the good or goods at stake and/or the relevant distributive pattern thereof. There is no better example of this than the educational sphere itself, whose marquee policy conflicts in areas such as finance, governance, and professional qualification admit of, to say the least, a high degree of variance. Is access to a certain level of educational resources a fundamental right to be guaranteed by state action? Or is it best distributed as localities or even private voluntary associations (e.g., religious groups) see fit? Or is it simply a commodity like any other for those who can afford it? Present policy in education is better described as, at best, a patchwork of compromises among competing conceptions of the "good" of education itself, rather than as an articulation of any shared sense of what that the good may mean per se. Indeed, given the number of parties potentially involved, these multilevel interpretive conflicts seem only to increase the complexities of complex equality, perhaps to a level that would nullify any normative force the theory might claim. It would simply be too relativistic and in practice too anarchic.

In *Spheres of Justice,* recognizing this problem, Walzer had claimed that while "boundary conflicts are endemic," and so there should be no utopian desire to transcend them, he also allowed parenthetically that when "people disagree about the meaning of social goods, when understandings are controversial, then justice requires that the society be faithful to the disagreements, providing the institutional channels for their expression, adjudicative mechanisms, and alternative distributions."[37] But this suggestion was widely seen (including eventually by Walzer himself) as inadequate because of its vagueness. The interpretive conflicts that are the stuff of politics are not just side issues but rather must be central to any plausible pluralistic account. As argued above, the precise nature of the available "institutional channels" are the sine qua non of any workable pluralistic politics.

The combined weight of commentary on complex equality has suggested a broad avenue down which plausible responses must proceed, and it involves outlining some sort of societal deliberative-dialogical-hermeneutical (one may take one's terminological pick) procedure whereby what I am calling the regulatory bounding parameters and the relatively autonomous spheres are mutually responsive. Walzer himself suggests as much when he opts for a model positing "citizens as agents of last resort," who are to be understood as distinct from "agents of the first resort": the makers, distributors, and recipients of the goods in question. The idea is that there are instances in which the agents internal to a sphere band together to oppose what they together perceive as a pernicious external influence (e.g., priests against simony, college professors against legacies, proponents of small town life against Wal-Mart). But when the internal agents disagree such that they cannot resolve their disputes on their own (or, perhaps, when the ramifications of their internal decisions are sufficiently relevant to enough other individuals qua citizens or qua "inhabitants" of other spheres whose core interests may in turn also be at stake), they make their appeals "to the state, and so to their fellow citizens, to intervene and adjudicate the dispute or help one of the sides."[38]

In the case of such an appeal there are two types of extraspherical interventions possible: (1) political domination, where citizens at large or an interest group impose their policies on more or less reluctant inhabitants of a sphere (e.g., McCarthy-era loyalty oaths for university faculty positions, increasingly restrictive HMO regulations on physicians or the provision in California's Proposition 187 requiring educators to report children in their classrooms whom they suspect to be undocumented immigrants [on which more below]); (2) a more honest attempt by all parties to attend to the shared meaning of the good(s) in question that somehow resolves the immediate issue and afterward leaves the sphere to its inhabitants.[39] An example of this might be, at its best, a school tax referendum in which there will be a "citizens voice" and voices from the "K–12 community." Each side—even the latter—may be severely internally divided but the issue will be resolved on election day up-or-down, one way or the other. The hope is that the larger dialogue antecedent to the resolution will be in some sense mutually edifying: citizens will learn something about the school district's needs and not just reject the referendum on its face without due consideration, while the educators will reflect on the justice of the request given the constellation of priorities faced by the community as a whole. Similarly, internal conflicts within a sphere might necessitate an appeal to the citizenry in order to help mediate a dispute (as in federally mediated collective bargaining) or come down on one side or the other in an intraspherical family quarrel, so to speak (e.g., when competing scientific proposals lobby for finite public resources or professional athletes and team owners look to the courts to solve a labor dispute).

At times it is even morally imperative that ongoing conflicts hidden within the spheres be surfaced and brought out into the light of public scrutiny and control, such as in cases of domestic abuse, historically considered to be outside of legitimate public concern as wink-and-a-nod private "family" matters. Indeed, it is fully consistent with—even demanded by—the project of complex equality to remember, along with Seyla Benhabib, that the

> original sense of res publica is the "public thing" that can be shared by all. Sharing by all means first and foremost that certain issues become matters of public conversation and that, in Hannah Arendt's terms, they leave the sphere of private shame, embarrassment, silence and humiliation to which they have been confined. In making public those issues and relations that had condemned us to shame, silence, and humiliation, we are restoring the public dignity of those who have suffered from neglect.[40]

Thus the overall concern for status equality can at times turn a sphere inside out by prompting the exposure of extreme forms of oppression or exploitation. This functions as a crucial guard against abuses of the "integrity of the spheres" argument that may operate as mere pretexts for hidden and immoral agendas. On equally as grand a scale as domestic abuse, one thinks of the bogus legal "states' rights" doctrine of "interposition" disingenuously advanced in the United States by some southern state governors to justify their defiance of post-*Brown* desegregation mandates in the 1950s. (Constitutionally nonsensical, interposition held that states could "interpose" themselves between a federal mandate and its state-level implementation.) In politics there is ample reason for a healthy skepticism toward those who claim to have merely local problems and want the larger public to mind its own business.

Yet sometimes the public at large should not intervene. And complex equality differs from some more comprehensively liberal theories (or "critical theories" such as Benhabib's or Jürgen Habermas's) in its recognition that the larger public is not always the best arbiter of every matter of collective interest. The public in fact should *itself* recognize this and impose limitations on itself, as when it refuses to interfere with the inegalitarian governance structure of a church or, perhaps from that public's point of view, the overly egalitarian governance structure of a university.

Indeed, as Stephen Holmes has proposed, the public's limitation of itself lies at the very heart of any kind of democratic constitutionalism, most centrally in what he calls a "paradox of precommitment" in which the founding constitution-making generation effectively binds subsequent generations to the constitution it has created. Yet an uncompromising populist stance might see this an illegitimate authority exercised by the dead on the living. Hence the paradox: were we truly democratic it would seem that we should be able to decide on our own rules and remain fallibilistic and in principle open to revising even our most fundamental political ideals. But the liberal constitutionalism we also embrace does not allow this and places certain matters off limits: the Bill of Rights is not eligible for plebiscitary revision, for example. Holmes's explanation is that while it is an Enlightenment article of faith that the public plays an important role in correcting the errors of fallible individuals and nonpublic groups, liberal constitutionalism adds the idea that the public itself is fallible since any decision it makes is made only as the *present* public and not the public for all future time. (There are many cases of one generation's public consensus being overthrown by another's.) The basic freedoms and liberties-protecting constitutional core is exempt, however, because "rather than merely foreclosing options, it holds open possibilities that would otherwise lie beyond reach."[41] The public in a constitutional democracy is therefore founded on the paradox of limiting itself in order to protect and preserve itself.

The public must also limit itself in more practical ways, too, especially when it intervenes within a sphere of justice, such as an effort to ensure that the intervention is not just a pretext for a hostile takeover, as in the case of the state using a stall in negotiations between, say, a city government and its municipal unions as an opportunity to take over, impose a settlement, and augment the power of the U.S. Labor Department. (The more dramatic examples are found in international relations, where belligerent powers will almost always locate and capitalize on some internal conflict in order to legitimize an intervention.) There is an important sense, then, in which spherical conflict resolution by a self-limiting public can be honest to the goods in question, and conversely, where an intervention honestly come by or not can function as a smokescreen for the pursuit of external agendas. It is the difference between doing someone a favor out of friendship and doing the favor for strategic gain. Just as if you do this too often eventually you will be without friends, if the interventions are too numerous and too hostile eventually there will no sphere left in which to intervene. An extreme example of this kind of bad faith intervention would be the absurdly ideologically driven and short-sighted behavior of the Soviets during the infamous Lysenko affair from the 1920s to the 1950s. Backed by Stalin, the geneticist Trofim Lysenko politically engineered the enforcement of a party line that pedaled his own discredited genetics theories concerning heredity (a neo-Lamarckian, Lysenko believed in the genetic inheritance of acquired characteristics), thereby controlling—by, among other means, imprisonment, torture, and murder—the direction of Soviet genetics research. As a result of Lysenkoism, the Soviets succeeded in crippling for themselves any areas of science having to do with heredity, including their programs in agriculture and biology.[42] However, from the point of view I'm advancing, the moral of the story is not that the state should never intervene *simpliciter*, but rather that limits must be maintained as to the scope and extent of those interventions. And while those limits should be set publicly, deciding on them should be the outcome of at least some kind of dialogue between that public at large and those honestly speaking for the culturally determined sphere-specific good or goods in question. From the point of view of complex equality, then, it is unacceptable to cede exclusive control over scientific research either to the political process or the scientists themselves. Whatever the particular circumstances, a mature democracy will recognize the wisdom of this kind of (partial) self-limitation.

Complex equality thus requires a moral and political balancing act sensitive both to pan-spherical bounding norm of status equality and also at the same time to the internal autonomy of a multitude of culture generating and conserving spheres. By extension, this involves a Walzerian appreciation of the ultimate dependence of the former upon the more ancient latter. If intraspherical distributions should remain as faithful as possible to the nature of their axial goods, then some sense of propriety (itself a cultural product) must be cultivated among citizens in order to guarantee the requisite border-preserving sensibilities. But ensuring this propriety is not easy, as it requires what one might call the complex edification of citizens to stand as a bulwark against the indoctrinatory schooling typical of totalitarian regimes (understanding, again, that for complex equality a totalitarian regime is to be identified with an illicitly sphere-corroding power accumulation *of any kind*). A key insight for pedagogy is that bringing about the person with these sensibilities is not to be achieved by political education in the narrower sense of the inculcation of a proper ideology—even a democratic one. Rather, complex edification is secured by two basic processes: first and semicircularly, the "thick" informal education of actually living in an internally heterogeneous society rich with strong value-begetting institutions and, second, a "thin" formal process of schooling that teaches the morality and habits of status equality—citizenship—yet which also respects and does what it can to foster the cultural heterogeneity that guarantees that our decorous politics are *about* something that truly matters to us.[43] On the pedagogical ground, this means, in a strong sense: civics *plus* spherical pluralism and, by extension, psychological and cultural pluralism as well, with a recognition that a successful transference of the virtues associated with the pluralisms is unlikely to be achieved wholly within school walls. In general terms, the thick education and the thin schooling very much lean on one another, together constituting a situation of dual allegiances. Recognizing this mutualism is the basis for grappling with the unique demands that complex equality and democracy in turn place on the educational sphere.

Following the underutilized work (in educational circles) of Joseph Raz, this pedagogically dual commitment can plausibly be framed as capturing a fuller meaning of the traditional ideal of autonomy itself. Raz rightly argues that true autonomy strongly demands true pluralism, on the grounds that "[a]utonomy is exercised through choice, and choice requires a variety of options to choose from."[44] In other words, the options presented must be *real* ones rather than those of the "Coke or Pepsi" "McDonald's or Burger King" variety; Raz says, if "all the choices in a life are like the choice between two identical-looking cherries from a fruit bowl, then that life is not autonomous."[45] Included also in the notion of a real choice is the idea that among the range of available choices must be morally acceptable ones. And the practical realization of this requirement demands, in turn, the existence of a healthy variety of spheres of justice. "One is autonomous only if one lives in an environment rich with possibilities. Concern with autonomy is concern with the environment."[46] Educating individuals toward autonomy in the fullest sense possible in modern pluralistic democracies therefore involves cultivating not only autonomy in the sense of the thin citizenship virtues grounded in equality (the uncoerced and informed "critical thinking" of every voter, tolerance of others' expressive rights, a willingness to bear the political "burdens of judgment," etc.) but also ensuring that the reality of social life—in Raz's terms above, its "environment"—allows for a wide range of attractive life choices. That this outward movement lies outside many traditional notions of pedagogy only illustrates those notions' moral incompleteness.[47] Walzer himself interestingly extends this same logic by indicating further that "Ultimately, what makes it possible for me to choose is the fact that other people *have chosen* . . . and so have kept alive a way of life, a community that I can enter (and exit). I can't be a political adventurer or a cultural vagabond unless other people are settlers. The commitment to freedom, then, requires support for settlement, or, better, for a variety of settlements."[48] Where the reality of social life presents few attractive options in, say, economically distressed inner cities "when work disappears," to use William Julius Wilson's depressing but accurate phrase,[49] or, to give a related example, in the situation of an individual facing debilitating ethnic or culture-based discrimination that evacuates possibility, all the critical thinking and civics education in the world will be insufficient for true autonomy.

Consider the self-understanding of the disability rights movement, in which the fight for access in both literal and figurative senses is pursuant to expanding disabled persons' life options, all of which is based precisely on a moral vision containing an augmented sense of personal autonomy (rather than love, pity, or even money).[50] Here it could not be clearer how individual autonomy presupposes a plurality of life options that are actually open to that individual, a plurality that when translated into social terms involves the maintenance and accessibility of a rich and healthy spherical variety. Wheelchair lifts on buses are good only instrumentally— *only insofar as there are worthwhile places to go*—a point that also holds, more generally, for all the statutory machinery of federal disability law (or any other universalistically driven civil rights initiatives). Recognizing someone's humanity means little in the abstract and only more so as the ideal is given dialectical substance in the mutual concession of need and responsiveness that is the history of democracy at its best. Yet the formal privileges and duties of citizenship only go so far toward realizing this more challenging autonomy ideal. An educator committed to complex edification recognizes the morally and politically dual mission such a conception of autonomy entails: first a thin set of citizenship capabilities and second a more holistic look outside school walls toward the compound social reality within which those capabilities are to be exercised.

Complex Equality and Education

Hence the need for a liberal contextualism, a theoretical account of how inclusive educational institutions can in fact serve their two normative masters: the relatively autonomous spheres (including, social conditions permitting, the educational sphere itself) and the trans-spherical equality of status that together represent complex equality's vision of democracy. Historically, these textured pluralistic demands create for education a relatively unique problematic with which most human societies have been more or less unbothered. For without a public commitment to the provision of education for all via formal schooling, the problem of how to answer to such a range of constituencies never even arises. To the extent there exists no public commitment, education remains domestic and as such will be determined ad hoc endogenously within the various distributive spheres or, just as likely, by some authoritative conglomeration of spheres that would map a particular subculture within a larger, more heterogeneous setting: a class, a religion, an ethnicity, a nationality or, perhaps, a gender. Without the democratic universalist commitment to equality, formal education remains an ethnoreligious and/or a domestic matter for the wealthy, requiring private tutors and the like or, more glaringly, a site for the unabashed reproduction of class interests, as in the British "public" schools of previous generations, as well as in any number of caste systems of differentiated schooling. These stratified systems, it should be remembered, supply the rule rather than the exception in world history. Within them education is justified not universally but with reference to the specific ideals and aspirations of a particular social group—even if those ideals are somewhat expandable in the abstract, such as the eudaimonistic notion of *paideia* in classical Greece (or for that matter the nascent commitments expressed at the inception of American constitutionalism). For complex equality this is a structurally simpler matter (though, of course, since the simplicity stems from the dominance of a narrow elite group it is morally problematic as well) because education's place is decided by religious or class elites who, although potentially internally divided, are not beholden either to a universalizing political morality or to any organized effort under the banner of "education for itself." Under these conditions the sphere of education remains fundamentally servile as the instrument of the few.

Historically, however, modern liberalism alters these traditional arrangements via its expanding commitments both to particular freedoms and, eventually, to universal education. Here a basic dual tension first arises that shapes and greatly increases the complexity of the demands that a justificatory account must satisfy. Of this portentous historical development, Ira Katznelson and Margaret Weir write, "The inescapable tensions between the public and private realms, and battles at this boundary about the extensiveness of equal citizenship and popular sovereignty, took place in and were moderated in part by the system of schooling for all. The commitment to educate all children in primary schools paid for by the government is the most distinctive American public policy of the early nineteenth century."[51] Not only must education now answer to many different interests from which before in the "good old days" of elitism it had been sheltered, but it must also weather the instabilities inherent in being a primary site for the public mediation among those interests. Health clashes with religion over condoms, religion with religion over the use of the King James Bible, business with the arts over taxation for aesthetic education, local governments with federal governments over racial integration, the working class with a managerial agenda over credentialing, legacies, or school funding, and on and on. Whereas before educational controversies were relatively contained within their narrower boundaries, the universalizing imperative causes what would have been formal education's internal controversies (cloistered within the monastery, apprenticeship, estate or elite boys' school) instead to reverberate exogenously throughout the entire society—and back again—with only those in the most remote pockets untouched by them. It is amazing how many now have a self-conscious interest in what goes on in schools and how schools understand their own interests to be inextricable from those same external interests, despite the latter's variety and, frequently, their geographical distance from the physical site of schooling.

Hence the problem for justifying this institution that is so multifariously in demand: given the need for a sphere-checking "citizenship" parameter based on some universalizing ideal of status equality, how are expanding educational institutions—whose very expansion is premised on that universalizing imperative—supposed to justify their own autonomy? Or, correlatively, their own self-assertion over and against any of the other spheres? In other words, what makes them still *educational* institutions and not just a subdirectorate of, say, the political (as in Soviet-style dictatorship) or business interests (currently, our own economic competitiveness agenda along with, historically, the hidden curricula of class reproduction)? If one accepts both the need for educational institutions to maintain some distinct identity over and against other societal interests and also the need for that would-be distinct entity to account for itself in terms that all of those interests can reasonably be expected to accept, then one has accepted the problematic I am advancing. How can universal public education—the promise of education for all—satisfy at the same time the public at large, its constituent groups (in the language of business its "stakeholders"), and also *itself*? Stated another way: How in a democracy of complex equality (let's say, one not yet completely homogenized by a fratricidal business sphere) is the public provision of universal education to be justified?

This situation of divided loyalties is helpfully developed in Amy Gutmann's highly elaborated democratic theory of education. Though a strong advocate of universalism, Gutmann takes what I'm calling spherical pluralism seriously, and she builds her theory upon a very perspicuous recognition of the need for democratic educational institutions to strike a just balance between, on the one hand, threshold equality-grounded moral norms (she calls these "nonrepression" and "nondiscrimination") with, on the other hand, the three bounded sources of educational authority most legitimate historically in the Western political tradition. These are: (1) "the family state," *in extremis* Plato's Republic, wherein the state itself as *parens patriae* may pursue by various means a nonneutral conception of the good life for all its citizens; (2) "the state of families," the basic though potentially highly particularistic rights of parents to direct the upbringing of their own children; and (3) "the state of individuals" which expresses the claims to some privilege for the educators themselves on the basis of their presumed authoritative expertise (an authority in turn based on their presumed disinterested pursuit of the *individual* child's best interest).[52] On Gutmann's model each of these bases of authority can and do conflict with one another and the story of educational policy in a liberal democracy is the necessary give-and-take among them, which in the best case results in a dynamic equilibrium of all three. Whatever resolution is (temporarily) reached, however, it must be bounded within the two negative *Grundnorms* of nonrepression and nondiscrimination: the former restricting any party's right to interfere with the deliberative capacities of the individual child, and the latter a distributive principle of the former extending it to all children.[53] When these nonneutral terms are adhered to the resulting configuration will be a properly "democratic state of education," one that may come in different forms depending upon the (bounded) balance of power achieved among the three sources of educational authority.[54]

An especially good example of this authority balancing is the participatory process involved in setting and implementing Individualized Educational Programs (IEPs) for students with disabilities as mandated by a line of federal statutes, most recently *The Education for All Handicapped Children Act* (1975), often referred to as Public Law 94–142, the *Individuals with Disabilities Education Act* or IDEA (1991) and subsequent reauthorizations. The IEP has become a veritable ceremony of the shared governance of democratic education in Gutmann's sense. For a child to be initially labeled in a relevant special education category and then "placed" in the appropriate environment (by statute the "least restrictive" one, which in most cases involves inclusion with nondisabled children), an official plan must be agreed on and then recorded by a deliberative group, the IEP team. Though it will vary somewhat as a function of the particularities of the situation, the IEP team is mandated to include, in effect, "representatives" from each of Gutmann's three states of education. These might include: the child's teacher or teachers (of the special education and/or regular classroom variety) along with school administrators, school psychologists/counselors/nurses, social workers, and importantly, the child's parents and, where age-appropriate, the child him- or herself. In difficult cases—particularly where there are disputes involving money—each side may also have their legal counsel present. Each "state of education" is present: (1) the family state in the less embodied but nonetheless real statutes mandating the IEP and its procedures in the first place (and perhaps to a secondary extent if a social worker is present), (2) the state of families in the child's parents, and (3) the state of individuals in the various school personnel and their presumed expertise. And whatever IEP is agreed on, it is bound by something very much like Gutmann's threshold principles of nonrepression and nondiscrimination. Corresponding to the former, for example, a "basic floor" of educational opportunity must be provided,[55] such that a child may be observed to be making academic progress commensurate with what is stipulated under the IEP. Corresponding to the latter, no matter what her disability, the school district may not decide, as often happened in the predisabilities rights era, to exclude the child from a free and appropriate public education—even if it is costly, as it often is. The IEP is thus justified by both the deliberative agreement of the relevant parties composing the IEP team and also in its boundedness by the universalistic threshold principles.

In general terms, the dual form of this justification is consistent with what I am arguing it must be: Gutmann satisfies the universalistic equality condition with her two threshold principles and then gestures toward the role of the more variegated sources of educational authority with her triadic balancing scheme. From the point of view of complex equality this balancing scheme succeeds in that it recognizes plural sources of axial authority (one might even call them so many spheres) and it bounds their squabbles and schemes within a framework of thin but forceful equality-based parameters.

However, Gutmann's theory still suffers from an under elaboration of these plural sources. Her state-parents-educators equilibrium is overly abstract in that it underestimates the degree to which claims arising from all three are made not simply by naked individuals but rather *from the standpoint of a particular sphere of justice.* While it is true that parents on occasion may confront, say, school district officials to pursue isolated and even idiosyncratic agendas for their own children, they are much more likely to advance their claims—and to be more effective in doing so—as a member of something larger: a church, neighborhood, disabilities group, ethnic coalition, and so on. (In fact, it could be argued that insofar as parents pursue their interests in an isolated fashion they are unlikely to be heard at all, particularly if they have low incomes or are immigrants.) Further, often parental agendas that may seem ostensibly to be isolated are in fact social movements of varying degrees of cohesion, for example, the home schooling movement which is overwhelmingly a creature of religious conservatives (though there are of course some "pedagogues" who home school for other reasons).[56] The group nature of these claims is also attested by the fact that it is also one of the main agendas of social activists in immigrant communities precisely to organize parents into advocacy groups so that they will be unintimidated by officialdom so as to press their concerns more effectively. Pierrette Hondagneu-Sotelo provides some supporting detail in her study of Mexican immigrant communities in the United States:

> Undocumented Mexican immigrants who participated in self-help groups, special classes, and civic and educational organizations gained two things. They consciously worked toward improving both the quality

of their own lives, and those of their families' members. Some groups were organized as self-help groups, such as the women's Alanon group, while parents' groups aimed at improving the quality of their children's public-school education, and the immigrant-rights groups targeted the problem more broadly shared by the local undocumented immigrant population. In all of these endeavors, members gained a sense of satisfaction at bettering the quality of life for themselves, their children and families, and others in the neighborhood.[57]

As clearly indicated in this description, the group nature of the efforts she describes were a necessary condition for their effectiveness. Often those most socially vulnerable, like Hondagneu-Sotelo's undocumented immigrants, are in the best position to shed a realistic light on the actual mechanics of social change.

Gutmann is not strictly speaking wrong to identify *in abstracto* the rights of individual parents as a basis of educational authority, but in practice the childrearing ideals those parents pursue are not derived so individualistically, but rather are constructed by the thick social forces that are constitutive of those parents' identities. They are in sum not so neatly divorceable from the various spheres that are constitutive of their "individual" identities and beliefs. When it comes to raising children, how many of us really get our ideas truly on our own? Or even more improbably, how often is political activity arising from the concerns of parents pursued apart from some social group that shapes and colors (and in some cases even directs) the agenda? To be clear on this potentially volatile point: it is not that parents are shills or stooges for more organized groups—though they sometimes are—or that their beliefs count less if they are derived from a larger group (one might argue that most all of our beliefs have this status). The point is that parents, insofar as they are pursuing particular educational policy agendas *as parents,* are overwhelmingly likely to do so as members of organized groups and so to the extent that they are politically relevant at all they are in fact pursuing their agendas this way. By contrast, when they make claims about education *as citizens* they are speaking as individual bearers of rights and are then claimants upon that very different basis. As citizens, however, their arguments must appeal to public reasons that are based on shared political norms (e.g., basic constitutional liberties) that tend to discourage public deliberation of the highly particularistic claims (often based on theological grounds) that many parents will advance on behalf of their parenting projects.[58] These have their place and must be duly honored. The point here, however, is that a lacuna of overabstraction in Gutmann's theory is filled by recognizing the political reality that parents tend to pursue their extradomestic parenting agendas as members of groups with *their* own normative agendas. Such claims are thus matters not only of individual justice but also of spherical justice; Gutmann's balancing act among parents, teachers and the state is less a balance of individual interests than it is of collective ones.

An analogous point can be made regarding teachers who insofar as they are politically effective tend to pursue their agendas via unions and professional organizations. This is true also of the political process (particularly the municipal and school district politics that are the most relevant for school governance) which at a practical level concerning particular policy debates is more appropriately viewed as an arena of clashing interest groups[59] rather than an idealized public square within which individuals press their claims qua individual citizens. Astute politically, Gutmann is well aware of this and she supplies compelling and well-considered analyses of much that I've mentioned here by way of critique. Still, she does not make the multiplicitous and sphere-specific nature of educational policy central enough to her justificatory account.

Providing some needed flesh on the skeleton presented in Gutmann's view, then, the position I'm advancing proceeds from the assumption that educational institutions must satisfy an even greater heterogeneity of different audiences. To borrow a phrase from Gerald Gaus's justificatory liberalism, my account aims at a greater degree of "wide responsiveness"[60] that takes the dynamic spherical pluralism of complex equality (itself grounded in the Razian notion of the preconditions for true autonomy mentioned above) as the locus of the response. For it is a doubly complicated (and then some) story. It is this complexity that liberal contextualism tries to capture.

In sum, liberal contextualism must respond to what I'll call two response sets: first the generalized public wherein individual equality rights are elaborated and interpreted. This might be called "the constitutional realm," on the model of the federal judiciary's interpretive role regarding basic individual freedoms. As such, the constitutional realm trumps, via the U.S. Constitution's Supremacy Clause, interpretive attempts that are adjudged false and applications of basic constitutional law anywhere in the system that are ruled inconsistent with its own constitutional premises and common law precedents.[61] This constitutional realm functions as the ultimate semantic guardian of Gutmann's democratic threshold principles. Political and even military pressure may certainly be brought to bear in enforcing a certain "interpretation" of what this realm entails (e.g., the indelible image of National Guard Troops desegregating Little Rock Central High during the civil rights era), but ultimately it is the judicial sphere which decides, via its interpretation of constitutional principle and precedent, on the legitimacy of the executive branch's coercion or the legislative branch's resolve.

But even if legitimate, the actual implementation of the judgment qua policy depends on myriad factors more pertaining to the second response set: the realm containing the spherical pluralism underlying complex equality proper. This second response set is where politics as we ordinarily think of it resides and it is constituted by a polymorphous and dynamic "group of groups" of potentially unlimited diversity: the spheres of justice themselves. These are the workshops of social identities and the manufacturers of meanings that individuals take to be ultimate in their lives and also determine to a large extent what possibilities are realistic for them (e.g., as a function of the resources actually available to them). Though the more formal world of abstract individual equality, rights, and the like is operative as an external restraining boundary, it carries no necessary weight within these spheres which correspond to the (probably indeterminate) number and kinds of socially valued goods with enough gravitational power to coalesce into spheres. Here, as alluded to above, the bedrock insight of the communitarian critique of liberalism comes into its own: the idea that among the conglomeration of attachments that make up my identity some are so deep and otherwise constitutive of that identity that to abstract from them would be to shed that identity, thereby in general positing a metaphysically naked unattached self that is oddly unrecognizable from a standpoint that any of us could actually inhabit.[62]

The difficulties arise when one of these identity-constituting institutions, rooted within its own normative sphere, reaches for power beyond itself and requests a certain fealty from other spheres. When the church stops rendering unto Caesar and starts busying itself with worldly political power it does just this (save political involvement truly motivated by self defense, for example, in a climate of religious persecution). When physicians from within the sphere of medicine make expertise claims to insulate themselves from politics and religion not only to practice medicine as they see fit but also to organize their services so that delivering them is highly remunerative (often by political means such as restricting medical licensing), they too reach beyond their immediate sphere. On a larger scale, when business qua capitalism, to use by far the most pressing example, colonizes and in so many cases obliterates other spheres—from the destruction of "the commons" in the land enclosures of seventeenth-century

England[63] to today's vocationalist and for-profit schools—it is exerting power that is, from the point of view of complex equality's sense of propriety, beyond itself. As Walzer writes, "In all the spheres of distribution, groups that defend internal standards—health care for the sick, housing for the homeless, education for all the children who are capable of learning—are increasingly challenged by the theory and practice . . . of the market price and the profit margin. But the market is incapable of helping the growing number of excluded men and women; it won't provide them with jobs or underwrite the autonomy of nonmarket spheres of activity."[64] This complex face of exclusionary injustice must be kept firmly in mind, as when the monetary inequalities generated by the market obstructs access to spheres where it has no business acting as gatekeeper, for example, where valid constitutional claims go unpursued for lack of money to pay the lawyers or where the assessed value of private property in one's neighborhood cannot adequately fund one's schools.[65]

This is not to say that all extraspherical power is illegitimate, however. Hardly. Much of it may be warranted and even welcomed warmly from the perspective of other spheres. Hence the difficulty in trying to assess the legitimacy of interspherical interventions and the hugely differentiated concentrations of power that are usually present. This problem is especially acute given that the universal claimant is necessarily embodied, catalyzing what ought to be a pervading anxiety in any reformer's policy prescriptions: to what extent is the agenda "really" universalistic and to what extent is it generated from the particular spheres of justice in which the reform proposer happens to be involved? The postmodern (and Marxist, actually) caveat about universal claims often hiding particular agendas offers no psychological assurances to the theorist.[66]

Restated in light of these intervening considerations, the proper way to extend the present inquiry becomes clearer. If it is to possess a legitimacy widely recognized in our society overall, the institution of education must make what Kenneth Strike has termed a "morally bilingual" appeal in the languages of the two response sets of citizenship rights and the spheres of justice.[67] This situation calls for two parallel justificatory accounts, one corresponding to the *thin-but-morally grounded* constitutional realm of individual rights, and the other to the *thick-but-morally bounded* spherical realm that is as internally variegated as are socially valued goods themselves. Attention to spherical pluralism shows the necessity for this bifurcated account of how schooling for all must be justified. A robust theory of the place of educational institutions in our pluralistic hoped-for democracy must as best it can aim at a harmony of this often tension-ridden dialectic, all the while working to ensure that the greatest present threat to social heterogeneity—the market for goods and services upon which our overall welfare depends—remains the servant of our visions of the good life rather than their master. In this sense, the notion of complex equality helps us both as educators and citizens better to see who we really are and who we aspire together to be.

THE CASE OF PROPOSITION 187

A vivid illustration of the above dynamic is the brief life and death of California's Proposition 187. This would-be state statute contained provisions to deny public services (including education and health care) to undocumented immigrants and their children. Though legally dead as of September 1999 (originally approved by voters in 1994, it never went into effect and was subsequently voided by federal courts) the key issues raised by the referendum live on in similar state anti-immigration initiatives and also in altogether different areas, such as educator opposition to the federal *No Child Left Behind Act* in the mid-2000s. (Progeny of 187 have been debated in California and actually passed in Arizona in 2004 as "Proposition 200," and are reported to be on the horizon for several state legislatures in the years to come.[68] Significantly, for reasons the below analysis will make clear, these progeny have so far not included education provisions akin to those of 187.) I'll focus on two distinct ways in which the opposition to Proposition 187 were articulated: the headline-grabbing universalism that focused on constitutionality, human rights and anti-racism and also the quieter, yet, I think, morally and politically powerful particularism heard most notably from California educators themselves.[69] Consistent with this book's overall argument, liberal contextualism attends to both.

Proposition 187 was designed to cut off public services, most notably health and education, from illegal or undocumented immigrants. The relevant educational provisions, which were to become part of the state's education code, read as follows:

(a) No public elementary or secondary school shall admit, or permit the attendance of, any child who is not a citizen of the United States, an alien lawfully admitted as a permanent resident, or a person who is otherwise authorized under federal law to be present in the United States.

(b) . . . each school district shall verify the legal status of each child enrolling in the school district for the first time in order to ensure the enrollment or attendance only of citizens, aliens lawfully admitted as permanent residents, or persons who are otherwise authorized to be present in the United States.

(c) . . . each school district shall have verified the legal status of each child already enrolled and in attendance in the school district in order to ensure the enrollment or attendance only of citizens, aliens lawfully admitted as permanent residents, or persons who are otherwise authorized under federal law to be present in the United States.

(d) . . . each school district shall have verified the legal status of each parent or guardian of each child [referred to in subdivisions (b) and (c)], to determine whether such parent or guardian is one of the following:

    (1) A citizen of the United States.

    (2) An alien lawfully admitted as a permanent resident.

    (3) An alien admitted lawfully for a temporary period of time.

(e) Each school district shall provide information to the State Superintendent of Public Instruction, the Attorney General of California, and the United States Immigration and Naturalization Service (INS) regarding any enrollee or pupil, or parent or guardian, attending a public elementary or secondary school in the school district determined or reasonably suspected to be in violation of federal immigration laws within forty-five days after becoming aware of an apparent violation. The notice shall also be provided to the parent or legal guardian of the enrollee or pupil, and shall state that an existing pupil may not continue to attend the school after ninety calendar days from the date of the notice, unless legal status is established.

(f) For each child who cannot establish legal status in the United states, each school district shall continue to provide education for a period of ninety days from the date of notice. Such ninety day period shall be utilized to accomplish an orderly transition to a school in the child's country of origin. Each school district shall fully cooperate in this transition effort to ensure that the educational needs of the child are best served for that period of time.

In short, the measure would have required schools to investigate children's citizenship status and report suspect students—and their parents—to the INS. One can only imagine what this might have entailed on a day-to-day basis for teachers and school administrators. In the words of a *Los Angeles Times* editorial, Proposition 187 would "make snoops out of teachers" because it "would literally force a school district to question young Americans about their *parents'* immigration status and report to authorities any parents suspected of being here illegally . . . Imagine requiring a teacher to quiz a pupil about whether her parents are illegal—what an ugly outrage."[70]

As stark as these predicted realities seemed and as much shock as they generated among many educators, the most effective arguments against Proposition 187 did not center upon the undesirable consequences it would have entailed for teachers and administrators. Rather, the clearest case to be made against it involved a relatively straightforward application of constitutional law, where the reigning precedent was the U.S. Supreme Court case *Plyler v. Doe* (1982). The majority opinion in *Plyler*, authored by William Brennan, invalidated a Texas statute that required local school districts to deny schooling to children not "legally admitted" into the United States and threatened to withhold state funds from those districts that did not deny the schooling. The Court held that the Equal Protection Clause of the Fourteenth Amendment, which states that no State shall "deny to any person within its jurisdiction the equal protection of the laws," prohibits Texas from denying something so basic absent any rational relation to any state goal (significantly, the Court discounted the argument alleging the debilitating cost of educating these children). It distinguished denying children education from the constitutionality of prohibiting the employment of adult illegal immigrants by noting the patent unfairness of imposing "a lifetime hardship on a discrete class of children not accountable for their disabling status. These children can neither affect their parents' conduct nor their own undocumented status." The children, at least, were regarded as "innocent." Many felt that the precedent of *Plyler* invalidated Proposition 187 on its face. The Equal Protection Clause's coverage of individuals (citizens and noncitizens alike) "within its jurisdiction" seemed obviously to apply to 1990s schoolchildren in California as it did to 1980s schoolchildren in Texas. And, indeed, pending the constitutional challenge, a temporary injunction placed the statute on hold almost immediately after voters passed it. In the end, Proposition 187 never actually went into effect and, as indicated above, was finally and officially, just this year invalidated in federal court. Ironically, the legal reasoning ended up having more to do with the priority of previous federal anti-immigration legislation with which Proposition 187 was ruled to be in conflict.

As a moral argument, the reasoning of *Plyler* is universalistic in form, relying as it does upon categorical claims about the rights not only of citizens, but anyone within the jurisdiction of the U.S. Constitution. Any "person" within that jurisdiction is entitled to equal protection under the law. And *Plyler* explicitly holds that illegal immigrants are, sure enough, persons. While education is still not viewed at the federal level as a "fundamental right"[71] (and thus one triggering a very high level of judicial scrutiny of statutory attempts to withhold it), it is given a pride of place as "not like any other governmental benefit" because it is held to be an indispensable precondition for living any kind of worthwhile life. Undocumented immigrant kids in California, Texas, or wherever, get free public education because they're human beings and as such get "protected" by the laws, too. It is probably safe to say, I think, that this kind of universalism accords well with most teachers' self-understanding, however much its implied commitment to human beings as such might clash with anti-immigration sentiments or simply, in this case, the specific requirements of legal naturalization. Except for cases of extreme prejudice, it is difficult for well-meaning people who deal closely and protractedly with small children to see those children's basic humanity as secondary to an abstract legal status. This implies a strong form of what one might call a lived universalism, although it is one that, in a peculiar way, as I'll try to show, also belongs internally to the sphere of education. This lived universalism, then, may be thought of as the experiential corollary to the high Court's reasoning in *Plyler*.

As in the case of medicine, education is one of those things whose practitioners (often as distinct from those *administering* the practitioners) are loath to limit their services as a function of exclusionary criteria that seem to come from outside their sphere. In contemporary medicine, the most pressing examples have to do with the ability to pay, the proverbial (and sometimes real) case of allowing someone to bleed to death outside the emergency room because they lack insurance. Whatever the Gradgrindian incursions of the HMO industry and the hospital bureaucrats, no true physician would fail to act in such a situation, compelled as she would be by a strong moral momentum internal to the practice of medicine: healing the sick unqualifiedly. This is not to deny that physicians can profit from their practice, that there are unscrupulous physicians, or that the practice of medicine is increasingly under the control "bottom-line" forces. Rather, it is to note that sincere practitioners of medicine themselves would in an intangible yet palpable moral sense withdraw the title "doctor" from one of their own who allowed the gratuitous emergency room gate exsanguination. In withholding care, they somehow seem to have stepped outside the bounds of their proper sphere, just as surely as if they refused to treat a criminal or, in another defining controversy, presided over state death penalty executions. Even more extreme, Nazi doctors who tortured prisoners in their hideous "experiments" violated both universal norms of human decency and rights, but also, more to the present point, internal norms having to do with the particular allegiances to which they were bound as doctors, a system of obligations widely recognized among physicians and medical researchers themselves (sometimes by custom, sometimes more formally in professional codes and the like).

In the educational sphere, despite its lack of internal agreement in many areas, there are still particular norms and obligations that are widely recognized and that, moreover, may cause spherical "border wars" when they come into conflict with the external exigencies of other spheres. Walzer retells a traditional Jewish story in order to begin illustrating this point. In "Hillel on the Roof,"

> An old Jewish folktale describes the great Talmudic sage as an impoverished young man who wanted to study at one of the Jerusalem academies. He earned money by chopping wood, but barely enough money to keep himself alive, let alone pay the admission fees for the lectures. One cold winter night, when he had no money at all, Hillel climbed to the roof of the school building and listened through the skylight. Exhausted, he fell asleep and was soon covered with snow. The next morning, the assembled scholars saw the sleeping figure blocking the light. When they realized what he had been doing, they immediately admitted him to the academy, waiving the fees. It didn't matter that he was ill dressed, pennyless, a recent immigrant from Babylonia, his family unknown. He was so obviously a student.[72]

In the ideal case this story represents—ideal in the sense that it is arguably closest to the most common conceptions practitioners hold of how education should be conceived—there is something about teaching and learning that resists its being distributed according to social distinction and even ability to pay, just as surely as would have been the case with doctors had Hillel been bleeding outside the emergency room.

It is not that simple need operates as a sufficient distributive criterion, as it seems to in the medical sphere. As Walzer points out, particularly with regard to what we would call a higher education context, "interest and capacity are at least as important . . . Teachers look for students, students look for teachers, who share their interests; and then they work together until the students have learned what they wanted to know or have gone as far as they can."[73] A properly functioning educational system, that is, one organized in ways that might be said to be true to the good of education itself, will have a certain relative autonomy as an institution. It will be capable of (and allowed to be capable of) functioning according to its own logic, even when that logic runs counter to that of other important spheres. In other words, it will mean something when one says that X, Y, or Z is an *educational* matter rather than a legal, financial, or political one. And while all spheres of activity may be viewed through the point of view of a contextually prioritized sphere (financial, political, aesthetic, etc.), as long as the inhabitants of a sphere are able to keep their specific "environment" intact, there will remain a sense in which the sphere must be understood on its own terms. The challenge within an overall social environment of spherical pluralism is to be able to cede enough autonomous space to the various sphere for them to maintain something like their own identity, while also guaranteeing the universalistic boundary conditions that in a constitutional democracy must characterize the system as a whole. This challenge may require action on different fronts simultaneously: in the manner of antitrust regulation, policing the borders among spheres in order to prevent a robust and expanding sphere from a hostile takeover of others (e.g., the religious sphere in contemporary Saudi Arabia or Iran or the pressing example of the sphere-corrosive dynamism of today's global marketplace) or, perhaps, the statist dystopia of the domination of the political over all of society. The project of a contextualist liberalism is to balance the relative and, in most cases, institutional autonomy needed for intraspherical richness with the basic rights and liberties that must characterize the system as a whole.

From this point of view, Proposition 187 is doubly problematic. Not only does it violate the basic rights and liberties side of the bargain as outlined in *Plyler*, but it also involves a corrupting incursion into the educational sphere itself. In general, considerations of the former type are recognized by arguments in the public arena that of necessity take on a universal, which is to say in our society, increasingly legalistic form. It is the educators themselves, however, who must speak for the latter in sphere-specific terms. And many of them did. One of the best available examples is contained in the documentary film "Fear and Learning at Hoover Elementary" by Laura Simon, a teacher at the school. Simon's film describes the effects of the threat of Proposition 187 on an inner city elementary school with a high immigrant (legal and illegal) population in the Pico Union neighborhood of Los Angeles. In many respects, even the *fear* of Proposition 187 among teachers and, most importantly, parents and students, significantly compromised the school's ability to carry on its educational mission. Among many other things, the film very poignantly shows how teachers and students had to start looking at one another in a suspicious new light—very un-Hillel-on-the-roof-like. In the following recent interview exchange with NBC's Matt Lauer, Simon explains:

SIMON: It was horrible. What we were supposed to do with this bill or this law that actually passed, is actually document, write a list, a black list of the kids who you thought were undocumented, and turn it into your principal who was then going to report them to the INS and have them taken out of the classroom.

LAUER: In effect, it was making teachers INS agents. So when you drove to school in the morning, the bill became the law . . . But when you knew this bill became law, and you're heading to school that day, a school which, by the way, is estimated to have seventy percent of the students possibly the children of undocumented aliens, what were you thinking?

SIMON: I was thinking I was going to have to report my kids. And I was thinking, I can't do this. And I think I might go to jail by the end of the day.

LAUER: You would have refused to do it?

SIMON: I didn't go—I didn't become a teacher to hurt children. And I was so desperate. I was desperate. My kids were so fearful of me that morning. One of my kids asked me if I was a cop, and if I was going to kick her out of the classroom. And when she did that, I was so devastated. I—I needed to do something . . .

[Proposition 187] never went in effect. But what it did was it made school a very cynical place. We were divided. A lot of teachers tried telling the kinds "You don't belong here." And the environment we created was so rough that we lost some kids. And [referring to one of the children central to the film] unfortunately, I lost my baby. I lost one of my most favored students.[74]

Simon's comments illustrate very well why so many teachers were so strongly opposed to the proposed law. (Most of the state educational groups, including the California Teachers Association [NEA], the California School Employees Association and the State Superintendent for Public Instruction [along with, incidentally, the California Medical Association] opposed the law and lobbied vigorously against it.) They seemed to feel, particularly of the enforcement provisions, that Proposition 187 would have forced them to act in ways fundamentally at odds with the moral underpinnings of their roles as educators: having to take names, draw up lists, or, just generally having to take up a new attitude of suspicion toward schoolchildren. These voices are not in this instance raising global concerns about the issue of immigration and neither are they necessarily concerned about the INS and its own enforcement mission. They are speaking from within the virtues of their own particular role as teachers and, by extension, the integrity of the educational sphere as such.

Significantly for a contextualist analysis, even proponents of the measure ceded this point, and attempted to make their case in such a way as to decrease fears that Proposition 187 would indeed require teachers to act in these unteacherly ways. Understanding the symbolic power of this issue, one editorialist, herself a former teacher, proclaimed, "It is a lie to say that the measure will make teachers "cops" or informants or agents of the INS. Teachers nurture and instruct all children assigned to them, without reservation; Proposition 187 doesn't change this in any way. Teachers do not determine eligibility for enrollment, so they would not be expected or required to identify children who are ineligible because they are in this country illegally."[75] National conservative leaders Jack Kemp and William Bennett were troubled enough by this (and other) aspects of the measure that they publicly opposed it, and in doing so went against their usual ideological constituents. Kemp told a disagreeing conservative audience that he could not in good conscience support a measure that would "turn teachers and nurses into agents of the INS."[76] There was such concern on this point that, during the days leading up to the referendum, California Attorney General Dan Lungren was forced to make a statement that he had "no intention of criminally prosecuting anyone" who refused to report suspected illegal aliens.[77] Perhaps even more powerfully than Simon's unapologetically oppositional stance, concessions of educational autonomy like these from Proposition 187's supporters and ideological fellow travelers show how widely accepted—at least regarding education and health care—is the concern with spherical integrity. Teachers and nurses making lists and turning in the young and the sick? It just doesn't *sound* right. From a contextualist point of view, we should worry if more and more of us are deaf to the sounds of these differences.

In conclusion, liberal contextualism attempts to balance the demands of the above-mentioned response sets and therefore recognizes that moral arguments for or against public policies may come in either form. The problem for liberalism is when, as examined in chapter 1, it gives undue emphasis to only one response set, usually by championing a proceduralist legalism (and, derivatively, the absolutism of "rights talk" [78]) that functions undeservedly as a juridical trumps. When there are "rights" to be asserted the messiness of debate grinds to a halt as the heavy artillery of judicial reasoning is wheeled up as champion to decide things for us. However much we need the artillery, though, the assault on truth needs many other kinds of weapons. *Plyler*'s legalism presents a compelling argument, but so do the somewhat different considerations emanating from within the educational sphere. Wise public policy demands that we listen to and learn from the intraspherical voices that possess their own traditions, sets of virtues, lived realities, and even, sometimes, uncompromising obligations. The next chapter concerns how the educational sphere can as a whole give greater volume to its voice, achieving the kind of autonomy democracy needs it to have.

Chapter Three

Education's Institutional Autonomy

The Question of Institutional Autonomy

On the contextualist view just described, the good society is best understood as a pluralistic one, where different social spheres are allowed as much free play as possible within democratic boundary constraints that are themselves based on relatively thin universal norms of social equality. Education and an indeterminate number of other areas of endeavor (e.g., law, politics, markets, medicine, policing, religion, journalism), constitute such spheres, which in their developed form are autonomous enough to possess norms, traditions, distributive arrangements, and whatever other particularities are appropriate to them.[1] The Rawlsian notion of a reasonable pluralism is to be understood in terms of these spheres: recognizing and preserving the irreplaceable thickness our spherical involvements give to our lives, while limiting their sovereignty if they become unreasonable, defined here as severely oppressive or otherwise inimical to basic democratic norms.

Consolidating the insights of the previous chapter, I would stipulate that liberal democratic educational institutions ought to be understood as strongly ensconced within a justificatory network of distinct and sometimes conflicting nodes of obligation. These fall into three main categories: (1) the multiplicitous realm of goods-environing social spheres with constitutive internal standards of excellence that give rise to local (i.e., sphere-specific) hierarchies and distributive patterns, (2) constitutionally enacted and morally universalistic ideals and principles that must bound and regulate 1, and (3) the "integrity" of a particular sphere that generates systemic tension via centrifugal momentum outward toward 1 and 2. Schooling, for example, as the dominant institutionalization of the educational sphere, must answer politically to those representing spherical interests such as business, politics, civil and criminal law, the family, and even athletics and public health (1). Yet it also must answer to the universalistic norms represented in constitutional law (e.g., civil rights and desegregation, disability statutes, compulsory schooling requirements) (2), 2 as well as satisfy norms, virtues, procedures, etc., that are unique to the educational sphere itself (3). These often-suppressed latter demands are experienced by educators as claims on them *as educators,* as opposed to the obligations they may feel as parents, neighbors, employees, citizens, and so on.

Properly contextualized, the political justification of educational institutions—the main instances of which are state-provisioned and/or regulated systems of public and private schooling—is therefore triply complex: Schools in pluralistic constitutional democracies must serve (1) universalistic ideals such as individual liberty and social equality, (2) the particularistic goods that are socially recognized as valid, and also (3) their own sense of pursuing a uniquely *educational* mission. Democracy seems to stretch schooling in impossibly many directions. Amid this push and pull of external forces, it would seem difficult for schooling to remain intact, let alone in any sense autonomous. Hence my guiding questions: Can schools in a pluralistic democracy be so many things to so many different constituencies while also standing for something themselves? Are they more than merely the sum of the demands made on them? And, ultimately, does democracy possess the moral capaciousness to accommodate its educational institutions with what one might think of as an institutional dignity?[3] Or, to put it in yet another way, can democracy allow itself to be served without servility?

Non-instrumentalism, Instrumentalism and Beyond

It is tempting to frame these questions in familiar traditional terms having to do with education's instrumentality or noninstrumentality. Partisans of the latter, for example, Michael Oakeshott and his conception of liberal higher education as an "interval" apart from its economic, political, or even moral use-value, partake of what R. S. Peters calls the "non-instrumental attitude," the perennial (though usually politically weak) cry of "education for itself."[4] Also exemplary in this regard among twentieth-century thinkers is Hannah Arendt who, in a widely cited essay, holds that education should not be regarded as a means toward political ends, however democratic or otherwise well-intended the reigning politics might be.[5] Less comprehensively and couched in more developmental terms, there persists a strong strain of this sort of thinking—from Rousseauian Romanticism onward to Deweyan progressivism—that cautions educators not to view childhood as merely preparatory to adulthood. There is something inherently valuable in childhood and so the educators who occupy so much of that time should never think of their enterprise as exclusively justified in terms of some future state of affairs, however bountiful the promised pedagogical harvest. As an explicit theoretical position, this noninstrumental voice is, it seems to me, mostly lost among contemporary educational theorists, though Peters's "attitude" still significantly (though not necessarily directly) informs, among others, the work of Nel Noddings on education and caring, Matthew Lipman on philosophy and children, and Nicholas Burbules's description of education as dialogue.[6] Despite their differences, common to all such views is a conviction that there is something to education that is not reducible to its serviceability to allegedly higher aims such as politics (even of the democratic variety), economics, or cultural identity.

Given the understandable centrality of social justice and democracy to many contemporary philosophers of education, noninstrumental conceptions are usually held to be overly aloof, if not elitist and therefore complicit in perpetuating societal inequalities. The aristocratic pedigree of many noninstrumental conceptions such as the classical Greek paideia or the Renaissance courtier ideal only heightens this suspicion.[7] So instrumental conceptions of education, from their less to more subtle versions, are the order of the day. Today, the most widespread instrumental view is also arguably the crudest: a vulgar economism that holds schools accountable for the value they add to production, consumption and market exchange. Education is to be supported because it helps "us" compete, both nationally in the global marketplace and as individuals seeking credentials, skills, and jobs. The rhetoric of "excellence," "quality," "efficiency," and the like are the watchwords of this influential view that marks the deepening colonization of all levels of the educational sphere by the sphere of business.[8] Either long or shortsighted, the economic bottom line, increasingly and in myriad subtle and unsubtle ways, dictates the terms of debate in education and all other spheres.

There persist other powerful instrumentalizers of education, though. One of these utilizes education toward goals of national or cultural identity creation and preservation. This stance has a long history, of course, beginning especially with the early modern period of nation-state formation[9] and continuing under guises such as ethnic assimilationism, racial segregation, anticommunism, and exclusionist policies in such areas as public services and the language of instruction. Sometimes these nationalist-patriotic projects have served liberal goals that have expanded public commitments to previously excluded individuals and sometimes they have been associated with nativist policies of exclusion. (In the U.S., the very birth and extension of compulsory schooling for all—the common school ideal—is exemplary of this ambivalence. A great deal of the support for it, along with its Jeffersonian civic and cold-eyed economic rationales,[10] was the patriotic sense that all *Americans* ought to have it. Simultaneously, this very expansiveness constituted a powerful push to exclude non-Protestant forms of religious affiliation—a momentum only halted in the 1920s by the recognition of a constitutional right to private schooling in the *Pierce* compromise.[11]) Whichever of these it has been, though, the nation-building and, most spectacularly, the indigenous and overseas colonizing uses of schooling are an integral part of the ancient and continuing story of the instrumentalization of education.

Hegemonic power is of course not the only puller of the national or cultural identity educational levers. Nonhegemonic groups, usually because they perceive themselves to be threatened in varying degrees—from Middle Eastern Kurds to African Americans to Francophone Quebecois to countless others—have sought and still seek to use schools to advance their particular cultural identities.[12] Needless to say, though, to lump together all of these varieties of education-as-cultural identity formation, particularly those advancing their agendas from positions of privilege and those clearly at the oppressed end of the spectrum, is not to establish any kind of moral equivalence among them. I simply mean to illustrate the power and near inexhaustible variety of instrumentalist conceptions.

There are of course religious conceptions, perhaps the most historically significant cases of assigning a higher purpose to school. For most of Western history, "religious education" was almost a tautology, from monastery to church and charity school to the Jewish *cheder*-schools of the shtetl and ghetto. In each case, from children's Bible stories to the most intricate theological and Talmudic disputation, like everything else in this world, education is conceived as an instrument of the divine, a gateway toward salvation, a practice of devotion (or, in excess, a Faustian temptation toward pride and other sins).[13] In addition to the religious view, there have been still many more influential instrumentalizing views, almost a catalog of all the views and philosophies of education that have ever been. There are those who link education to the advancement of science and technology for *their* own sakes, aestheticizing philosophies that link education's primary purpose with the creation of great art or great individuals, psychological theories associated with schooling's role in promoting mental health and hygiene, biological, if not eugenicist, theories seeing schooling as a force for purifying the gene pool or as an arena of Darwinian struggle. The list is as endless as there are philosophies in the grand sense.

Still another extremely influential instrumentalization, especially enduring among academics, is what one might call the political conception. This view is doubly interesting in that so many of its partisans understand themselves by advancing it to be fighting the narrowness of the economistic, cultural identity, or religious picture. Here education is seen as a distinctly political instrument, and therefore as radically regime-dependent. Notable among these are the adherents of many Marx-inspired views, the crudest among them positing schools simply as sites for disseminating or reproducing the correct ideology. More subtle but cut of the same cloth are educators who see the ultimate goal of their teaching as the raising of their students' political consciousnesses (usually construed as educating students "up" out of false consciousness to, presumably, the educator's own superior consciousness). Subtler still would be pedagogical views like those of Antonio Gramsci, who famously defends a counterintuitive coupling of a rather old-fashioned traditional pedagogy with politically revolutionary politics.[14] But it is not just the old-style left that has such designs for schooling. Any "political fundamentalist" holds by self-sanctioned definition a trump that subordinates education to pre-approved political ends. Certain fascists, conservatives, environmentalists, feminists, localists, multiculturalists, even some self-contradictory anarchists and libertarians all want schools to instill the political convictions and/or "virtues" they take to be necessary for the preservation, extension, or advent of their chosen political worldview. Sorting out one's politics is the royal road to the reform and reordering of all the social spheres, especially those so "obviously" subordinate such as education.

Despite the lip service they often pay to the noninstrumental conception, most prominent civic republicans, strong or "participatory" democrats, as well as many more classically liberal thinkers fall into this politics-as-fundamental category as well.[15] Among the more straightforwardly comprehensive liberals, for example, Gutmann forthrightly declares herself to be an educational "relativist" owing to her assumption that any system of schooling must always be relative to a society's regnant regime.[16] But the level of self-awareness on this point that Gutmann displays is rare. I would venture that most liberals, in fact, actually see themselves as noninstrumentalists, upholding civic ideals of equality, humanity, freedom, and so on against what they take to be cruder instrumentalisms like those mentioned previously, such as economism, religious fanaticism, and the allegiance to nationalistic or subaltern identity politics. Liberals tend to see their Kantian commitment to humanity as ex hypothesi placing them outside the instrumentalist camp. Nonetheless, when they do venture school plans, they champion particular pedagogical goals that are the result of deliberate and nonneutral choices; no matter how humane, open hearted, great souled and tolerant, what these kinds of liberals require of their schools is still radically dependent upon what they require of their politics. Figuring out what schools should do is in principle as simple as it is for any other form of instrumentalism: ascertain what we need for political life—competencies, literacies, virtues, and so forth—and then harness the schools to plow toward the externally-set goals. Such accounts are diverse only insofar as their chosen civic requirements differ; yet they are uniform in their allied assertion of the political sphere as the ultimate ground of educational authority and their consequent reluctance to cede education the degree of autonomy traditionally granted, for a variety of political, historical, and pragmatic reasons, to spheres such as religion, law, medicine, and basic science.

Whatever the appeal of the better versions of instrumentalism and noninstrumentalism, I describe them only as preparation for discarding them both. The either-or they represent is a false dilemma that debilitates contemporary liberalism's ability to manage coherently the institutional pluralism that complex societies require. In this sense, it is important for practical and moral reasons to appreciate just how dead are the ends in which either alternative terminates.

To elaborate, let me fine-tune the terminology. In a critique of Alasdair MacIntyre, David Miller suggests a distinction between what he identifies as "purposive" practices (which corresponds to instrumentalism as described above) and those that are "self-contained" (corresponding to noninstrumentalism).[17] (For his part, though he differs substantially from Miller on other germane matters, MacIntyre in response implicitly accepts this basic distinction.[18]) At issue is the moral and political status of the two kinds of practices, namely, those that are self-contained and valued from the "inside" by practitioners and those that are purposive and valued from the "outside" by nonpractitioners and practitioners alike. An activity, say, chess, generates internal goods that are only meaningful within the context of the history, traditions, rules, and so on, of the game of chess. This is true apart from any external utility chess may serve, like the money Bobby Fischer may make from it or the national self-esteem it procures for Russians. That one can easily imagine chess apart from fame, fortune and nationality suggests that the practice of chess is relatively self-contained.

On the other hand, there seem to be inescapably purposive practices that cannot truly be understood in isolation from the external goods they generate. Clear examples would include agriculture and medicine, where the generation of external goods is necessary to the meaning of the practice itself. In what sense could a physician be practicing medicine if the patients always got worse owing to her efforts? Only trivially would one be farming if one's crops were perpetually so horrid as to be unusable by anyone. Such practices would be eviscerated due to their failure to generate the requisite external goods. In extreme cases, they might even become hopelessly deformed via a sort of spherical involution, where practitioners become overly immersed in purely internal imperatives that occlude the just-as-necessary externalities.[19] For Miller this can and does happen. In medicine, for example, the artistry of rare and spectacular surgical procedures might actually become deleterious to a patient's—and patients' in general—long-term best interests. I will risk the suggestion that an additional, directly educational, example is commonly found among certain segments of the humanities faculties of U.S. research universities, where devotion to increasingly inbred forms of scholarship proportionately inhibits the achievement of externalities long popularly associated with the humanities: inspiring students through teaching, cultivating public aesthetic taste, and so forth. One might speak of both as cases of *internal* institutional corruptions.

Such corruptions come in many forms, though. As he reminds Miller during the exchange from which I am drawing, MacIntyre, in *After Virtue*, had previously outlined a more external form of corruption. For MacIntyre, this is, in fact, the most common form of institutional corruption in our increasingly money-driven society.[20] Here, intra- and inter-spherical interactions are no longer motored by the realization of internal goods (which may become the dimmest of memories) but rather by the satisfaction of ascendant externalities, creating a sort of Weberian iron cage where erstwhile means effect a master-slave reversal to become ends in themselves. Contemporary medicine (unfortunately an irresistibly fertile field for these examples) would for many count as corrupt in this sense. In the United States, Health Maintenance Organizations (HMOs), once envisioned as a judicious way to provision care equitably and efficiently, have now pretty clearly become ends in themselves. Once a relatively unobtrusive servant of medical practitioners, health insurers have now become masters in the medical sphere, issuing bottom line and hence alien directives to physicians. Through them, the business sphere has more conclusively "taken over." For MacIntyre, this master-slave reversal signifies the external corruption and degeneration of a once-sovereign (or at least relatively so) sphere, an event that is regrettable to the extent that the internal goods at the core of the sphere remain valued.

Beyond a certain point, however, and *pace* both Miller and MacIntyre, it is difficult to sustain the self-contained-purposive distinction. The exigencies of schooling in a democracy, I will argue, illuminate this extremely well. For despite the relative popularity of dichotomous either-or instrumental-purposive conceptions, the category to which schools belong seems undecidable. Are they self-contained or purposive? Instrumental or noninstrumental? The choice is forced. Clearly, schools fit into both categories at once, both as a sociological fact and as a matter of normative and conceptual coherence.

Despite their disagreements on other pertinent matters, in this instance Miller and MacIntyre both erroneously assume the false dilemma that social spheres must be *either* self-contained *or* purposive. This rules out the possibility of Walzerian relative autonomy,[21] that is, the idea that spheres might have both internal and external momentum simultaneously as, indeed, a great many of them surely do. Spheres may vouchsafe something of their own, retain a distinct identity, administer distributive arrangements pertaining to "their" good, and so on. But right alongside this, they may also maintain a network of relationships with other spheres and work to ensure their own consistency with society-wide and, in the case of a democracy, universalistic constitutional principles.

Democratic schools are certainly like this. While maintaining—albeit imperfectly at times—a sense of themselves as distinct from, say, banks, strip malls, hospitals, prisons, and so forth, schools are also quite useful to the spherical interests embodied in those neighboring institutions. Though they are not strip malls or banks, they are extremely useful to the sphere of business and markets. Though they are not hospitals or prisons, they serve as useful sites for the promotion of public heath and the prevention of criminality. Though they are not exactly public squares or legislative assemblies, they are eminently useful for producing the citizens needed by the democratic political sphere (or, *mutatis mutandis*, individuals with the characteristics required by whatever regime). As indicated previously, the list of uses to which external spheres may or may not try to put schools seems inexhaustible. But the mere existence of all these purposive elements does not entail that the school system in any given case necessarily lacks self-containing qualities. Nothing could be further from the truth. For in a healthy spherically pluralistic democracy, this is precisely what we ought to require of our schools, namely, that they pull of this balancing act of managing their usefulness to other spheres while maintaining some sense of themselves, some consistency and integrity as *educational* institutions. They must serve other spheres; political, fiscal, moral, aesthetic, and other spherically instantiated human interests form a legitimate response set for a pluralized form of educational accountability. Still, however, education cannot be *reduced* to these loci of accountability or their sum. This would kill the goose that lays the golden eggs by robbing it of its reproductive organs, that is, of the structuration of goods internal to the practice that enables it to do what it does in the first place. Without that internal distinctiveness, education becomes merely politics, markets, religion, and so on by other means.[22] So, at least for large and complex spheres like education, the purposive/self-contained and, by extension, the instrumental/noninstrumental distinctions appear misleading, if not spurious altogether.

Attempting, in the Deweyan manner, to bring to light and remove a false opposition like this usually reveals some unjustifiable metaphysical *eminence grise* as the culprit. In the present context, I would lay much of the blame on an unexamined Aristotelian teleological conception of spherical justification where there is assumed some overarching, telic conception of the human Good to which all social spheres must demonstrate their relatedness. Or, alternatively, a sort of anarchy of the good in which each sphere is understandable only on its own terms and so intercourse with any other sphere can only be understood as a corruption. In either case, there is a conception of the Good or Goods as being written into the fabric of the universe and as such impervious to interactions among sublunary human beings. In such a picture, justification is tethered to one big metaphysical entity or to several smaller ones. It is, in a word, a foundationalist account. It provides the major premise, ultimate grounding, sine qua non, etc. for any attempt to justify the place of a social sphere. The sphere is either to be valued because of its proximity or indispensability to the Good or it is a stand alone good in and of itself whose justification needs no exterior supports. But unless one is prepared for the leap of faith needed to posit an underlying metaphysical substratum (monotheistic or polytheistic), one is left unsatisfied.

As a result, one is left wondering about the project of justification itself. If there is no solid and self-supporting foundation for our attempts to justify the social spheres and their goods, perhaps there is no sense in chasing after justification at all. Maybe the concern to justify a social sphere is itself a metaphysical anachronism, the vestige of an age prepared to grant legitimacy to its own foundations via an unconditional faith.

EDUCATIONAL AUTONOMY IN CONTEXT

It seems to me, however, that giving up the task altogether would be an overreaction, not unlike the excessively nihilistic rebound against theology that Nietzsche expected and ultimately feared.[23] For, as I will use the remainder of this chapter to suggest, there is an alternative, more pragmatic way of giving form to institutional justification that keeps the implausible metaphysics to a minimum. Proceeding from the reasonable pluralism assumption outlined above, there is an indeterminate number of socially valued goods around which coalesces a correspondingly indeterminate number of social spheres and institutions.[24] Although democracy appeals to universalistic norms such as equality to bound and "discipline" the extent of its endogenous and exogenous spherical diversity (this is the "reasonable" part of reasonable pluralism), the commitment to pluralism means that there can be presented no overarching Good capable of carrying by itself all of the hydra-headed justificatory weight. (The Rawlsian notion of "overlapping consensus," while having many practical merits in the context of intercultural disagreement, is, as a justificatory story about liberal institutions, ultimately only as strong as are the groundings for each of the consensus's individual points of agreement.[25] For example, one could imagine overlapping areas of consensus among different but equally monstrous parties.) Justification therefore cannot succeed if it is conceived foundationally, that is, as the unilinear project of establishing convincing entailments between source and social sphere. Postmodernism has been salutary in at least this respect: neither God nor Nature nor Man nor any other metanarrative suffices to ground all the social spheres because we now lack the requisite faith in them. "Whither is God?" cries Nietzsche's madman, "I will tell you. *We have killed him*—you and I."[26] So there is no convincing appeal to a Platonic, comprehensively-radiating Good or to any other imagined self-supporting basis on which a particular sphere might rest. Both the instrumental and noninstrumental extremes of "Education for God or Humanity" or "Education for itself" are equally problematic in this regard. What is left, then? Nothing solid, it seems, but the pluralism itself. In other words, there is nowhere for justification to turn but to the array of socially constructed goods and practices themselves—to the very *variety* of them.

In many respects, this only seems to compound the problem. And indeed it does. But, on my view, compounding the problem is precisely the proper approach. Those concerned to protect the identity, integrity, and autonomy of a sphere should not look to the Good above or the Good within, but should look to the very instrumentalities that the sphere generates and from which it has become inextricable. For this is how any spherical autonomy at all must arise: through a criss-crossing of lines of instrumentality that connect a sphere, via relations of use-value, to a range of similarly ensconced and similarly useful spheres. The justification of spherical autonomy should be reconceived accordingly. A sphere has standing to speak for itself when it is useful to enough other spheres such that each have their own agendas and so "tug" against the sphere in question from enough competing directions. If both my arms are pulled in opposite directions I will be able to stand much steadier than if only one of my arms is being pulled. A left arm tug jerks me to the left. A right arm tug jerks me to the right. If they are properly calibrated (and, obviously, not *too* strong!), though, both tugs simultaneously leave me standing relatively still. Following this logic, better yet would be a multiplicity of forces pushing and pulling me in so many different directions that, in effect, they—or at least a large enough proportion of them—cancel one another out, not unlike the pushes and pulls of various natural forces that allow molecular, atomic, and subatomic particles to attain that most basic of physical equilibriums. If there are enough of these mutually canceling forces and they are positioned properly, there arises a kind of autonomy—relative autonomy—wherein it is possible to imagine a kind of self-standing freedom that is not obviously dependent on any metaphysical buoy.

With regard to social spheres and their interrelations, I would suggest as highly appropriate a metaphor of nesting. One might call it justificatory nesting. Allow me to mix in a few additional metaphors to develop the idea. The social map would look somewhat like a vastly more complicated and dimensioned road atlas.[27] The various relatively autonomous social spheres would look like major city hubs, extremely brachiated and otherwise complex networks of use-value whose strands connect to other extremely complicated hubs that are similarly constituted. Some of these hubs will be so large with connecting use-value strands that they will look like nests, the connecting strands having achieved a certain density that would itself represent a proportionate amount of relative stability or, again, in that sense, relative autonomy. Any society with any complexity and history at all will contain a significant number of these spherical nests, of varying degrees of size and stability. The resulting constellation of them will describe something very basic about the society itself and its priorities. Under totalitarianism, the connecting threads will look neat, coercively "combed," as the lines of justification will tend to be straight and ever-straightening one way or another in the direction of the all-encompassing spherical Good or Goods. One finds a striking historical example in the Nazi ambition toward *Gleichschaltung*, where all social institutions were to have been aligned with the Single "Good" as declared in Party ideology. Here institutional justification is more or less unilinear, a relatively simple matter of showing how X, Y, or Z sphere promotes the officially sanctioned One True Good. By contrast, a healthy pluralistic society will be much harder for anyone in authority to comb. It will abound in kinks and snags of various sizes and kinds as it will proliferate and foster as many justificatory nests (i.e., relatively autonomous social spheres) as possible. Spheres will seek to maximize and multiply their usefulness across a sufficient range of other spheres, thereby attaining a relative autonomy that does not allow any single external sphere too much control over its own internal affairs. Spheres would thus be able to construct themselves to the extent that they are useful in the constructions of others; "nested" spheres would be those that achieve this multifaceted usefulness. As in the moral-existential paradox common across the major world religions, in serving others they find *themselves*.

This account provides an attractive basis for considering how schooling for all might be justified under conditions of pluralism. It is also a great deal less cynical than some of the competing pictures, for example, those who view the development of public schooling solely through the jaundiced eyes of a social class reproductionist view, or the even more jaundiced eyes of human capital theory. It is admittedly no coincidence that public schooling and its permutations coincide with a certain stage of capitalist accumulation and production. But this does not tell the whole story. Schooling was and is certainly useful to the capitalists and to economic agendas of various kinds, but the counterweight to this powerful force is that schooling is also useful to democratizing, aesthetic, nationalistic, scientific, and other agendas whose internal goods are not reducible to economics. To deny this claim is to embrace the indefensibly reductionist Althusserian thesis that everyone engaged in whatever sphere is fooling themselves in their "false consciousness" not to realize that the High Truth of their activity is to be found only in understanding its place in the relations of production. While there are these places and Marxist functionalism helps us see them more clearly, it does not follow that the relations of production should automatically—metaphysically—receive all the explanatory honors. Education's very usefulness to these often-competing spherical titans grants it a certain autonomy that has not often enough been appreciated, let alone seized on and exploited by those "within" the educational sphere.

Less appreciated still has been how to carve out more autonomy where and when it is needed. As a strategic matter, the momentum should always be outward, a restless figuring out of how best to serve spherical constituents old and new. On the schematic I am advancing, spherical death is most likely facilitated by an excessively defensive set of mind, perhaps a fearful reaction to the encroaching dominion of a particular sphere. (Throughout most of Western and probably world history, such spherical imperialisms emanated mostly from religion and from the state, whereas today's successor spherical tyrants seem to be business and, especially in complex constitutional democracies, law.) Instead of forging mutualistic alliances and seeking to multiply use-values to potential counterweights (e.g., embracing a civic agenda pleasing to politicians or a technoscientific agenda pleasing to nationalists, as in the anticommunism of the Sputnik era, and using these agendas as fulcra against the vocationalist onslaught of big business), educators have all-too-often simply imploded into an anachronistic nostalgia where education was once upon a time supposedly valued for itself[28] or, at the other and more common extreme, collapsed into an abject sell-out to the hegemonic spherical interests of the day.[29] If trying to foster a robust societal commitment to some meaningful sense of education as such is the goal (and this is certainly not everyone's goal), these strategies fail because they do not appreciate how that societal commitment—and the educational autonomy that will ensue—is purchased by multiplying spherical loci of instrumentality rather than severing them or, equally disastrous, strengthening one tie to the exclusion of all others. The former dooms one to a shrinking irrelevance while the latter subordinates the enterprise out of existence. Only a much more judiciously equilibrated dynamism can secure the necessary delicate balance. Following the title of David Tyack and Larry Cuban's history of U.S. educational reform, "tinkering" seems an apt verb, so long as the utopia toward which that tinkering aims appropriately balances education's external uses and internal needs.[30]

Two Objections Considered

One objection to the foregoing account of institutional autonomy is that it may appear to be excessively Machiavellian, in that the concern to multiply interspherical instrumentalities would commit educators to an agenda of underhandedness.[31] In a democracy seeking to provision and determine the nature of public schooling as fairly as possible, this kind of institutional strategy, if pursued in a certain way, might devolve into a distasteful realpolitik, where educational institutions gain relative autonomy via cynically covert interspherical "deals" behind closed doors and outside public scrutiny. To take matters further, such a posture might lead not to autonomy but, Trojan horse–like, may serve only to make more decisive the conquest of schooling by the business sphere. As sounds all too familiar these days, educators would be counseled to make themselves indispensable to the powers that be and, consequently, to strategize in terms of advertising, market share, consumer preference, and the like, in short, to behave much like a business corporation seeking to garner wealth and influence by convincing others to buy its products. Stated thus, the strategy of multiplying instrumentalities would seem a more apt description of the Dutch East India Company or Microsoft Corporation's rise to power (or of the accumulation of capital itself) than it would point toward a morally defensible strategy for educational autonomy. While many free marketeers on the educational policy scene would forthrightly argue that education should indeed make itself over along business lines and so would be unbothered by this objection, the perspective of spherical pluralism needs to take it seriously. Given the current context, where the economic sphere appears to be by far the greatest threat to spherical heterogeneity, any move that would so decisively aid in the business takeover of so central a sphere as education is to be strongly resisted. So there are two objections, really. The first is a matter of democratic principle, the second a matter of intraspherical integrity: (1) The realpolitik of interspherical ingratiation may be inconsistent with the principled openness required by the democratic procedures that must govern interspherical interactions (2) For reasons indicated above, a strategy of multiplying instrumentalities might actually erode educational autonomy rather than build it.

By way of response, beginning with the first objection, there is often a fine line between what one might call political maturity and political cynicism, crossings of which are greatly facilitated by the media-blitz nature of contemporary political processes. There is widespread acknowledgment, I think, that what one gets through the televised glare of political reportage and official pronouncements is some ways distant from what must *actually* be going on, behind the closed doors, through unofficial channels, in the inner circles of power, and so forth. One who earnestly believes everything politicians say (and that tell her the whole truth) is properly regarded as akin to a child a little too old still to believe in Santa Claus. Does such skepticism represent a welcome maturity or a regrettable cynicism? I suspect it reflects a little of both. And so it would be with my imagined interspherical instrumentalities. As those pursuing relative autonomy negotiate the variegated social topography of complex societies, there will inevitably be trade-offs, compromises, long- and short-term strategic concessions, hard choices, even intractable, perhaps even tragic moral dilemmas. This, after all, is why the operative phrase qualifies "autonomy" with the word "relative." Like its British, Berlinian, cousin, Walzerian spherical pluralism does not aspire toward a world in which moral conflicts are necessarily solved or smoothed out. It revels in that Walzerian "art of separation" of different spheres from one another, following in a way Kant's characterization of the Enlightenment itself as at bottom the kind of maturity needed in order to appreciate the differing involvements and obligations accruing to our public and private selves.[32] As in many other areas of life, in such a pluralist environment of perpetual separations, political stewardship of the educational sphere would require a judicious mix of sphere-rooted idealism, political realism, and a host of more technical skills such as dialogical agility and intercultural adventurousness. A pluralist strategy for institutional autonomy would thus require the psychological and social maturity to tolerate the subsistence of differences within and among different spheres. It would correspondingly tend to discourage political purists with more pan-societally unifying ambitions, including so-called strong or participatory democrats whose highest good is universal political engagement.[33]

There is in addition a further and more substantive response to this first question. Along with the maturity and the ability to tolerate conflict and ambiguity, amid all the negotiating, the compromising, the dialogue, and the realism, there must also exist in sufficient quantity a simple and strong sincerity regarding the universalistically grounded public procedures that in a democracy must govern interspherical interactions. Here I will lean on the emerging school of "deliberative democracy" and its account of the nature of "publicity" requirements for political discourse concerning public policy, particularly in the work of Amy Gutmann and Dennis Thompson.[34] When debating, advancing, or implementing policies that significantly affect others, as do a large proportion of even intraspherical matters (particularly in a hub sphere like education), basic constitutional norms prohibit the backroom deals, the secrecy, except under very special and restricted conditions (for example, certain wartime military operations). Consider the case of a school official under pressure from the local business community to implement a school-business "partnership." The Walzerian perspective I am defending would certainly involve a presumptive suspicion against such a move as a familiar symptom of undue business influence on the educational sphere. However, it would be a clumsy application of a general rule and, in fact, as implied above, run counter to a mature consideration of social complexity to dismiss a priori all such collaboration. As posited in the Aristotelian virtue tradition, there is no rulebook for seeking educational autonomy; one hopes at best for the relevant exemplary person or persons of practical wisdom to be in the pivotal decision-making positions. Given all the variables involved in managing a school district, educators may, for example, see a series of long-term/short-term trade-offs that make the benefits of a given instance of business influence worth suffering a temporary and localized cession of direct authority. There may even be a bit of gamble involved, but one that is carefully judged to be worth taking by the educators on the ground. The devil—or the angel—will lie in the details of the proposed arrangement. The various tasks of discernment will be located neither in any disembodied universal bureaucracy nor in the invisible hand of the market nor, indeed, in the university researcher, but rather as firmly as possible within the relevant sphere and according to its own norms, traditions, standards of excellence, and so on.

But this does not mean there cannot be trans-spherical principles that bound and shape such decisions. Among the foremost of these will be a general policy of openness, as counseled in the deliberative framework regarding the publicity of the policy process, enjoining interspherical operators to consider decisions as openly as possible—to lay out their hands for all to see, as it were. (Though, as in the limited military exception to the general rule above, there will remain instances where even in the schooling context this rule may be laid aside ad hoc. Examples would include preparations for certain real estate negotiations, where complete transparency may enfeeble a public school district's deal making ability, or certain kinds of personnel deliberations that require confidentiality.) The imperative toward openness in the policy arena will stand as a key safeguard against the betrayal of both the public interest and also interests that are more peculiar to the educational sphere as such. At the very least, everyone involved, from the generalized public to partisans of particular spheres, will stand to be alerted as any matters potentially dear to them will reliably surface (or at least not be deliberately concealed).[35] As conflicted and strife-ridden as it may then be, the ensuing political activity will thus get off to a fairer start.

The second objection, the more internal concern about strategically multiplying ties of use-value to other spheres, is somewhat simpler. Here I will flatly appeal to an analog of the Churchillian aphorism about democracy being the worst form of government save all of the others. As I have argued, simultaneously valuing educational autonomy in particular along with spherical pluralism in general precludes both instrumentalism and noninstrumentalism from serving as moral or practical bases for institutional justification. The failure of either extreme suggests a middle passage of sorts. The pluralist view retains from instrumentalism a salutary pragmatism that places educational institutions alongside other institutions and otherwise situates them full-bloodedly within the context of human interests. Yet it also possesses the end-in-view closest to the heart of noninstrumentalism that there is something worthwhile and sustaining about education not reducible to its serviceability to any particular external interest. It is appropriately idealistic and realistic simultaneously.

While one may legitimately worry about a sphere potentially losing itself to extrinsic usefulness (or usefulness*es*), becoming corrupted by an excess of cynical machination and so on, in the broader context it may actually be salutary that this kind of corruption is always present as a possibility. For whether corruption is to be avoided in a given instance is *itself* a contextual matter; it depends on the relative worth of that which corrupts and that which is being corrupted. Mercy and compassion might "corrupt" in this way and nonetheless be welcome. In fact, it is probably desirable for the project of winning and maintaining relative institutional autonomy to possess a degree of instability, a subjectedness to a pack of simultaneous threats from many directions, lest a sphere become too autonomous, too incorruptible. Integrity should perhaps not come too cheaply. It is arguably overly easy in today's rapacious globalized marketplace for a CEO to be impeccably "responsible" to his or her profit margin or shareholders, even at the cost of incalculable human suffering. Perhaps there are worse fates than for CEOs to "sell out" from time to time to external interests such as education, health, and even beauty.

More generally, as the contextualist account of relative autonomy begins to show, for the institutions of a pluralistic liberalism, autonomy and dependence are locked together and inseparable. Institutional autonomy, currently threatened by the homogenizing forces of the market, is a precious achievement that must be self-consciously defended by those who value the endangered spheres and seek to sustain the cultural and personal capaciousness that in the ensemble those spheres enable. But this needed autonomy is only available as relative autonomy; as the truism has it, the only way out is through. As it has always recognized at its best, for democratic education, to serve and serve everyone is also to secure its own survival. And this is where the going gets tough. For claiming to serve others implies a promise actually to do so, to show that the promised serving is in fact taking place. Thus arises an entirely justifiable concern with accountability across the totality of legitimate interests in the polity as a whole. This means politics and like all politics it is a dirty business. Pure hearts beware.

Chapter Four

Accountability in Context

ACCOUNTABILITY AS SELECTIVE PREFERENCE SATISFACTION

Accountability is an inescapably value-laden notion, one that must have particular features as a regulatory component of a system of democratic education. In general, accountability, like "justice" or "equality," is something that responsible parties are all for, at least in the abstract, before a particular accountability regime is specified. Who could be against monitoring whether or not desired ends are being achieved? But we are strangely prone to forget the inherent normativity of accountability, that the ends to which it is hitched are socially desired ends rather than natural ends written somehow into the fabric of the cosmos. We prefer instead to treat accountability as if it were one with its attempted specifications: standardized test scores, parental satisfaction ratings, or the school's financial efficiency. Accountability thereby becomes a form of accounting.

This magic trick of quantification then allows for a "no nonsense" attention to be paid to the polling data, "adequate yearly progress" based on kids' reading and math test scores under The *No Child Left Behind Act* (NCLB), school "report cards," Standard and Poor's ratings, or whatever else might allow marking off a numerical threshold.[1] Above this threshold lie the accountable, the saved, and below it lie the unaccountable, the damned, their mutual fates then subject to whatever rewards and punishments the accountability regime has in store for them. Unsurprisingly, then, much of the discourse surrounding NCLB centers on the punishments to be meted out for falling below the enumerated testing thresholds. While NCLB is a very large law—a reauthorization of the omnibus *Elementary and Secondary Education Act* of the 1960s—where there is talk these days of "NCLB" it is sure to be talk of the accountability and accompanying enforcement mechanisms directed against schools not measuring up. While NCLB itself does not use the word "failure" or the phrase "failing schools" and instead relies on the more anodyne "needing improvement," everyone is clear that falling into this category puts one at the wrong end of the regulatory gun.

Yet it seems that even as the stakes rise and as more and more education policy discourse centers on accountability, the very idea of accountability gets more and more obscure. When the rhetorical and budgetary bludgeoning pauses, one wants to ask: Accountability *to whom,* exactly? The public? Which of "our" desires for our school system are being certified by the regnant accountability regime? And why these desires and not others? These are large and difficult questions, especially in a large and complex polity. But anyone wishing legitimately to employ the notion of accountability must give answering them a good and thorough try. Democracy demands this effort. If the people are really to rule, there must in most all cases be (save extreme and transient situations such as certain wartime emergencies) a certain justificatory transparency regarding key public policies. This transparency requires at minimum that those in positions of authority own up to and articulate the honest reasons behind X, Y, or Z policy.

As a general rule, with relatively few and unusual exceptions, democratic leaders should not hide from us the truth, or any significant part of it, when they act in "our" name, particularly when they are trying to publicly justify a policy. Consequently, among the rhetorical ploys ideally to be ruled out would be the kind of political manipulation where I try to sell you on an idea by deliberately appealing exclusively to one thing I know you want and excluding from your view considerations relevant to other things I know you also want. To get you to go along with my proposal for a post-9/11 security crackdown, I might play exclusively to your perhaps well-founded fears about terrorism while deliberately excluding from the discussion other things I know you care about, such as personal liberty or the equal treatment of persons. However commonplace in product advertizing campaigns, artificially narrowing the range of public deliberation in this manner is surely impermissible from a democratic point of view. We may indeed come to differing conclusions about how best to balance security with liberty or thorough safety measures with the avoidance of racial profiling. In a democracy, though, where the people are in some important sense presumed to rule, it is illegitimate to exclude a priori important desiderata that are in fact widely and deeply embraced as such. If as a public official I wanted very much to assure a draconian security crackdown, I would violate an important norm of democratic deliberation by deploying resources so as to play exclusively on everyone's fears while ignoring everyone's love of liberty and justice. This manipulative constriction of deliberation would constitute an antidemocratic form of demagoguery. As a matter of liberty, individuals can say what they want about a policy proposal, even it if means weighing in one-sidedly. But a public policy has democratic legitimacy in large part owing to the inclusiveness of the deliberative process leading up to its adoption, both in the straightforward distributive sense (was anyone excluded from participation?) and in the related sense of the deliberation including a reasonable range from among the *whole* of what citizens do in fact value. Everyone must be able formally to participate in the debate and the debate itself must not exclude reasonably widely shared values that are in fact held by the citizen-interlocutors. The totalitarian dictator who justifies the police state with, "You wanted security and so I gave it to you" is, by the selective honoring of this one preference, surely revealed for the enemy of democracy that he or she is. Though rhetorically useful to those desiring to get their way, *selective* preference satisfaction lacks democratic legitimacy. Robust deliberation may not exclude relevant ideas any more than it may people.

So why do we allow this patently undemocratic model of selective preference satisfaction to underwrite our public debate about something so crucial as the performance of our education system? It is, I think, intolerable that we do so. A defensible accountability scheme must include not just one or some of the things that "we the people" care about, but *all* of the things that collectively we care about, at least as far as all of those things can be considered under one accountability scheme. Raising the largest questions about educational accountability is thus a philosophical enterprise, because we have to take into account so many very different things if we want to ask how our education system is doing in an *overall* sense, rather than continuing to think that we have exhausted the accountability question by ascertaining how the system is doing with exclusive regard to X, Y, or Z thing that we or some particular interest group care about. Raised in the way it needs to be, democracy in this way throws us into the unsteady arms of philosophy, the arena where large and general questions are pursued at a sufficient level of abstraction. If we were simpletons or fanatics, there would be no need for this move. Fortunately, we do need it. As individuals and as "we the people," we are complex. For something so vast yet so close to heart as the education of our young, we want, inevitably, many, many things, not just one, two or three things. Any truly legitimate accountability scheme must encompass this variety.[2]

As I see it, then, these are the chief theoretical challenges for a defensibly democratic framework for educational accountability: (1) to keep at the forefront the inevitably moral nature of the very idea of accountability, and (2) to be able broadly to accommodate the wide range of values that are in play when we try to make an overall assessment of our education system. In contrast, much of today's accountability justified "standards" movement seems both amoral and narrow. As selective preference satisfaction, it at best attends to some things we care about—particularly those things that are amenable to quantitative measurement, such as basic literacy—but ignores others.

It stands to reason, though, that the best accountability scheme would take into account the whole range of what we value. But what might such a more encompassing alternative look like? Could there be a framework for educational accountability that is premised upon accountability's moral nature and also the diversity of our desiderata? I believe there could be. Though rightly seen as wildly impractical from the measurement point of view, such a framework would perhaps help us not to forget that a thing's measurability counts neither for nor against its legitimacy as an educational aim. Toward articulating such a framework, I will draw from the liberal contextualism developed thus far, a summary and extension of which follows below. On this basis I then describe an appropriately normative account of educational accountability.

LIBERAL CONTEXTUALISM AND DEMOCRATIC EDUCATION

As developed in previous chapters, a contextualist picture of schooling and social justice resists the reduction of educational value to any single good. It proceeds instead on a eudaimonistic assumption of value pluralism that there is no One Best Way to live a worthwhile human life. Contextualism recognizes value pluralism at both individual and societal levels. As an individual, I may care for family, music, and nature without any ready scheme for reducing any of these to any of the others. My social group (or groups) may contain a diversity of allegiances to particular conceptions of, say, wealth, sexuality, and the sacred. As a theory of social justice, contextualism holds that a good society will, overall and through its particular "spheres" and institutions, *do justice* to the many goods that are valued in such a society, and will do so in a way that accords with how those goods are actually valued (not necessarily how someone might say they *ought* to be valued, as against the relevant social understandings as they actually exist).³ Important areas of our individual and shared lives have their own logic and aims; what "works" in the world of commerce may not "work" in the world of science. The same applies for romance and art, politics and friendship, family and warfare, or whatever combination. From a contextualist standpoint, much of the work of social justice is to make sure that one sphere of life does not illicitly override or infiltrate other spheres. Contextualists wage such battles as keeping money apart from politics, politics from religion, religious identity apart from equal legal protection, and legalism from overtaking pedagogy.

The most obvious problem with contextualism as a guide to social justice, however, is that it seems overly reliant on social convention. If contextualism is pledged to maintain the integrity of the various social spheres (and because of this postures respectfully toward the traditions embodied in those spheres), it would seem to lose its ability to provide a critique of them at obvious points. For example, Susan Okin argues that sheltering one sphere of life, such as the family, from externalities that might otherwise impinge on it may win protection for the sphere, but at the cost of allowing patriarchal injustices to persist within it.⁴ Even worse, one cannot help but note how often racial inequality (even unto slavery and genocide) has been justified by an appeal to "*our* way of life," American, English, German, Serbian, Hindu, and so on. One who worries about such problems must therefore qualify contextualism with an appeal to trans-spherical norms that constrain and discipline certain kinds of injustices wherever in the sociocultural topography they may appear. My own variant of contextualism, liberal contextualism, attempts to do this by emphasizing the fate of individuals, as opposed to practices, religions, subcultures, or traditions as such. It thereby brings to the fore classically liberal ideals of individual liberty and equality, such as those manifest in the constitutions of liberal democratic states and certain international organizations like the United Nations. So liberal contextualism, while admitting of significant variation, represents a moral compromise between universalizing liberal ideals growing from root commitments to liberty and equality and the diversity of social spheres where human beings manufacture their most enduring meanings.

In the famous terms of Isaiah Berlin, a liberal contextualist account of schooling is committed both to negative and positive freedom.⁵ It must adhere to classically liberal human rights of suffrage, speech, conscience, equal protection, due process, and so forth, while also sheltering, perhaps even nurturing, the social spheres wherein positive freedom is enacted—those aspects of our lives that are, though interrelated, not normally reducible to one another: religion, art, commerce, science, politics, romance, sport, ad infinitum. The ambitions of liberal contextualist schools, then, are high, as they aim to help create human beings committed to freedom and equality for all, and who are, *in fact*, pursuing happiness. On the current scene, the freedom-and-equality educational goals are most notably championed in theories of democratic education that feature citizenship, some of the most subtle being those of Amy Gutmann, Eamonn Callan, and Stephen Macedo.[6] Yet liberal contextualism differs from such citizenship-centric theories in that it takes more seriously the "pursuit of happiness" part of the equation, avoiding the assumption that the universal ideals have universal priority. In an adaptation of Kant's famous epistemological dictum that "thoughts without content are empty, intuitions without concepts are blind," a liberal contextualist holds that liberty and equality without meaning is inhumanly empty, meaning without liberty and equality is inhumanly blind.[7]

This is part of what it means to say that contextualism is eudaimonistic, because it holds that, on the whole, life will be richer where social spheres are able to maintain their distinctiveness (more on this in chapter 7). One implication is that contextualists are inclined to worry about homogenization of *whatever* type, instances in which one sphere of life and its characteristic aspects come to dominate other spheres. Whereas in previous eras contextualists would worry about religious or political dominance (the earlier-mentioned Nazi policy of *Gleichschaltung*, or "alignment" of all societal institutions providing a nightmare example), today's contextualists are more likely to worry about the commercial or juridical domination of spheres of life, including education. For liberal contextualism, democratic education at its best manifests a kind of harmony between, on the one hand, a universalizing morality of schooling for all individuals (regardless of race, gender, class, disability, etc.) and, on the other hand, the particular involvements through which those same individuals make for themselves lives they are able to find meaningful. This requires an integration of the commitment to the trans-spherical, universalizing norms of liberalism with the recognition of the equally indispensable particular social spheres with traditions, norms and symbolic ecologies of their own. Broadly conceived, this eudaimonistic integration—a kind of harmony, perhaps—is reminiscent of Walzer's complex equality, as discussed in previous chapters. It is a moral vision of bounded heterogeneity. A contextualist picture of accountability thus faces a severe challenge. Not only must it raise as its standard "the moral" against an amorally reductionistic accountability status quo, but it must also recognize the heterogeneity of that standard. Little would be gained by merely reinscribing a new monomania to replace the old one.

LIBERAL CONTEXTUALISM'S
THREE REALMS OF ACCOUNTABILITY

Consistent with the foregoing, a cardinal contextualist assumption is that the Good to which democratic education should be held accountable is morally composite. This assumption prohibits any simple reductionist or foundationalist account, that is, one where the education system would ultimately be normed according to one overarching good, however widely hailed (examples of popular candidates would include "moral virtue," "autonomy," "equal participation," "economic productivity," "culturedness," "salvation," and "understanding"). Tying education's value to any one good runs afoul of the assumption of edaimonistic pluralism by effectively denying the diversity of human moral and symbolic life which, *ex hypothesi,* democratic education must positively acknowledge. Yet, partially because of the pluralism itself (that is, the concern to preserve the pluralism against the perpetual threats from homogenizing forces), and also because of the set of commitments to individual equality and freedom required by liberal democracy, the eudaimonism must be reigned in, to a large extent in some instances, in order to find a balance with which "we the people" can live. Any number of specific settlements would be acceptable in this regard. Liberal theorists, I think, often go too far in trying to deduce, as if from the principles of first philosophy, the correct "answer" to particular policy disputes. Defensibly liberal regimes may come down on different sides of some of recent years' marquee policy conflicts along these lines in education policy: *"l'affaire du foulard islamique"* in France, the *Mozert* and creationism federal court cases in the United States, the religious and spiritual curricula in the U.K., various nations' experiments with school choice, and the like. What I am after is more general, namely, the basic *kinds* of considerations that any set of such settlements should satisfy, what the moral shape should be of any system of democratic education, an outline of the desiderata which any educational accountability scheme must serve.

This moral shape, I contend, should have three basic contours, or realms of accountability, as I shall call them.[8] I propose a liberal contextualist categorization of these realms of accountability according to the following scheme: a tripartite division composed of moral attention to realms of Right, Association, and Meaning. Alongside other keystone democratic institutions, democratic school systems are beholden to each of these realms. In the order of the above list, they shade, qua obligations, from thinner to thicker, negative freedom to positive freedom, universalistic to particularistic, globalized to localized, liberal to non- or extraliberal, and explicitly political to less political (in the sense of being within the direct power and competence of governmental authorities). Refracted through received genera of Western moral philosophy, the realm of right tends toward a deontological articulation, association toward a utilitarian account, and meaning toward a virtue-oriented elaboration. Let me elaborate on these all-important realms, the basic elements of a defensibly democratic picture of accountability.

Right

Herein lies the liberal part of liberal contextualism. At the global level this is a concern for fundamental human rights that accrue to every human being without qualification by nationality, citizenship status, race, gender, religion, and so on. An emblematic document here is the United Nations "Universal Declaration of Human Rights (1948)," whose Preamble recognizes "the inherent dignity" and "the equal and inalienable rights of all members of the human family."[9] One also sees important variations on this theme in certain national constitutions, notable historical examples being the French Revolution's *Le Déclaration des Droits de l'Homme et du Citoyen* (1789) and the U.S. Constitution's Bill of Rights (1791). There are of course a great many of these national constitutional statements of basic rights, and they are usually quite terse, at least, certainly, relative to their judicially elaborated application (i.e., the body of constitutional law) and their national legal code as a whole. The realm of right comprises the set of basic obligations that we owe one another as human beings, no matter how near or far away we may be from one another geographically, ideologically, physiognomically, and so forth. Liberals of various stripes will of course disagree about the details (e.g., the precise circumstances under which a human rights violation obligates a response, the question of intervention), but by definition no liberal will say that there is no such universalistic moral substratum. Failure to recognize all human beings as inside the morally charmed circle of humanness or failure to extend *some* relatively substantial (in world historical terms) rights-oriented substratum to all human beings automatically disqualifies one from being a liberal. Liberal philosophers certainly debate the nature and extent of rights, but even if they find that they are "artificial" (to use David Hume's term) and/or hardly sufficient by themselves for a defensible political life, they will not ipso facto cease to defend some version of them. In whatever packaging they come, for liberalism these are moral givens.

The realm of right should, I think, be understood as occupying something of a moral middle ground between, on the one hand, even thinner norms often considered appropriate vis-à-vis nonhumans such as the preservation of nature, humane treatment, and noncruelty to animals and, on the other hand, the thicker norms that one begins to see as one approaches most national legal codes, which, qua intranational and intraconstitutional, end up having much more to do with the realm of association (as discussed a few pages hence). However desirable it may be to adopt them (along with many other liberals, I myself would endorse versions of them), the even thinner norms that apply to nature and nonhuman animals are, I believe, currently not accurately described as being necessary components of liberalism. Generally speaking, radical environmentalism and moral concern for nonhuman animals lie outside liberalism, at times as antagonists (e.g., radical nonanthropocentrists who welcome epidemic disease as population and hence environmental damage control) and sometimes as supplementary (e.g., those who argue that there are circumstances where human beings should limit economic development to preserve an endangered species for the sake of science and aesthetic enrichment). I am convinced by Franz de Waal[10] and other "cultural" primatologists that chimpanzees and other apes indeed have their politics, and that this gets them pretty close to human political concern (as they are close to us physiologically), but still they are not human beings and they are therefore not directly spoken for in liberalism, which is a political philosophy (a statement that does not touch the question of whether it has metaphysical elements or not).[11] It may be right to say that a bald eagle has dignity, is worthy of respect, that it should have freedom, and so on, but saying so takes one beyond (anthropocentric) liberalism.

Especially important for my present thesis is the quasiparadoxical nature of the liberal ideals of equality and liberty characteristic of the realm of right. The near paradox is that, curiously, these universalizing ideals somehow seem most palpable and most visible in their *absence*. Freedom and equality are most clearly defined in their denial; they are, I think, at their purest essentially negative phenomena. To study the history of freedom is to study its denial and the overcoming of that denial. Could one imagine a (Western) liberal account of the development of freedom without coverage of such matters as the persecution of religious minorities in Europe or the American civil rights movement, where the *denial of the denials* lent greater substance, respectively, to norms of toleration and equal legal protection? As Stuart Hampshire elegantly summarizes:

> The essence of a liberal morality is the rejection of any final and exclusive authority, natural or supernatural, and of the accompanying compulsion and censorship. In this context, freedom itself is felt, and is cherished, as a negative notion: no walls of dogma, no unquestionable rules from priests and politicians; the future is to be an open field for discovery. Openness is a negative concept, appropriately therefore an indeterminate concept. The liberal's adversary is disgusted, or made nervous, by this negativity, by the openness and emptiness, by the looseness of undirected living. The ensuing conflict is stark and often bitter.[12]

I take as corroborative evidence of the nature of this "negative concept" the commonly observed phenomena where those who appear most deeply to *feel* their political equality and freedom are those who have experienced its denial, whereas those who have not truly experienced this may take it for granted and assume it as "natural."[13] These are lessons learned less well, I think, from philosophical treatises than from battered wives, refugees, political prisoners, slaves, and survivors of genocidal regimes. The great hope of human rights requires such persons' nightmares for its own symbolic sustenance.[14]

It is no surprise, therefore, that many of the great liberal statements of rights have been framed in essentially negative terms. Many of the individual amendments making up the U.S. Bill of Rights begin with the phrase, "Congress shall make no law . . . ," underscoring how the enumerated rights are to be understood as protection of individual citizens *against* the federal government (and, later, via the doctrine of incorporation, against all governmental authority at whatever level). In the grand liberal tradition, these are negative rather than positive freedoms. As applied to education, for an exemplary statement, we turn once again to Gutmann's *Democratic Education* and the two guiding principles of her "democratic state of education," namely, "nonrepression" and "nondiscrimination," the former signaling an ideal of education governance where no party (the state, parents, professional educators) is permitted to act such that it inhibits individual student-citizens from developing the ability competently to deliberate rationally concerning competing conceptions of the good life. The latter principle, "nondiscrimination," prohibits nonrepression from being restricted to any class of individuals; it functions as the distributive principle of nonrepression.[15] Gutmann's two principles capture well the scope of liberalism's commitment to universal schooling within the realm of right: as a distributive principle of equal schooling for all and as a rejection, in Hampshire's terms, of "compulsion and censorship."

In sum, education is to be defended within the realm of right because some level of it is a sine qua non for the exercise of individuals' basic political rights, which themselves, as per the UN "Declaration," are necessary components of human rights. Yet there is not much by way of a story of positive freedom to tell here. Education shows up in the realm of right mostly as a distributive ideal of schooling for all (e.g., school finance equity) and as a matter of equal legal protection (e.g., substantive and procedural due process protections against morally arbitrary exclusions, such as those made on the basis of gender, race, or disability). In its more developed forms, such as Gutmann's, liberalism also supports pedagogical aspirations toward the promotion of autonomous choosing, again pursuant to basic political and human rights, but also to the pursuit of happiness in a form consistent with others' like freedoms. These basic competencies and capacities are essential to any form of liberalism. Yet they are largely negative freedoms in that they resist the supplying of any real determinate content. What they provide is a set of guarantees that enable the operations of liberalism's free choosers. But what might these choosers choose to do? Who might they choose to be?

Association

Within criminal boundary constraints, what the choosers choose to do takes place largely within what I am calling the realm of association. Here, one enters into the political realm proper, where, under normal conditions, politics actually happens (as opposed to happenings in the realm of right, where the *conditions* for actual politics are themselves assured, the "constitutional baseline").[16] This is the realm of civil society, where there exist all sorts of associations large and small, political and nonpolitical, intense and casual, religious and secular, service-oriented or narcissistic, credentials-requiring or not, and so on. In the language of contextualism, this is the realm of the interrelation of the various social spheres, and we would expect a very large degree of complexity concerning those interrelations in any modern democracy. This is what we are as human beings: we are associates with our fellow human beings, in all sorts of contexts and in all sorts of ways. Some of these associations are chosen in a fairly straightforwardly voluntary way (e.g., I started showing up at the park on Tuesdays and became over time one of the regulars of the chess club), others are less obviously voluntary (e.g., as a child, a parent, a member of the religious group within which I was brought up, etc.). Yet on balance, in a liberal democracy, these associations will be voluntary at least in the sense that I am in principle free to exit from them if I desire, a right of mobility that is guaranteed by the realm of right. (There are of course exceptions: I may be drafted for military service; it will be hard to exclude myself from more or less mandatory associates such as my fellow taxpayers or jurors.) My basic citizenship assured by the realm of right, I am able with others to work, play, worship, shop, love, and so forth. as, in principle, a free agent (again within criminal boundary constraints that are themselves ideally based on considerations of right, e.g., if I choose to leave my spouse and children, I must see to their material support).

Within this realm, I believe, belongs educational accountability as it is typically understood (i.e., qua selective preference satisfaction), the arena wherein democratic schooling must justify itself according to the aggregated demands issuing from adjacent social spheres, demands commonly manifest in sets of competencies or literacies: technological, mathematical, cultural, scientific, even moral, religious, and spiritual.[17] There is nothing nefarious in these demands per se. Hardly. All associations in a liberal democracy are obliged to one another in some way. For some this is a minor matter: my chess group may need to share in some fair way public park space with the poets, and make a case for ourselves if that park space is scarce. For larger but still private associations, such as churches or businesses, while there will be debate over how much public responsibility, usually manifest in regulatory schemes, they ought to have (left-statist liberals leaning in the direction of more, right-libertarian liberals in the direction of less), there is typically understood to be some proportionately larger degree of mutual obligation as a quasi-utilitarian function of how many lives they effect and how significantly they do so. (An industry whose mistakes may kill people is subject to greater regulation than an industry whose mistakes result in mere inconvenience.) The web of mutual obligation is even tighter, however, for the large-scale associations that have a public face, particularly those that are recipients of public funds, such as public education, the military, the health care system, the police, the justice system, museums, libraries, and so forth. Like the other key democratic institutions, the education system must be responsive to the demands arising from within the realm of association, namely, the demands of *other associations*. These range proportionately across all spheres of society, most notably, families, businesses, government, medicine, even sports and the arts (along with indeterminately many others) who all legitimately queue up to make more or less reasonable demands on schools—just as education, in turn, queues up to make its own demands on others. This is where liberal contextualism lives and breathes: in the interchanges, gives-and-takes, interrelationships and dependencies, and the hot and cold interspherical "wars." Contextualism revels in the dynamism of the interspherical conflict. Although justice requires that certain key battles be joined, rarely does that much hang in the balance regarding a particular dispute (e.g., religious authorities aghast at an artist's provocation), for, in the ensemble, there is comfort in the very persistence of disputes. Where contextualism starts to worry is where there are no more conflicts, or they seem overly lopsided on the way to the comprehensive victory of one sphere of life over all of the others. A nightmare for the realm of association is when some sphere like business, religion, law, or, certainly, "the Party" gets to tell everyone else what to do. For contextualism, this is the very face of tyranny and injustice.

A crisis in educational accountability, then, is not generated because schools are made to answer to the public, business, parents, or whomever. On the whole, in fact, this answerability is all to the good, as schooling must be justificatorily on all fours with everyone else, particularly other public institutions. The crisis occurs when those calling the question represent inappropriately narrow interests. Contextualists would be concerned, for example, where accountability seems too closely allied to a "standards" rhetoric pushed by business interests who want competent workers and seem blind to much else.[18] As I argued in chapter 3, I think the way out of this problem is for institutions across the board to pursue a strategy toward a certain kind of institutional autonomy, one that is built up out of the very dependencies and demands that surround them (rather than a circle-the-wagons or purity-at-all-costs mentality where the institution tries to escape these demands).[19] A lineup of healthy institutions, autonomous yet responsive in the above way, will ensure that the accountability question is not raised exclusively by any overly narrow hegemon. In this way, the ideal of the realm of association becomes one of public service, where the various institutions "win" a nonzero sum game by becoming akin to good neighbors; they gain power and prestige by their demonstrable contributions to other social spheres. There should be no option of exit from this network of reciprocity for key social spheres (which could be disastrous, e.g., a military coup); they must all stay and play. But the reciprocity is necessarily complex. It cannot mean mere unidirectional answerability to the powerful, for this would defeat the wider civil society purposes served by the realm of association. For a contextualist vision of democratic accountability, such a self-defeating devolution of reciprocity is to be avoided at all costs.

Meaning

In the intimate realm of thick meaning, as individuals and collectivities, we link education and our other activities with our reasons for living. If the locus of the realm of association is among interspherical interactions, the realm of meaning represents an intraspherical move inward. This is the place where we make final sense of our lives according to some comprehensive doctrine—or the shards thereof—that we have embraced either as individuals or in concert with others (our church, say). I stress that this is an "intimate" realm rather than necessarily an individual one, as for many and perhaps most people the search for moral, aesthetic, and/or spiritual plenitude is inextricably intersubjective and bound up with a particular tradition. Indeed, the traditional conceptions of the many world religions are probably the most widely adhered to. But there is infinite variety: forms of consumerist hedonism, *volkische* fascism, communism, anarchism, Deweyism, Kantianism, Stoicism, Nietzschean self-creation, conceptions involving human liberation and authenticity (e.g., in Sartre, Heidegger, Freire), celebrations of cultural coherence that verge into having a quasi-mystical element (e.g., Zionism, U.S. Afrocentrism, Pan-Serbianism, etc.), totemism, animism, paganism, some forms of radical environmentalism, New Age feminism, Enlightenment deism, and so on, ad infinitum.[20] What all these belief systems have in common is that they have something to say (where "say" should be defined broadly) about the final ends of our lives—they directly weigh in concerning the worth and point of it all.

It is important to be mindful that the realm of meaning is not neatly divided from the realm of association (for that matter none of the three realms neatly separates from the others). Different societies, qua so many distinguishable symbolic orders, are in fact characterized by the integrative contours and "borderlines" they establish in this regard. Good examples of interrealm border relations are found in the many instances where the realm of meaning's private comprehensive conceptions of the Good provide the normative foundation for, not only houses of worship, but also many, many other key institutions: schools, hospitals, nursing homes, neighborhood parks, children's sports leagues, underground dissident operations, soup kitchens, decolonization and civil rights movements, therapeutic circles of self-help, publishing concerns, and on and on. There is also a strong sense in which the thick normative commitments of the realm of meaning also underlie, though very often in a much less direct way, the basic political structures of a society. To venture a fairly standard historical example, modern democracies depend on some conception of human equality, if only "one person, one vote" at its barest. This conviction in turn rests upon a conviction that every person has singular value which, though it would be logically possible to defend it on other grounds, as a matter of history is pretty well bound up with human beings as reflections of the divine, having souls, and so on. Sometimes this debt is explicit (e.g., in the American Revolution) and sometimes less so, even at times posturing as a radical historical break (e.g., in the French and Bolshevik Revolutions). But like every other ideal, human equality is a human product that has not come from another galaxy (as far as we know) but from the culture and traditions—in this case religious ones—of the human beings who gave rise to it. One need not sign on to the whole of Hegel, Nietzsche, or Marx to see this "dialectical" or "genealogical" development. So a very good historical case to be made (maybe even an obvious one) that comprehensive commitments to the Good, most notably Judaism, Christianity, Enlightenment theism and, I'm sure, others, have in crucial ways premised the basic constitutional commitments characteristic of today's democracies. This alone gives one reason to worry, *for the sake of democracy*, over a situation in which the products of the realm of meaning are not given their due.[21]

Just as in the case of rescuing someone from death or illness, the ultimate reason formally to educate someone has traditionally been attributable to some comprehensive conception, rooting the appropriate pedagogy in the ultimacy of that conception: the Protestant drive for Biblical literacy for personal salvation, a cultural ideal such as classical Greek *paideia*, Romantic conceptions of human liberation and authenticity, Hegelian-cum-Marxian conceptions of inevitable historical progress, and so forth. There is great power in this kind of instrumentalization of education. Inspired practitioners with a vision before their eyes of "final things" can often undergo great material deprivation and other formidable obstacles in discharging their mission, for what their vocation has become is indeed in the literal sense a mission, a calling. For such educators, being a "good teacher" means something in an ultimate sense, not just a pay raise, expanded career opportunities, or the often transient psychological grati-fication of helping people. It means playing a role in a larger drama, one that retrospectively makes sense of the small-scale chaos and frustrations of the quotidian. Since schooling has often been linked closely with reli-gious and other institutions animated by comprehensive conceptions, and also since teaching has only rarely been highly remunerative or prestigious (particularly the "dirty work" of teaching small children), the educational sphere has always drawn a great number of its practitioners from the ranks of those motivated by deep and fervent convictions.[22] This phenomenon underscores an important social function of the realm of meaning, which is to ensure a supply of true believers for some of the tougher jobs.

Any variety of liberalism must manage this intense and unruly Pan-dora's box. The challenge is especially acute for liberal contextualism, since it has as a distinct aim the conservation and even cultivation of a robust realm of meaning; this is why, after all, as a liberal one signs on to the con-textualist project. But the realm of meaning can mount severe challenges to the entire tripartite structure, calling into question the integrity of the social spheres in the realm of association and the legitimacy and authority of the constitutional principles of the realm of right. Examples are legion, with democratic schools frequently providing the sites for these conflicts, which are typically reflections of larger societal fissures. There are religious sects and cults that abuse children in the eyes of the law, racists who teach pernicious and incendiary doctrines, religious enthusiasts who scorn the basic elements of political citizenship (or, perhaps even worse, do so for a portion of their members, such as their women). Wearing the banner of human rights, liberal "enforcers" from the realm of right will face hard choices regarding intervention in such cases, usually intervening on be-half of what are perceived to be vulnerable members of the subgroup like women and children.[23] More commonly, there is a wide range of milder conflicts where partisans of various comprehensive conceptions fight it out on the policy arena, the conflicts being settled, more or less amicably or bitterly, via politics, the courts, or both. Almost every day brings news of these sorts of education policy tensions: religious education, corporal punishment, students' extracurricular activities, requirements regarding teachers' "moral character," national and local curriculum choices, text-book censorship, team mascots and symbols, and so on. Yet liberal con-textualism offers no blueprint for solving these cases, merely a monitoring of them in a manner more keyed to larger social trends than to ad hoc resolutions. If there are in place fair and open political processes, working alongside robust and relatively autonomous social spheres and institutions containing wise parents, judges, politicians, clergy members, educators, police, and others, then these kinds of disputes will remain at the level of "normal" politics and take care of themselves. Liberal contextualism eschews political micromanagement as leading to disproportionate accretions of power, including the state's police power, where liberal commissars bully other spheres and in doing so become merely commissars.[24] Like the trite saying about the opposite sex, one cannot live with all meanings, but at the same time one cannot live without the meanings. In the end, there is little by way of "correct" political decision regarding particular cases, only an imperative toward decisiveness itself, in effect, a need to dig the trenches *somewhere* reasonable so as to establish an identifiable set of front lines. Only when these front lines between and within realms are too widely overrun is there a case for contextualist intervention.

A Contextualist Picture of Educational Accountability

As in much of life, it is the monolithism of the extreme that is to be avoided. For example, the realm of right becomes monstrous when it tries to make over in its own image all of a society's associations and intimate meanings. One might adduce Soviet-style communism as the last century's most significant example of such a grave mistake, where all aspects of civil society and intimate thought and expression are madly sacrificed to a formally consistent ideal of human equality. By the same token, the various historically significant fascist movements might be thought of as the reverse, where an evil genie of meaning escapes its bottle and enforces on everyone its *mythos* of national greatness, racial purity, blood and soil, and the like, where "human rights" is regarded as at best a degenerate nuisance to be overthrown in the pursuit of "higher" ideals.[25] Each form of totalizing move initially aims to capture the realm of association in order to make it over in its own image, to align and purify.

The raison d'être of the liberal contextualist model is to resist such moves. Regarding the realm of right's possibly imperialist ambitions, the liberal contextualist recognizes right's negativity and formal emptiness, its "slave" status vis-à-vis the other realms. Actual human beings cannot commit themselves to human rights in a free-floating manner, find themselves willing to sacrifice anything of value—let alone fight or die—unless that commitment to rights is part of some comprehensive conception, one of many that might support the value of human equality and liberty on its own terms. People who voluntarily give of themselves for human rights do not do so for pieces of paper or for syllogisms supported by international statements or elements of national constitutions. This would require a very strange and counterintuitive theory of motivation. People do things on account of money, love, coercion, moral ideals, and on behalf of infinitely many motive besides these.[26] My supposition is that anyone claiming to be motivated out of a concern for an ideal such as human rights is bound to be expressing that concern as an outgrowth of *some* comprehensive conception or other; I just cannot imagine someone caring about rights *simpliciter*, rather than caring about them instrumentally on behalf of some comprehensive conception, secular or religious, in which rights are part of some larger moral, spiritual, or aesthetic equation. In this sense, as will be greatly elaborated in later chapters, to adapt and paraphrase Hume's famous point about reason being the slave of the passions, it might be said that right is and ought only to be the slave of meanings, and can never pretend to any other office than to serve and obey them.[27]

So there is no true battle between right and meaning. The commitment to right is typically supported by some comprehensive conception that is necessarily intimate and meaning-laden. Though the latter admits of a great variety of forms, if the realm of meaning is resected altogether, the realm of right will be left directionless and unable to motivate moral adherence from actual human beings who, ex hypothesi, require meaning for significant voluntary action (via some form of democratic consent, the only kind of political legitimation that a regime of human rights can countenance).[28]

Liberal contextualism's composite normative picture of the realms of accountability is importantly internalist as well, in the sense that it does not obviously require a justification formally outside the system, a metaphysical buoy, if you will. Consistent with contextualism's eudaimonistic assumption of value pluralism, there is no room for any overarching meta-perspective that gets its way across all realms and social spheres (e.g., the stricter Wahabbist forms of Islamic *sharia*, or any such totalizing theocratic vision). The closest one gets to this is with the basic liberal principles emanating from the realm of right. But even these are limited. No right is absolute, since any list of basic liberal rights will require a scheme of constitutional interpretation that works out compromises among the basic rights themselves, for example, between individuals' freedom of association and equal legal protection,[29] nonestablishment and the free exercise of religion, freedom of speech and a right not be harassed, and so on. Some basic scheme of liberal rights, though, is trans-spherical and transrealm. But this is different from its being metarealm or meta-spherical. This is because the system of rights will be supportable, qua a Rawlsian overlapping consensus of comprehensive conceptions, in multiple ways from the realms of meaning and association.[30] There are Christian, Islamic, Kantian, Wiccan, Nietzschean self-creationist, liberal ironist, and so forth ways to support basic liberal rights. Liberal rights, in fact, as per the above discussion of their sources of commitment, need such supports if they are actually to be consented to by individuals. Individuals and groups holding particular comprehensive conceptions may indeed see their commitments as in an important sense transcendent, that is, beyond politics. But the contextualist system *itself and as a whole* does not allow for any such metaphysical self-catapult. Justification must proceed from the actual reasonable (that is, accepting of some form of liberal principles of equality and liberty) traditions and beliefs of the individuals and groups that actually inhabit the system; it is committed in this crucial sense to a kind of internalism. As the last century's horrors demonstrate far better than any logical proof, externalist political systems, that is, those that assume too thick a conception of what is ultimately worthy for human beings (these often accompanying highly exclusionary definitions of who are the human beings), are the ones to be most wary of. Admittedly, every political system must rest on certain assumptions, take some stands, and make some exclusions. As noted, as a species of liberalism, liberal contextualism nonneutrally champions individuals' equality and liberty. But, as an internalist system, it seeks legitimacy from its actual inhabitants and what they in the ensemble are able to find supportable.

There are further implications here for educational accountability. By recognizing and accommodating the great range of legitimate demands on the education system, liberal contextualism would feature democratic education's diverse normative underpinnings and also illuminate its centrality to our public life. Consider the accountability question raised as broadly as it must be under liberal contextualism: How might we evaluate our education system *overall*? Liberal contextualism would argue for a tripartite answer corresponding to the three above-described realms, and in so doing championing a more holistic understanding of accountability. Satisfactory accountability to the realm of right would involve the structure and delivery of education and how these two would adhere to basic principles of equality and liberty, perhaps in the form of a liberal democratic nation's constitutional traditions, and perhaps supplemented by some further liberal principles such as Gutmann's nonrepression and nondiscrimination.[31] Accountability in the realm of association would involve a complicated map of the institution's responsiveness to other associations, that is, other institutions and social spheres. Much of the current accountability regime that seeks to satisfy demands from the business and political spheres would probably survive, but there would be more of a premium placed on responsiveness to other spheres that currently lack the coercive power of these two. Maybe the artists would have something to say. The military. International aid workers. Who knows who else? Much of the citizenship agenda of civic liberals would flourish here, as a set of legitimate demands on education to do its part in providing for civic commitment and competence. In addition to being just in the strict sense of the realm of right, education must also play the role of the good neighbor and public servant within the realm of association.

But this is not all. Liberal contextualism additionally brings a focus on the realm of intimate meaning. Education in a democracy also demands citizens who have substance and depth, such that they will be able actually to pursue happiness and so be able voluntarily to make social justice a heartfelt and therefore durable aim.[32] As I have noted, liberal contextualism can morally tolerate a sizable range of policy configurations so long as each configuration respects the "prerogatives" of each of the three realms of accountability. But it cannot tolerate a situation in which it is common for individuals *not* to possess some comprehensive conception of whatever type. A world where people are so shallow that they cannot be said truly to have comprehensive commitments at all (maybe they are drugged by consumerism or a soma-like pill, to borrow the Huxleian image[33]), or one in which they are coerced into someone else's commitments—perhaps through lack of any option but the One Officially Sanctioned comprehensive conception—is a dystopian nightmare for liberal contextualism because it is a defeat for eudaimonistic pluralism. An education system that on the whole neglects the fostering of depth and substance in individuals' development of intimate meanings is a system as unaccountable as one that does not provide satisfactory achievement test scores and employable skills. Educational accountability must be defined in terms reflective of the *whole range* of what we actually care about in our complex and heterogeneous democratic societies. An education system fails if it does not connect with all three realms robustly and in good measure.

So liberal contextualism would situate educational accountability squarely as a matter of social justice, rather than as a *method* of accounting designed to satisfy business interests and ever-manipulable public opinion. This understanding of educational accountability harkens back to ancient notions, such as Plato's, of justice as a certain kind of proportionality. But, in a Humean vein, there is also a sense in which progress may be marked, sympathies corrected. The criterion here would be a coherentist "satisfaction" of all three realms, where any one realm being too far out of line or out of balance with the others will be corrected by emphasizing another as a counterbalance. So, for example, if a school seems so bent on enhancing a child's propensities toward critical thinking that it is endangering family involvement and connection with the school (and child), then there will need to be some new attention paid to the way the school is relating to family in general. Consider also an unfortunately pressing example of a world out of balance, the rash of U.S. school shootings now symbolized by the 1999 Columbine High School massacre. By all accounts, Columbine High largely passes muster in the realm of right (except perhaps for the fact that as a well-funded suburban school it is out of the reach of poor city children in nearby Denver). Though there can always be more resources, this school is reportedly well-provisioned, open to all members of the immediate community, full of conscientious teachers, and so forth. It seems similarly satisfactory with regard to its associations: community members are generally happy with their local schools, which seem reasonably well integrated with the larger social life of the community they serve, families seem involved, students' test scores are high, and so on. But, as in many other places, all the while in this "perfect" suburban world there seems to be a horrifying deficit somewhere in the realm of intimate meaning, such that suicides and random lethal violence are so prevalent (one-fifth of American high school students report that they have "seriously considered taking their own lives during the previous year"[34]) and disturbed children seem so easily to fall unnoticed through the cracks of the school system. The liberal contextualist sees this situation as demanding attention from any morally defensible scheme of educational accountability, though it will admittedly be harder to "get at" for schools alone. A school system that is just both in the distributive/critical capacities sense and also in the community/public service sense may at the same time be complicit in the spread of a chilling nihilism. To my mind, this is a problem to be addressed and accounted for just as urgently as would be a school system that is formally discriminatory (racially, say) and therefore in violation of liberal principles of right. It is certainly worse than where the problem is merely that the test scores are flat.

Accountability thus *becomes* a question of social justice. There will always be standards and concomitant measurements of schools' and students' selected performances. This is part of what accountability must mean. But surely it is only a *part*. A more defensible notion of accountability adheres to eudaimonistic pluralism in recognizing that the only road to collective improvement is in satisfying the multiplicity of what we most value, rather than arbitrarily singling out just part of what we value. We ultimately progress by enlarging our sentiments such that we might come, in Hume's terms, "to fix on some *steady* and *general* points of view,"[35] that is, achieve a kind of eudaimonistic equilibrium across the realms of accountability. The ongoing challenge of liberal contextualism is to make something livable out of our unavoidable contemporary involvements in fairness and freedom, our shared projects and traditions, and our need to make sense of it all in terms that we ourselves can accept. This itself is a kind of moral education writ large, where social progress is measured by the extent to which we collectively satisfy and make cohere across the board the demands to which our most significant involvements give rise. Insofar as some of these demands are neither measurable nor quantifiable, and insofar as we must still decide in any event where our priorities among them lie, the question concerning the overall quality of our schools will remain intractably philosophical. The inescapably philosophical dimension of liberal contextualism is even more apparent when we focus less on institutional structures and more on the individual persons who make them up.

Part Two

Persons and Passions

Chapter Five

Cartesian Inwardness
Doubting Democrats

> I resolved one day to undertake studies within myself and to use all the powers
> of my mind in choosing the paths I should follow.
> —René Descartes, *Discourse on Method* (AT VI 10)[1]

AUTONOMOUS CHOOSERS

Like all conscientious democracy enthusiasts, liberal contextualists must
defend educational programs aimed at creating people capable of independent thought. If people are to be sovereign decision makers they—every
last one of them, ideally—should, in the Kantian formulation, "dare to be
wise" and think for themselves.[2] But what precisely does this mean? Vague
and magisterial, "autonomy" has been the watchword in philosophy, but
other words leap just as much to mind, some popular among educators at
large and some particular to the literature on democratic education: "critical thinking," "critical deliberation," "self-determination," "detachedness,"
"independence (of mind)," the exercising of "free speech," even "Socratic
questioning." Those of more exotic, extraliberal tastes may prefer "negativity," "consciousness raising," "critical pedagogy," Freirean "critical consciousness" or "*conscientização,*" "freeing our minds,"[3] and such like. As described in earlier chapters, Gutmann's nonrepression principle exemplifies
a commitment to autonomy by proscribing education system stakeholders
from repressing others' abilities to deliberate among competing conceptions of the Good.[4] There are many ways to run afoul of nonrepression,
some obvious, some not. Lobotomizing someone would probably do it.
But so would, say, my substituting fairy tales for science, where I would
violate nonrepression insofar as my curriculum would withhold the tools

123

of thought to be acquired via science education and so hampers students' abilities to become competent and conscientious citizens. By contrast, I might equally violate nonrepression by *withholding* fairy tales, perhaps by stifling the imaginative powers to be released through a salutary immersion in literature. Pedagogical sins of both omission and commission might therefore cause the requisite damage.

At this level of generality there is little controversy. Everyone not patently illiberal thinks it a problem if citizens cannot think for themselves. If one cares about democracy, more or less by definition one desires an educational outcome in which students-as-citizens have the capacity and disposition to utilize their intellectual powers so as not fundamentally to depend on others to interpret for them how the world is and how they ought to lead their lives. One might (and should) worry about possible conflicts with other important ideals, such as liberty, parental rights, cultural diversity, and so on, but one would still be balancing these additional concerns with critical thinking/autonomy. While there is robust debate about its priority and place, and huge areas of disagreement about the policies associated with it, I know of no relevant discussant simply *against* it.[5] Yet despite this ecumenical acknowledgment, autonomy and its synonyms are as educational aims almost mysteriously underexplored. Not wholly unexplored, as there are important studies, such as Gutmann's, that wade into these waters, as does her focus on the ability to deliberate among competing conceptions of the Good.[6] What one mostly gets, though, are fairly brisk accounts followed by the author's real object of attention, namely, whatever might be the policy ramifications. What about families? School choice? Religion? Ethnic identities? Curriculum? Or whatever else might be the policy controversy du jour.

In this literature, the "critical" part of the thinking is typically resolved into a quasi-existentialist imperative toward choosing, where one's freedom and/or autonomy consists in one's ability to choose one thing or course of action over another, particularly where important choices about one's life overall are involved. This, as Donald Kerr emphasizes, is where the connection to education is made: "a belief in the right of all to participate in democratic life, and to be able to choose for oneself—at least in some sense—how to live one's own life, that is, what constitutes a good life and to pursue it, is a prime justification of education."[7] Beyond this, there are often disagreements over *who* gets to choose (parents? students? local communities?), but "choice" is still sacrosanct. Almost by definition, though, liberals emphasize the need for *individuals* to be the choosers, absent some compelling reason otherwise (e.g., childhood, severe mental disability).[8] This follows the Rawlsian "political conception of the person," which holds in pertinent part that democratic citizens are to "conceive of themselves and of one another as having the moral power to have a conception of the good," which they are "capable of revising and changing," both of which is made possible by their seeing themselves "as self-authenticating sources of valid claims."[9] In addition to the individualism, this focus on the choice of a conception of the Good strongly implies a priority, not for the everyday acts of choosing that continually go on (like when to tie my shoe), but for the larger, life-orienting kinds of choices that are presumably made on a less continual basis.[10] Indeed, the smaller choices often turn out to be either morally arbitrary or functionally dependent on the larger eudaimonistic ones. For example, whether to select peas or corn is arbitrary (in most small-scale contexts) but is made morally relevant by virtue of the larger decision scene created by the prior choice to be a vegetarian. Similarly, my small choice whether to go to the nine or ten o'clock church service is derivative from my/our larger choice to attend church, to want to live in a godly manner, to adhere to a particular religion, and so on.

Because of this dependency of the smaller choices, it is the large-scale choices that enjoy priority in most conceptions of democratic education. While critical thinking as a curricular item is commonly defended as that which helps one figure out the best way to build a bridge, read a map, or plan an investment strategy (perfectly valid pedagogical objectives) such abilities are not especially morally relevant per se. Perpetrators of genocide build bridges, read maps, and plan investments, too, sometimes "problem-solving" very creatively. So it's about the larger-scale, more fundamental choices, those concerning what Charles Taylor calls our "hypergoods,"[11] and not so much the smaller-scale, everyday ones, or even the oftentimes very important technical ones—except insofar as these derive from the larger-scale fundamental choices.

But what are these kinds of choices? In what sense do we make them? It seems accurate to the phenomenology of such choices that they often are experienced as something more nearly the other way around, as making us more than we make them. Adhering to a particular religion, for example. As communitarians and others (even the most radical devotees of individual freedom-qua-choosing, the existentialists) have long pointed out against an overly simplistic free choice picture, the traditions that shape us into our identities or, if you like, in more general Sartrean or Heideggerian terms, our "facticity" or "thrownness," render it undecidable who or what is doing the choosing, where, when and how the choosing takes place and, really, whether there's any sense to talk of choosing at all. It is strange, almost paradoxical: the choices that appear most choice-like are sized S, M, and perhaps L. But when one follows the bases of those choices toward those that are XL, the *choicedness* of the XL choices and then, consequently, the choicedness of all the other-size choices seems remarkably to recede. Just like approaching a desert mirage: at the moment of maximum size it vanishes.

This, then, gets us quite close to a deep and mostly hidden problem that lies coiled within democratic education and its prioritization of our critical choice-making capacities. In his discussion of avoiding "ethical servility" in education, Eamonn Callan expresses this priority well: "Each of us must learn to ask the questions of how we should live, and the way we answer this question can be no servile echo of the answers others have given, even if our thoughts frequently turn out to be substantially the same as those that informed our parents' lives"[12] [or, one might add, any other authoritative source]. The problem thus has to do with the most fundamental, XL-size choices, those made with respect to the general outlines of what sorts of lives we choose to lead, our conception of the Good, the "questions" and "answers" we have given to ourselves, to the extent we have given them, concerning the ultimate meaning of the smaller things we do in the course of our daily lives. So if the choicedness of the XL choices is at risk, so too is the choicedness of all those others. Unless it is content with superficiality and trafficking in illusions, any ethical system with individual choosing at its center has to deal with this philosophical difficulty. By definition, every vision of democratic education wants people equipped to be making, in a sense as crucially important as it is frustratingly hard to grasp, *real* choices about *fundamental* aspects of their lives. If this is absent, then so is democracy and, a fortiori, democratic education.

How, then, might it be conceived that individuals make choices about the most fundamental aspects of their lives, those having to do with their visions of the Good, with God, freedom, immortality, Truth, Beauty, and so forth, in short, all those having to do with that XL realm of meaning that constitutes the terminus for choices of lesser scale? *Can* we even make choices about the XL? And if not, are all our educational efforts—both on behalf of others and of ourselves—doomed to being instrumental, technical and, really, as Callan says, *servile*, in the double sense that they serve ends not only outside of ourselves but also utterly obscure to us? If we cannot know why or what we do, yet we continue doing, how critical or deliberative can we really be? How much *conscientização* can we have?

What seems required is some way to "catch up" with ourselves, some method by which we might render the ends of our activities graspable, in both the sense of understanding them and also (potentially) manipulating or otherwise altering them. Perhaps this might comprise only the briefest orienting glimpse, as when one pauses on a hike to ascend a bit of high ground in order to survey the lay of the land and gain direction. Or maybe it will result in a more perspicuous and abiding vision. Whichever, if we are to participate in the large-scale choices that shape our lives most generally, our most basic beliefs about why, what and who we are, we would need some reliable way, not necessarily to ascertain final answers, but to gain at least some sight of what we ourselves happen to be accepting at this moment, now, at the time of our asking. Autonomous choice with regard to our own lives requires at a minimum that we at least *assent* to the general direction we are taking. Harry Brighouse amplifies this point with his suggestion that even "commitments generated by nonautonomous processes become autonomous when the agent reflects on them with an appropriate degree of critical attention."[13] Although it may, this "critical attention" plainly does not necessitate altering our course; it may turn out we affirm the course we happen already to be on. A hearty self-congratulation in that case! But even this minimum option, that is, assent without alteration, asks much more than may at first appear to be the case. This is for the simple reason that an authentic assenting-to-X (where X = my life as I perceive myself to be living it or my life as I'd like to be living it) demands that I have true (or true enough) knowledge of X. I qualify "knowledge" with "true" because it clearly would be unsatisfactory if I were to base my choice of what life I wish to live (or am living) on an illusion. As Kenneth Strike argues, autonomous choosing has informational requirements.[14] If I were deluded or, say, mad in some way comprehensive enough to make false my opinions about the life I wish, then my assent to that illusory life would itself be illusory and therefore no assent at all.

For both small-scale and large-scale choices, insofar as the choice is based upon false information, it is an illusory choice or, really, no choice at all. It may *feel* like a choice, but feelings unadmixed with knowledge are notoriously untrustworthy. I say I crave one of those apples. Unbeknownst to me, the Evil Queen has poisoned them all. She gives me an apple. As I die, she says, "It was your choice!" Is the Queen to be exonerated as an innocent choice-honorer? Hardly. Even though I did indeed say I wanted one of *those* apples, had I known their true nature I would not have so chosen. My alleged preference was bogus because I did not possess (enough) truth about the object of my choice. For my choice to have been a real one, I would have had to have known the truth about those apples, at least in all the relevant particulars.[15] Further, though it may save me from the bad apples, the mere having of the truth is insufficient for what democracy requires of us, namely, our own active individual involvement in the truth-seeking process. Arguing for a Cartesian understanding of the "voluntariness" of belief, John Cottingham articulates this desideratum in his suggestion that "what we want is not just that we should be passively led to the truth, but that we should play an active role in searching for that truth, in scrutinising the candidates for truth, in devising procedures for eliminating the faculty candidates and establishing why the sound candidates are reliable. In short, we want a methodology of inquiry that is within our control as epistemic agents."[16] From the point of view of the requirements of democracy and democratic education, this need to "play an active role" is nowhere more true than where the object of inquiry is *ourselves* as, I've been arguing, it must in some crucial sense be. I may accept in the end someone else's assessment of myself, but *I myself* still have to make the internally experienced, volitional assent that "acceptance" implies. On such an important matter, democracy cannot accept even the results of "my own" subconscious happenings; it needs my deliberate attention and not simply my experience of emotive directedness. Neither can it accept too high a degree of what Anthony Appiah calls "intellectual outsourcing," where others do all the hard thinking.[17] At a minimum, the imperative is that *we ourselves* be present as we are being directed toward an XL conception of the Good. It may sound simple in the abstract but it is in reality a tall, tall order. Thus my preliminary point: if we aspire to be truly critical, autonomous, and "by our own lights" concerning the most fundamental matters, then we must possess self-knowledge sufficient for us to give *real* assent to our own beliefs. We will not acquire total knowledge, an impossible and probably incoherent aspiration. That is not the goal. Needed is the willingness to see ourselves as part-authors—but still authors—of our own stories. We must win for ourselves by our own agency some nontrivial self-knowledge—at once the easiest yet severest of all epistemological problems.

CARTESIAN DOUBTING

Descartes's famous confrontation with this problem is still unrivaled. Of particular interest is his conception of how doubt and knowledge are inextricably intertwined, how the latter needs the former in order to become what it is. Ostensible appearance would have it that doubt and knowledge are opposed—to have knowledge is precisely to banish doubt, it would seem—but Descartes shows that true knowledge must be preceded and in a certain way accompanied by doubt ever after. One may in the end gain knowledge, but if and only if one first somehow becomes hyperbolically dissatisfied with what one had always taken to be the truth of one's experiences. It all begins with that ancient, nagging and still-mysterious Socratic epistemological hypochondria that pulls one out of the ordinariness of immersion in everyday life, makes one worry whether what one has been assuming one "knows" is in fact *really* true, where there is perceived to be a novel and urgent "oomph" to the "*really*" qualifying the "true." I wonder anew—or for the first time—if "perhaps what I take for gold and diamonds is nothing but a bit of copper and glass (AT VI 3)." Frustratingly, this epistemological crisis does not seem to be ameliorated by teaching and learning in the formal sense; even the finest schooling lies helpless to stop this hemorrhage of epistemic confidence. On the contrary, it may help precipitate and/or exacerbate the situation. As Descartes relates, "For I found myself beset by so many doubts and errors that I came to think I had gained nothing from my attempts to become educated but increasing recognition of my ignorance. And yet I was at one of the most famous schools in Europe, where I thought there must be learned men if they existed anywhere on earth" (AT VI 5). So it may be that the fingerprints of formal education are all over the scene of the crime. Yet it is not clear that there exists any necessary relation between, as it were, book learning and the experience of hyperbolic doubt. Common experience teaches that while formal learning may be an enabler of the experience, hyperbolic doubt may be occasioned by agencies outside formal learning as well, for example, a life-altering event of bad (or, more rarely, good) fortune, a bizarre coincidence, or simply an undifferentiated feeling. I will return to this problem, but I emphasize it here to introduce an immediate caveat for any educator wishing deliberately to produce hyperbolic doubt, to create a pedagogy of it: it seems not at all to be the kind of thing reliably produced by deliberate means. It is an outcome, but of what?

Descartes himself is unclear on this question of origins. At times it seems as if the doubt is merely an extension of the same sorts of doubts one encounters in the course of everyday life when common sense is proven wrong. Sometimes it seems a mere rearrangement of common sense. It is possible that Descartes would if pressed for an explanation, avail himself of the same *deus ex machina* that serves as the final epistemological guarantor of the *Meditations*, where error is avoided via simple faith "that

God is not a deceiver" (AT VII 90); perhaps analogous to the acquisition of virtue in Plato's *Meno,* it is ultimately to be conceived as an inexplicable "gift from the gods."[18] But mostly the question of the doubt's origins is passed over in silence, immediately eclipsed by Descartes's enthusiasm for what the doubt, once acquired, might achieve; a gift from somewhere, it is instantly instrumentalized in the service of building reliable knowledge. Above all else, from the moment of its being announced in the preceding "Synopsis" of the *Meditations,* the occasion of Cartesian doubt is conceived as a fundamentally *constructive* event wherein, "[a]lthough the usefulness of such extensive doubt is not apparent at first sight, its greatest benefit lies in freeing us from all our preconceived opinions, and providing the easiest route by which the mind may be led away from the senses. The eventual result of this doubt is to make it impossible for us to have any further doubts about what we subsequently discover to be true" (AT VII 12). It may be a temporary "demolition" of received opinion and the personal convictions we "have begun to store up since childhood" (AT VI 481),[19] but the point of the enterprise is unequivocally to accomplish something positive, viz., a sound foundation for science.[20] In this light, Descartes really wasn't a skeptic at all, no matter how much we speak of "Cartesian skepticism" and the like. He was simply using it as a tool. Gail Fine relates a telling episode in the *Seventh Replies*: when "Bourdin mistakenly views Descartes as a patient, suffering the disease of skepticism; Descartes replies that he is the doctor with the first sure cure."[21] What then did this "cure" involve?

Descartes provides another memorable image in the *Seventh Replies,* where the doubting process is likened to someone attempting to select unblemished produce. "Suppose he had a basket full of apples and, being worried that some of the apples were rotten, wanted to take out the rotten ones to prevent the rot spreading. How would he proceed? Would he not begin by tipping the whole lot out of the basket? And would not the next step be to cast his eye over each apple in turn, and pick up and put back in the basket only those he saw to be sound, leaving the others?" (AT VI 481). In the service of separating false from true beliefs, it is best for those concerned with getting at the truth "to reject all their beliefs together in one go, as if they were all uncertain and false. They can then go over each belief in turn and re-adopt only those which they recognize as true and indubitable" (ibid.).[22] This then is the reason for rejecting all of one's beliefs via hyperbolic doubt: not a mere gesture of refusal where one clears out one's mind in order to remain empty and "free" from outside influences, like some romantic visions of "authenticity" would have us believe, but rather a cognitive clearing out that is preparatory to a potentially unlimited cognitive putting back. As Descartes writes in his earliest published work, "there is no need to impose any restrictions on our mental powers; for the knowledge of one truth does not, like skill in one art, hinder us from discovering another; on the contrary it helps us" (AT X 360).[23] In the terms utilized above, I therefore provisionally "hold back my assent" (AT VII, 18) in order that I should be able truly to give it; the propositions I accept, the small and large assumptions under which I operate, are thereby given the volitional stamp that "criticality" requires. "[R]egarding the opinions to which I had hitherto given credence, I thought that I could not do better than undertake to get rid of them, all at one go, in order to replace them afterwards with better ones, or with the same ones once I had squared them with the standards of reason" (AT VI 13–14). Examining, rejecting, revising, or readopting in part or whole are the kinds of mental house-framing that need to be done. But it is the doubting that clears and grades the lot, even before the building's foundation can be erected.[24]

Such is the (temporarily) destructive Cartesian skepticism that individuals exercise not merely vis-à-vis governmental and other authoritative truth claims but also, and perhaps most importantly, with regard to their *own* truth claims, the "paths" they have determined for themselves to follow (AT VI 10).[25] The apotheosis of this skepticism, the famous hyperbolic doubt of the *Meditations,* has several noteworthy features. A description of these premises my later argument about the dependency of democratic education on something very like this Cartesian radical doubt.

First is its episodic nature. Descartes often emphasizes this and, just as tellingly, does *not* emphasize it in others. The polymath's intellectual corpus itself testifies to this; the philosophical part of his writings is but a small fraction of the whole. As Janet Broughton observes, "Descartes gave many more pages, and much more time, to describing methods of inquiry that did *not* begin with radical skeptical doubt, than to describing one that did."[26] It is clearly not the only or even the most likely productive method of inquiry that situations might dictate one should use; there is something special and singular about hyperbolic doubt over and against what one does in the course of ordinary investigations or, to continue with the analogy guiding this discussion, in the course of the more ordinary choices confronted in life. This is apparent from the famous descriptive context beginning the *Meditations*: "I realized that it was necessary, once in the course of my life, to demolish everything completely . . ."(AT VII 17). As if to dispel any ambiguity on this point, in his later *Principles of Philosophy*, Descartes proffers as his first "principle of human knowledge," that the *"seeker of truth must, once in the course of his life, doubt everything, as far as possible* [emphasis in the original] " (AT VIIIA 5). Engaging in hyperbolic doubt "once in the course of life" would seem to place the hyperbolical doubting operation alongside other things one does but once or rarely, such as birth, death, a bar or bat mitzvah, graduating high school, a pilgrimage to Mecca, a baptism, undergoing a religious conversion, losing one's virginity, and the like. In short, it is construed by Descartes to be an *event,* something bounded temporally with a beginning and an end, as opposed to an occurrent situation, some state of being or ongoing quality characterizing one's existence, character, or both. Though it may have consequences once it is initiated, Cartesian-style doubt is something one might be found doing at Time A but then decidedly *not* doing at Times B or C or D. It *begins* and *ends.*

This leads to a second and related aspect. I follow most commentators in viewing Cartesian doubt as decidedly non-Pyrrhonian. The adjective "Pyrrhonian" refers to the ancient branch of skepticism named after Pyrrho of Elis (c. 360–270 B.C.), and associated with his pupil Timon (c. 320—230 B.C.) and, much later and most importantly, Sextus Empiricus (c. 160–210 A.D.) and his *Outlines of Pyrrhonism,* the most influential Pyrrhonian Skeptical treatise.[27] The eponymous Pyrrho's name has become an adjective owing to how he is reputed to have *lived* his skeptical convictions, which amounted essentially to attempting to live a life precisely *without* convictions. There are many tales of the life of Pyrrho, which may or may not be true. But that the stories were told reveals something of the Pyrrhonian Skeptic's mind-set. For example, the great philosophical gossip Diogenes Laertius writes that when Pyrrho's fellow skeptic "Anaxarchus fell into a slough, Pyrrho passed by without helping him; and while others blamed him, Anaxarchus himself praised his indifference and his freedom from emotion."[28] Though "calm and gentle," as a man liberated from convention and other dogmas, Pyrrho could also be found engaged in truly shocking activities (for a free Greek male of his time) such as house cleaning, grocery shopping, and pig washing.[29] As is the case with other ancient philosophical schools such as Stoicism, the goal of the Pyrrhonian Skeptic is *ataraxia* (Gk. "tranquility," "lack of disturbance"), and the "procedures" advanced by Pyrrhonians such as Sextus consist largely of philosophical "modes" or arguments of a point-counterpoint form designed to deliver the Pyrrhonian aspirant to the doxastic state of *ataraxia* via liberation from strongly held beliefs.[30]

For the present purpose of contrasting Pyrrhonian and Cartesian skepticism, this idea of "life-guiding" is the key point, that is, the expectation that one will live one's life consistent with one's philosophical beliefs. The Pyrrhonian Skeptics really meant it. They wanted actually to achieve *ataraxia* and be purged of life-guiding beliefs altogether (though, as Martha Nussbaum points out, it is perhaps inconsistent for the belief in *ataraxia* itself, and also in the causal efficacy of the recommended means to it, to enjoy special immunities from an otherwise all-consuming skepticism).[31] Following David Hume's lead, it has frequently been questioned whether it is possible really to live such a life and it has been common, as does Hume, to dismiss the possibility out of hand.[32] As always handy with the memorable slogan, Hume has it that

> Nature is always too strong for principle. And though a Pyrrhonian may throw himself or others into a momentary amazement and confusion by his profound reasonings; the first and most trivial event in life will put to flight all his doubts and scruples, and leave him the same, in every point of action and speculation, with the philosophers of every other sect, or with those who never concerned themselves in any philosophical researches. When he awakes from his dream, he will be the first to join in the laugh against himself, and to confess, that all his objections are mere amusement, and can have no other tendency than to show the whimsical condition of mankind, who must act and reason and believe . . . [33]

Hume and others have long thought it impossible to *live* Pyrrhonian Skepticism, as per the above quotation, and "the Skeptic" in the history of philosophy exists largely as a literary device, an epistemological foil. There is for all that little scholarly dispute—at least following the "stunning" rediscovery of the work of Sextus made possible by its Latin translation in 1562[34]—that skepticism exercised a real attraction for many of Descartes's contemporaries and near-predecessors, even among those with pious intent (who often saw greater threats to faith from rationalist theologies), including surprisingly, such faith-besotted figures as Savonarola.[35] As did the Church in confronting this Sextus-induced *"crise pyrrhonienne"* of the early seventeenth-century, Descartes himself saw skepticism as something more than just an imaginary philosophical position. In the *Seventh Replies* he writes: "Neither must we think that the sect of skeptics is long extinct. It flourishes today as much as ever, and nearly all who think that they have some ability beyond that of the rest of mankind, finding nothing satisfies them in the common Philosophy, and seeing no other truth, take refuge in Scepticism" (AT VII 548–549).[36] This, combined with the availability of biographical information about the ancient Pyrrhonists themselves, underscores how vivid this school of thought must have been to those of Descartes's era. For despite its initial implausibility as a realistic worldview, as Burnyeat explains, "Pyrrhonism is the only serious attempt in Western thought to carry skepticism to its further limits and to live by the result . . ."[37] It was a doctrine that "lived large," as they say. Thus, given its clear imaginability along with the then-known actuality of it as an ancient ideal, Pyrrhonism was indeed likely actually to have been feared by Descartes as a clear and present competing conception of the Good. It was a way of life to be *opposed*.

That a Pyrrhonian alternative so clearly existed for Descartes helps place into relief how Cartesian doubt is most definitely *not* to be taken on similar terms.[38] Descartes does anticipate it to be an important event in the autobiography of the one who undergoes it.[39] It might even be deeply satisfying, as Descartes indicates that it was for he himself, for whom the experience of doubt him led him to feel "such great satisfaction that I thought one could not have any sweeter or purer enjoyment in this life" (AT VI 27). However, he is explicit that doubting is not to be thought of as a guide for how to live one's life. Those who see skepticism in this way should be corrected. Descartes distances himself from the layabout skeptics of the ancient Pyrrhonist type "who doubt only for the sake of doubting" (AT VI 29)," "reached no certain conclusion from their doubts" (AT II 38) and did not understand "how one can make use of such doubts" (AT II 39). Even more pointedly, he considers it a cardinal normative principle, number three, in fact, of the *Principles of Philosophy*, that the "*doubt should not meanwhile be applied to ordinary life.* This doubt, while it continues, should be kept in check and employed solely in connection with the contemplation of the truth. As far as ordinary life is concerned, the chance for action would frequently pass us by if we waited until we could free ourselves from our doubts . . ." (AT VIIIA 5). Amidst the doubting process of the First Meditation itself, he avers that "the task now in hand does not involve action but merely the acquisition of knowledge" (AT VII 22). For Descartes there may be a life of faith, a life of science or many other "lives." But there is no life of doubting per se.

Ironically, almost immediately upon their publication, his clear statements to this effect were not enough to prevent Descartes himself from being attacked as, in Popkin's words, a "sceptique malgré lui," and "the culmination of two millennia of Pyrrhonists from Pyrrho of Elis onward, all of whom had tried to undermine the foundations of rational knowledge."[40] Analogous to Milton's notoriously alluring depiction of Satan in *Paradise Lost* or, if you like, the contemporary stock character of the FBI profiler who must try to "think like the killer" in order to catch him, Descartes's deep appreciation of the gravity of the skeptical challenge necessitates his imagining it so vividly that the villain ends up inadvertently stealing the show. Descartes's and his contemporaries' clear awareness of this danger helps make still more understandable his concern to distinguish his own skepticism from the Pyrrhonian life-guiding type; they were to be in effect compartmentalized as specialized and theoretical, to use Burnyeat's term, "insulated" from ordinary life.[41] As Broughton rightly puts it, "people are to use it only when they want to discover and establish various fundamental truths. Good cognitive life goes on outside the practice of methodic doubt."[42] The question then becomes whether or not the insulation can be maintained.

So can Descartes's meditator really remain, to use Hume's descriptor, non-"actional" and thus non-Pyrrhonian?[43] There is a compelling line of interpretation that in effect says "no," primarily by emphasizing the literary form and long tradition of "meditations" as spiritual exercises aimed at self-improvement. Pierre Hadot suggests that "it was no accident that Descartes entitled one of his works *Meditations*. They are indeed meditations—*meditatio* in the sense of exercise—according to the spirit of the Christian philosophy of St. Augustine, and Descartes recommends that they be practiced over a certain period of time."[44] And further:

Each *Meditation* is a spiritual exercise—that is, work by oneself and upon oneself which must be finished before one can move to the next stage . . . For although Descartes speaks in the first person (evoking the fire before which he is sitting, the robe he is wearing, and the paper in front of him), and although he describes the feelings he is experiencing, what he really wishes is that his reader should traverse the stages of the inner evolution he describes.[45]

This seems reasonable to me. As a prudent principle of interpretation when dealing with an author of Descartes's genius, one should assume that both the content and form of the text in question are deliberate. Can this experiential aspect of the *Meditations* then square with the anti-Pyrrhonian aspiration to keep the radical doubt insulated? My answer is that it can, if we wed it with the account of the episodic, event-like nature of the doubt rendered above. In short, it is a lived experience but a *special occasion*. It does not guide life in the sense that one constantly has it in mind, striving to live up to it qua perfectionist ideal, but it is to be practiced episodically every once in awhile, perhaps a *long* while. This does not mean its temporal borders will always be easy to pin down; one might not be able to tell exactly when one started to reconsider a fundamental belief about, say, a life devoted to moneymaking and when one finished that reconsideration.

Harry Frankfurt helpfully likens the event to that of the decision to give up smoking.[46] Even though one may think in terms of "Day 1, Day 2, Day 26, etc.," it will sometimes be tough (though not always) to determine when exactly the *decision* was made. Was it made exactly at the moment one crushed out the last cigarette? When one had the *idea* that, "Okay, I'm really going to quit . . . *now*"? But what if I told myself I was going really to quit . . . now . . . and then I lit up two minutes later? In that case, would I have *really* made that decision to quit two minutes before? Probably not. If I made it a month or a year, though, we would probably grant that the decision was *really* made. The point is that there are good examples of significant reconfigurings of our ideas that do seem to be experienced fairly unequivocally as temporal events although their precise temporal borders may be difficult or impossible to establish with precision. A further apt analogy, given the present context of democratic theory, might be with the classically liberal notion of a "periodic" consent, rather than an original or hypothetical one, where citizens are periodically *actually* to grant consent—as opposed to tacitly, or hypothetically; for example nonemigration implies consent—to basic political arrangements.[47] Practically, it might be conceived as a sort of holiday ritual of renewal, but for the necessary volitional imperative that entails an expectation that things might well turn out to be different *this time*. I imagine it as a less fun, philosophically introspective sort of holiday. Whatever it is, it is coherent to imagine the doubting itself as episodic and eventlike, yet lacking precise temporal boundaries and largely insulated from the run of everyday life. It may change our lives, but it need not do so directly through the everyday conduct of those lives but through acting on our most fundamental beliefs, be they philosophical, scientific, religious, or in whatever packaging they may come.

Nonetheless, "largely insulated" cannot mean completely insulated because, however episodic, an event is still "in" life. This leads to a third key aspect of Cartesian doubt, one to which I gave focus earlier, namely, its ultimately instrumental and *constructive* purpose. As Broughton has it, Descartes "is saying that we are somehow to *use* our doubts constructively . . ."[48] Though radical doubt is not, à la Pyrrhonism, directly to guide our lives, our *reaction* to the experience of such doubt may indeed do so; life is to be lived on the *rebound* from it. What is truly interesting is the meditator's *response* to it. Detectable in it is a sort of creative anxiety, to be stilled only by further inquiry. It is instructive to recall that Descartes, qua the meditator of the *Meditations,* does not at all linger at the scene of the crime he has just committed, that being his description of an all-encompassing skepticism. He strikes his blow and then runs away from it very rapidly. In inverse proportion to their prominence in the history of philosophy, the famous arguments comprising hyperbolic doubt, from lunacy to dream to evil demon to "fate or chance" are very briefly stated, taking up only a handful of pages. An average reader peruses them in minutes. No doubt intended by the author, the reader's experience—certainly the seventeenth-century reader's—is one of sudden dramatic suspense followed by an equally sudden deliverance from "the inextricable darkness of the problems I have now raised" (AT VII 23). In important respects, the initial energies released via this cathartic situation are reflective of Descartes's general purpose of *utilizing* doubt to fuel his and others' scientific inquiries more efficiently; this is a restive sort of doubt that leads not to Pyrrhonistic indifference but instead to discovering, creating, building, and so on. It's like an epistemological itch that one has to keep on scratching. And so one does, through inquiry into the nature of things.[49] After all, the "eventual result of this doubt is to make it impossible for us to have any further doubts about what we subsequently discover to be true" (AT VII 12). Ironically, given his vilification at the hands of "the pragmatists" as the source of debilitating dualisms, Descartes in this respect reveals himself to be a kind of pragmatist *avant la lettre.* It's all about what you *do* with the doubt, and it is Descartes's special merit to recognize that sunny can-do optimism may lead less well to meaningful inquiry than the disorienting fright of that apparently "inextricable darkness." I'm scared therefore I think.

The constructive stance provoked by Cartesian doubt leads, perhaps counterintuitively, to an appreciation of the ineluctably individuating and otherwise *personal* nature of the enterprise. A caveat must preface this claim, however. Despite the meditator's intimate voice, the *Meditations* are not simply autobiographical. It is clear from his other writings, including his correspondence, that Descartes did not himself undergo radical doubt in the same manner as is represented in the text.[50] (This is the main reason why it is prudent when discussing the *Meditations* to refer to "the meditator" rather than unproblematically to "Descartes.") One should be mindful once again that this is a work of literature as well as philosophy. But that does not mean intimacy is lost. On the contrary. Released from the strictures of autobiography, Descartes constructs a persona closer to that of an "everyman," perhaps the person of "common sense"[51] or, a bit more precisely, someone who has simply not yet undergone hyperbolic doubt. I say "more precisely" because I follow Broughton in finding it difficult to see how the person of common sense would be motivated to engage in something so noncommonsensical as hyperbolic doubt; doing so would seem ipso facto to render the person of common sense *not* such a person.[52] Though the text is written in the first-person singular, strongly implied by trappings of the *meditatio* context is a didactic second person "you, dear reader" who ought to be doing the prescribed workbook.[53] One is therefore reading more than a collection of epistemological arguments. One has in hand a playbook to follow, that one *has* to follow in order to understand three-dimensionally the plays that are sketched two-dimensionally therein. The point is to *do* the meditations for oneself.

For those not theologically inclined, an effective aid for comprehending what this kind of meditating might mean may be found in Edmund Husserl's inauguration of phenomenology in his classic and appropriately named *Cartesian Meditations*.[54] Nowhere in the history of philosophy is this *meditatio* imperative seized upon with more brio: "And so we make a new beginning, each for himself and in himself, with the decision of philosophers who begin radically: that at first we shall put out of action all the convictions we have been accepting up to now, including all our sciences."[55] Epistemologically jaded as are all sensible contemporary theorists, it's still hard not to admire the sheer chutzpah of this announcement, which is really just the refracted chutzpah of Descartes himself. I find it admirable, in part because it captures so well something of the universality of the Cartesian doubting operation, the sense that not only *can* we—you and I—engage in it, but in some unspecified yet compelling way we *should* do it, we should think for ourselves and "make a new beginning." This is the voice of the Enlightenment itself, speaking through one's gut-level intuition that however apart and out-of-touch may be professional philosophy, everyone thinking for themselves still involves an imperative for everyone to philosophize. "Accordingly the Cartesian *Meditations* are not intended to be a merely private concern of the philosopher Descartes, to say nothing of their being merely an impressive literary form in which to present the foundations of his philosophy. Rather, they draw the prototype for any beginning philosopher's necessary meditations, the meditations out of which alone a philosophy can grow originally."[56] Husserl later appends to this an imagined Cartesian reply to the critic who would object to the implied individualism of such a view by wanting to acknowledge the collective aspects of the community of scholars in philosophy, science or any academic field. This reply is telling and it is right on the point of my present argument: "Descartes's answer might well be: I, the solitary individual philosophizer, owe much to others; but what they accept is true, what they offer me as allegedly established by their insight, is for me at first only something they claim. If I am to accept it, I must justify it by a perfect insight on my own part. Therein consists my autonomy—mine and that of every genuine scientist."[57] Thus Husserl brings my own argument full circle by illuminating the linkage between radical, Cartesian doubt and autonomous thinking. If democratic citizens are to make choices for themselves, which is to say think for themselves, there is no other way than to become Cartesian "genuine scientists," at least of themselves and their actions. That this is a pedagogical undertaking almost goes without saying. Learning, particularly qua schooling, has many collective aspects. Despite this, however, there is still a personal, existential component to learning that is as unavoidably first-person as accepting moral responsibility or, ultimately, confronting one's own mortality. Viewed from the "inside," that is, the experiential qualia one undergoes with regard to it, no one can learn it *for* me any more than they can die my own death. The question is, "Do *I* get it?"

To clarify, I do not intend an endorsement of the entirety of phenomenology, which in any event would be far beyond my present scope. Husserl's meditator aids in the illustration of three germane points concerning Cartesian doubt. (1) It has a deliberately constructive nature, which for Husserl (and Descartes) does not mean mere destruction and "therefore does not leave us confronting nothing."[58] In the Cartesian manner doubting what it is possible to doubt, what Husserl calls the "phenomenological epochē," or simply "bracketing," rather "lays open (to me, the meditating philosopher) *an infinite realm of being of a new kind* [emphasis in the original]."[59] Sound inquiry begins when, during an appropriately structured episode, as much as possible assent is removed from the pack of assumptions comprising some object of inquiry—including when that object consists of oneself and one's own set of experiences, there being no license "to restrict the method to any particular subject-matter" (AT VI 21). (2) It is ineluctably personal in the existential sense that no one can experience it for me, however much the surrounding natural, cultural and interpersonal environments may enable it. It is an event *I* must undergo, precisely in the psychological sense that I experience a *gestalt* "aha!" on figuring something out. No one can have that experience on behalf of someone else; all the mechanisms of the world may lead us horses to water but we still have to drink. (3) The surprising extent to which the previous points (1) and

(2) are linked. Following the Cartesian "reduction" (Husserl's term) of experience to the *cogito,* which must by definition constitute an eminently "personal" experience, a certain clarity arises. Since all but one "tag-end" of the world is dubitable for me, namely, that doubting is being experienced, the perceptual world shrinks to a very manageable circumference: that same experience of doubting. (Try and doubt it without experiencing doubting!) "You cannot deny that you have such doubts; rather it is certain in fact that you cannot doubt your doubting. Therefore it is also true that you who are doubting exist; this is so true that you can no longer have any doubts about it" (AT X 515).[60] There is no greater epistemological austerity. Here, stripped down to nothing but my own raw experience of doubting is where the meditator finds salvation: the Cartesian meditator finding hers in scientific investigations whose objects' existence is ultimately God-guaranteed, and the Husserlian meditator in a disciplined study of perception, where the indubitability of the *appearance* of my appearances provides the field for study. Much of course can and has been said about these strategies. What I note here is their *structure*: a reduction of the world *in mente* to what is *mine*, an introspection, energetically pursuant to an active, even aggressive research program "to direct the mind with a view to forming true and sound judgments about whatever comes before it" (AT X 360).

DOUBT AND DEMOCRATIC EDUCATION

Cartesian inwardness thus highlights for democratic theory how autonomy as self-direction requires attention to the selves that do the directing and to what those selves' giving of direction would have to involve. True choice-making requires a volitional stamp at the location of the alleged choice, otherwise if it exists it's located elsewhere and hence someone else's choice. This includes, crucially, fundamental choices about the conception of the good we embrace; we ourselves, as individuals, must somehow stamp those large-scale choices as *ours*. With regard to this specific imperative it is not pertinent whether individual choosers end up with choices that are conventional or idiosyncratic or anywhere in between; what matters is that the individual choosers *choose* and that, correlatively, the range of their choice-making must encompass what is fundamental to their lives as they see them. Democracy in this way contains a broad imperative toward the maximization of such choosing behavior, where the limiting n = the number of individuals available in the polity.[61]

I would caution that this is not simple advocacy of critical thinking in the pedagogical problem-solving sense. It is not the steady-state occurrent disposition that is a main goal of many curricular reforms. Not that there is anything to be said against such a disposition. But Cartesian doubt is something different and it is important not to lose that difference amid the busy shuffle of educational buzzwords. Though its scope is potentially unlimited, it does not provide a guide to the conduct of everyday life. This is its non-Pyrrhonian quality. For it operates on one's most fundamental XL sorts of beliefs in an episodic manner as opposed to, self-defeatingly, every waking moment. One takes some time—a day, a week, who knows exactly?—in some appropriate venue and season of one's life to examine *for oneself* the assumptions about the world that one has been accepting. To the best of one's ability one tosses out the basket full of apples and starts to pick through them. As many rightly have, epistemologists will question whether one can really throw out all the apples at once and really be able to doubt as hyperbolically as Descartes's meditator. Perhaps a more sensible image of cognitive self-reform might be Otto Neurath's ship, where one repairs the ship while sailing in it, maybe over time gradually constructing a completely new ship. But one does so while at sea, and so always standing on some assumption-planks while working on others.[62] That may be a more accurate picture of what we can hope to achieve. But even if it were possible, 100 percent success seems to me far less important than the volition itself, the *personal will* to initiate the introspection and potential corrosion (or reflective maintenance) of those large-scale beliefs. Yet from where exactly this will come strikes me as something of a mystery.

As it was, I believe, for Descartes. Recall that one of the great perplexities of the experience of Cartesian doubt is how it can get started. What starts a person on the road to questioning his or her large-scale and often quite hidden major premises? What would motivate the "common sense" person to do such a thing? One answer might be that anomalies in everyday life lead one toward larger-scale questioning. These could be natural, such as scientists' reports of heliocentrism, evolution, or the universe's vastness. Or ethical, observing occasions where the wicked prosper and the innocent suffer. The daily news is certainly full of these. Or, perhaps most powerfully, personal: a radical change in material circumstances, the initiation or collapse of a marriage, experiences with one's children, the death of a loved one, sudden public acclaim or obloquy, and so on. All these could provide thoughts and experiences disorienting enough to "see" or question things one had not previously. It seems likely that this sort of thing does happen. But there is a difficulty in associating such occurrences too strongly with Cartesian doubt, which is that potentially disorienting experiences like these seem just as likely to lead *away* from anything like Cartesian doubt as they are to lead *to* it. One may be shaken into questioning one's theodicy by the suffering of innocents, but one may be just as likely to reinforce one's preexisting view that justice must await the afterlife. The untimely death of an intimate may lead one to new doubts about aspects of life but it may also lead one to cling with desperate nonreflective vigor to what one already believes. So it is hard to see even the most jarring actual experiences of life as especially likely to give rise to hyperbolic doubt. They may but then again they may not.[63]

Such doubt occurs, but its causes remain opaque and so too is how to predict or deliberately bring it about. All Descartes's meditator says is that "[s]ome years ago" he was "*struck* by the large number of falsehoods that I had accepted as true in my childhood, and by the highly doubtful nature of the whole edifice that I had subsequently based them on [emphasis added]" (AT VII 17). "Struck"? That isn't the most revealing formulation. By way of consolation to the would-be Cartesian, this is a problem of a very basic quantity-converting-to-quality type and as such it has very distinguished company. For example, it compares with the problem of consciousness, namely, how is it that "stuff" can turn in on itself and become *aware* of itself? Or with that of life itself: How to explain the quantum leap from a certain organization of chemicals to an entity with the qualities associated with being biologically *alive*? So it is with the generation of Cartesian doubt. How can the materials of everyday, nondoubting experience rearrange themselves such that they all of a sudden and in the ensemble become doubtful? How does one get "struck"? A mystery.

If this difficulty were not bad enough, it gets worse. It might be said that for the Cartesian the only problem as vexing as how and to what extent one can get *into* radical doubt is the problem of how and to what extent one can get *out* of it. Once in, is there any way to get back? Descartes provides some warning signs of this problem when he likens himself as doubter to "a man who walks alone in the dark" (AT VI 16), who is "able to lead a life as solitary and withdrawn as if I were in the most remote desert" (AT VI 31) or, if you like, "It feels as if I have fallen unexpectedly into a deep whirlpool which tumbles me around so that I can neither stand on the bottom nor swim up to the top" (AT VII 24). Though disturbing, these images underscore the episodic nature of hyperbolic doubt, and as such clearly imply the potential to get both in *and* out, though the whirlpool image leaves one less than sanguine about escape. But it is hard to see how to accomplish either, particularly when one (attempting to remain true to the relevant texts) recalls the non-Pyrrhonistic insistence on insulating the doubt vis-à-vis everyday life. The doubt episode is supposed to be intense enough to touch large-scale assumptions while *not* directly affecting everyday life. But, given his other commitments, it would seem to be hard for Descartes wholeheartedly to have believed this. As detailed above, one of the signal aspects of Cartesian doubt is the near-immediate, constructive, science-engaged response the experience generates. (Recall that Descartes is in large part motivated *to* hyperbolic doubt by his scientific concerns.) The conduct of scientific inquiry, one supposes, will normally take place outside the episode of hyperbolic doubt. So if, as Descartes indicates, the doubt episode can have an effect, presumably a salutary one, on scientific investigation, then there is at least one aspect of everyday life capable of being affected by it. It is clear that Descartes gives great pride of place to the observation of "ordinary experience" in his radical doubt-founded vision of science. In fact, as Desmond Clarke demonstrates in his studies of Cartesian science, Descartes was extremely distrustful even of scientific experimentation conducted in overly complicated settings. Too many potential variables. Such mediated observations contain too many potential sources of error for Descartes to place too much stock in them, for example, reading and then interpreting the readings of some instrument. Clarke concludes that "the source of Cartesian doubt about experiments is not their empirical character, but the fact that their relative complexity makes them more liable to errors and misinterpretations than the common experience of unscientific observers of nature."[64] So far as everyday life may be indispensable as the setting for scientific investigation, then, score one for the Pyrrhonist. But keep the scorecard out. There may be more points to add. For what justification could there be for removing the insulation from one area of everyday life (viz., the as-ordinary-as-possible observations of Cartesian science) and not from others? Why not remove it from psychology? Sociology? City Planning? Art? Interpersonal relations? Sports team allegiances? Morality? Grocery shopping? Or—heaven forbid—theology? Once it is admitted that one area of life might be affected by the doubt episode it is hard to bar the possibility that others might be similarly affected. Why couldn't they be?

The cost of this admission is that it slides Cartesian doubt a little ways toward Pyrrhonism. But it buys a considerable mitigation of the above problem of entry and exit from the doubting episode. This means that the doubting episode can indeed have an effect on everyday life; the insulation simply cannot be airtight. This does not by any stretch make Descartes into an out-and-out Pyrrhonian, though. It is a perfectly coherent position to hold that the doubting episode could be a special occasion and also effective in the normal course of life that lies beyond the episode. Many religious rituals are like this, for example. Even an academic course could be. So to experience radical doubt one does not need to become Pyrrho of Elis and attempt to live without any beliefs. The doubt can be contained and compartmentalized. But not completely. And that's the rub, especially for those with the pedagogical ambition deliberately to bring it about: the extent to which it can be contained and the areas to which it might be compartmentalized seem to be undecidable in any given case. It is unpredictable just where and when the insulation will thin; it will depend on a thousand variables about a person, almost certainly too many for any educational planners to account for with any reliability. It is possible that empirical studies could eventually reveal patterns and probabilities, but by and large there is simply no telling who might fall into it or where it might pop up in somebody's life. The educator would seem consigned mostly to a debilitating ignorance about whether or not the would-be learner is "ready" for the doubt episode, a kind of developmental uncertainty presenting a daunting obstacle for any educator seeking deliberately to bring the experience about. To draw on the Aristotelian notion of *phronesis,* this may simply be one of those noncodifiable situations that calls on practical reason, where a wise and experienced philosophical teacher could somehow "sense" this ripeness in a way impossible to pin down pedagogically. That is possible and even likely, in my view, in particular cases where everything is "just right." However, given the resource-intensive nature of such pedagogical interactions, requiring as they would a *phronemos* of sufficient philosophical acuity, pedagogical skill, *and* intensive knowledge of his or her individual charges, this almost aristocratic tutorlike model is unpromising for the universalizing requirements of democracy, where mass schooling is a practical necessity in a polity of any size.[65] So any plan to make "the occasioning of Cartesian doubt" a curriculum objective for school or college classrooms would likely be ineffective. There are also, to say the least, many prudential problems associated with what would undoubtedly be perceived by many as head-on challenges to received conceptions of the Good, especially families' religious views. For schools to be "detached" from parents' conceptions of the Good is one thing; for them explicitly and directly to aim at undermining those conceptions is quite another.[66]

But classrooms are not the only venues for securing educational objectives. The wider world is a venue, too. And it is there the democratic educator should look for maximizing the possibility that individuals will experience occasions of Cartesian doubt. I would suggest an indirect strategy consisting of augmenting the availability of relevant cultural tools. Traditional mainstays of democratic education policy would be indispensable preconditions for the use of such tools, and so such initiatives as universal public education, affordable access to college, and well-stocked and -run public libraries would be part of any effort. A more determinate and perhaps more novel approach would be an emphasis on citizens persistently encountering (directly or indirectly) vivid and diverse examples of individuals who have undergone episodic doubt and have as a result committed themselves to whatever form of life or conception of the good, in short, to paraphrase Descartes, people who *have* chosen the "paths in life" they should follow. One assumes that under conditions where basic civil liberties are secure, this will mean a rich diversity of such voluntary path followers. There are many of these now and they are certainly not just academic philosophers who, in fact, as individuals might not embody voluntary path following in the requisite sense. They could, but there is no special reason to expect them to excel at it; many if not most professional philosophers probably inhabit roughly the same eudaimonistic ruts as everybody else.[67] At any rate, at issue here is not so much the existence of such individuals because they have to be assumed already to exist. There's not much point to any of this if they don't. As per the above argument, doubt experiencers can't reliably be intentionally created, so let us hope for them. Needed, however, is our paying a greater level of attention to them. To be sure, we already do some of this through our many entertainments: books, films, plays, storytelling, music, and so forth. But one could easily imagine a new genre (maybe I should say "revived") explicitly *about* reflective lives worth living. The reader will have to play along here to some extent by imagining nonboring and nonsanctimonious examples of such a genre, but it is clear to me that the materials currently exist, particularly in literature and film. There is certainly no reason why the vivid depiction of a life cannot be fiction. Maybe that's the best vehicle of all. One might object that vivid lives are portrayed and passed on to the point of surfeit, say, through Bible stories and other religious narratives. *Lives of the Saints* and the rest of it. This is true. Yet the curriculum objective here is not just to secure the portrayal of a life or two or of any one "type" but to secure a *diversity* of portrayals. From the Cartesian perspective, the need for this diversity is to provide materials that are hopefully conducive to episodic doubt. By long philosophical tradition back to the pre-Socratics, the mere existence of a variety of ways of being human or, in this case, the living of an examined life, is itself a potential catalyst for the questioning of the large-scale assumptions by which we have been ordering our own.[68]

Along these same lines, there are other cultural tools one could try to provide for the individuals who might be ready to use them. Pedagogically, the age-appropriate teaching of philosophy to children would probably have the effect of legitimizing that sort of inquiry for individuals later on and in the culture generally. People tend to think of the subjects they studied in school as the "real" subjects. For those inclined to charge the castle head on, the "philosophy for children" movement associated with Matthew Lipman and the Institute for the Advancement of Philosophy for Children at Montclair State University (NJ) could be promising in this regard.[69] Religious education of the type required in the United Kingdom, where students learn *about* different religious views would have some of the same effects, at least showing the different ways in which people give ultimate meaning to their lives. In my view one of the best ways to pursue developments along these lines is to emphasize juvenile literature in which the theme of "other worlds" plays a prominent role, such as may be found in C. S. Lewis, Richard Pullman, and, yes, J. K. Rowling.[70] For adults (though a famous feature of Lewis, Pullman, and Rowling is their suitability also for adults), and in any event more directly to be billed as "philosophy," one could do much worse than recognize the media-savvy efforts of an outfit such as *No Dogs or Philosophers Allowed*, which tries to make philosophy entertaining (and hence more accessible) to a wider audience via public access television, yet retains a serious, substantive and challenging core.[71] In this same vein, one can also only applaud the efforts initiated by Christopher Phillips, author of *Socrates Café* and, just as importantly, his hundreds of actual "Socrates Cafés" in the United States and worldwide.[72] In very much an extra-academic (but not anti-academic) spirit, Phillips has inspired individuals to create in their own communities voluntary groups who convene to discuss philosophical questions they themselves have chosen. There are also magazines, such as *Philosophy Now* and *Philosophy Today* and, of course, numerous websites, blogs, and other online attempts to fill the same niches.[73] There are, I'm certain, many, many additional hyperbolic doubt-relevant cultural tools beyond these bare suggestions, tools that may or may not have the "look" of traditional philosophy.

SUMMARY AND CONCLUSION

By way of conclusion, let me rehearse the Cartesian rationale for the "cultural tools" idea and thereby summarize the overall argument. Democracy calls for citizens to think for themselves about the lives they want to lead and so democratic education must bring about citizens who can do this. Toward this end, it is less urgent that we exercise autonomous thinking regarding the smaller things in life than it is regarding the larger ones. The largest choices one can make include those concerning the *overall* shape of one's life and its *overall* meaning, one's conception of the Good. And in order really to choose such a conception, because it is part of the meaning of "choosing," one must exercise volition regarding it. It must be a choice that one makes *for oneself* in some nontrivial sense, otherwise it is someone else's choice or no choice at all. So democracy contains an imperative for a citizen's personal involvement in his or her choice of a conception of the Good, at least a movement far enough down that path for it to be said that one has reflected on it.

The Cartesian method of doubt is a highly compelling way to understand what this might mean. But it is no ordinary activity. As a study of the relevant texts reveals, Descartes provides a highly specified model for engaging in a kind of radical doubt where one attempts to remove assumptions that one has simply been given or has otherwise unreflectively assumed. In a way, one tries to gain volitional control over one's fundamental beliefs in the sense that one makes them explicit, examines them and either rejects, alters or retains them; one strives to pass one's own judgment over what one has in one's head. Cartesian doubt contains several noteworthy features. In particular: the episodic nature of the doubting experience; its non-Pyrrhonistic qualities; its constructive, active and investigatory implications; and the experience's necessarily "inward" and personal nature. A potential flaw in Descartes's conception is the degree to which radical doubt can be insulated from ordinary life, and this is the key to a revised, neo-Cartesian conception amenable to democratic education. But from the point of view of democratic education, this flaw is more a virtue, in that it allows for experiential congress between the (rare) episode of doubt and the life that lies beyond it. A serious pedagogical difficulty arises regarding the getting "in" and "out" of the episode of doubt, an account of which is needed for anyone, namely, an educator, who wishes deliberately to generate it and then "return" to everyday life, to psychological and social functionality. I believe this "getting in and out" problem remains unresolved and would constitute an interesting area for further research.

What does seem clear is that while episodic doubt can and does take place, it is unlikely deliberately to be pedagogically engendered, particularly under the conditions of mass schooling that education policy-makers must realistically expect. Direct instruction is unlikely to succeed at actually occasioning the episode of doubt (as opposed to learning *about* it, say, by studying the texts and arguments of Descartes or whomever). Thus indirect instruction is the most promising option. My main suggestion here is that the goal of occasioning the episode of doubt might best be achieved by populating our public and private lives with relevant cultural tools, such as various media whereby other worlds and other lives can be examined. The study of philosophy itself might be considered such a tool, both inside and outside the academy. It may not always be the best available tool, but given philosophy's track record of raising big questions and unearthing hidden assumptions, I think it's still a good bet, one whose odds improve as a function of philosophy's ability to enlarge beyond its current academicist constraints. Philosophical reflection must not be thought of as unavailable to citizens of a country with a reasonably thorough and efficient system of public and private schooling. To scoff at this sentiment as unrealistic or too demanding is to scoff at the highest aspirations of democratic education. Instead, let us candidly admit that the aspirations are indeed high. So counsels the Cartesian in us, realist and unrealist both at once.

Chapter Six

Humean Outwardness
Reasonableness As Civic Friendship

The One-timer Problem and Doubt's Social Dimension

A serious problem remains from the Cartesian account, at least for the democratically minded educator. Let's say someone has undergone the requisite hyperbolic doubt and has emerged with the promised genuinely reflective basic commitments. The problem is that it is easy to imagine such a person subsequently becoming, over a period of time, as rigidly dogmatic as the person who never touched doubt with a ten-foot pole. This person I'm imagining we might call the "One-timer," who, say, in her radical days in college ragingly challenged much around her, experienced a Cartesian-style doubt episode and then settled into a set of life-orienting, comprehensive views. Maybe as a Marxist radical. Maybe as a born-again Christian. Maybe as a dogmatic liberal. Having *at one time* engaged in doubt, she carries the conviction that whatever she believes is sufficiently justified because of that once-upon-a-time period of radical doubt. She may have rejected her religious upbringing or the received wisdom of her community about politics and economics, thus preserving her in her own mind from the category of "the duped" ever after. Having doubted Packet-of-Beliefs A and then having embraced Packet-of-Beliefs B, she can safely ignore future occasions where Packet-of-Beliefs C, D, or E beg for her consideration. She's already done all that doubting. Why bother with it *again?* What to do about this one-timer?

Required is something more long-term dispositional than the initial willingness to jump in and engage with Cartesian doubt, as indispensable—and mysterious—as that initial willingness is. It is equally necessary to be disposed to *keep on* jumping in, to stay open to doubt while also keeping sane and getting on with life. The doubt must be episodic in the Cartesian sense, and as such temporally bounded, yet the doubting episode must remain at all times a possibility. It cannot be conceived merely as a stage of life that one passes irrevocably and safely beyond. This implies a need for a both a corrective to Cartesian inwardness, with its propensity for solipsism and self-regard and also a likely generator for it. (One cannot say "reliable" because, as argued in the previous chapter, what exactly causes it remains mysterious.) The stereotype of the Cartesian thus has a grain of truth. Autonomy requires a degree of self-consciousness and democracy requires that individuals possess a degree of autonomy. Continual (or continual enough) self-consciousness, however, paradoxically requires something beyond the self that is doing the regarding, otherwise it becomes a static self-regard, a narcissism. The corrective is of course other people. One gets by with a little help from one's friends—and enemies or whomever. Other people are the key. Nothing occasions a fresh look at ourselves, in either the personal or intercultural sense of "ourselves," like being made to see ourselves from the perspective, or from what we imagine the perspective to be, of others. A continual propensity to look outward toward others is just as indispensable a requirement of robust doubt as is the searching individual gaze inward. As Sartre and others never tired of pointing out, when it is all said and done, other people are the only real mirror we have. It may be hell or it may be heaven. But there it is.[1]

So liberal contextualism will place a high premium on a certain openness toward others, one characterized not just by politeness or civility or even moral regard for their dignity but by something more robust: taking others seriously as at least potential bearers of meanings that may be important not just to them but to *me*. They could actually have something to say. This is of course far easier stated and embraced in the abstract than it is in real life, where aspects of actual others may render them boring, obnoxious, stupid, or otherwise insufferable. A psychological challenge for the liberal contextualist is thus to maintain that disposition toward intersubjective openness in some robust manner even in the face of our fellows' foibles and flaws. In my view a serious obstacle to the maintenance of this disposition is a kind of liberal dogmatism to which noncontextualist liberals are often prone. This is a propensity to draw an exclusive circle with the extremely overused and very fuzzy notion of "reasonableness," where those who accept certain basic principles are deemed "the reasonable" and those who don't aren't. Admittedly, my own liberal contextualist view is guilty of this to some extent, as evidenced in previous chapters, where signing on to basic liberal *grundnorms* of liberty and equality is the ticket into the charmed circle of reasonableness. The contextualist liberal, however, is exceedingly sparing about what is required to sign onto the liberty-equality gestalt and, owing to the constant pull of the meaning-generating centers from outside the realm of right, he or she is prevented from putting too much determinate content into that gestalt, from building the walls of reasonableness too high. More comprehensive liberals have less restraint and can be found utilizing the notion of reasonableness more recklessly, as a way of making it sound as if *their values themselves* are the reasonable ones, that in effect they have reason on their side. *Ipso facto* those who disagree are unreasonable, lacking in that essential human quality of reason and therefore less fully human, even. This sort of rhetorical bullying has got to stop. Liberals need a way of understanding how those who disagree with them—most of them, anyway—are not simply lacking in reason.

They need, in other words, a new notion of reasonableness, one that is more intersubjectively attuned to the meaning-generating needs and capacities of others. For it is a better notion of what it is to be reasonable that ultimately defeats the one-timer problem, the one who conceives herself the epitome of reason in the flawed and overly dogmatic sense. To develop this better notion, thereby supplementing the previous chapter's Cartesian account, I turn to this study's other main bookend of democratic personhood, David Hume, the modern-era's patron saint of other-directed virtues such as conviviality. For Hume, passion is in an inescapable sense prior to reason; the former motivates the latter and not the other way around. If we are to understand what moves us to act in the first place, we must grasp this, even more so if we are to attempt to understand what moves others. Hume's model for how reason and passion interact allows us to see in microcosm how what I termed in Chapter 4 the realms of "right" and of "meaning" interact at the social level. Hume helps us recognize how it is not, literally, their unreasonableness that causes others to be differently motivated from ourselves. This realization allows us to take others on terms that are likelier to be healthy both for the others and also for ourselves and our own autonomy as well. As indicated above, other people—generally speaking, the more different the better—are the ones who will save us from wallowing in nondoubting unreflectiveness. Since ex hypothesi democracy requires autonomy of us, democratic education requires a kind of intersubjective continuing education. If an impoverished notion of reasonableness has led democratic education into a conceptual dead end, Humean reasonableness offers a way out, a rehabilitation of reasonableness where the notion is less a rhetorical bludgeon than a social ideal. It becomes an imperative for how we should interact with one another as meaning-kneaders and needing-makers. Later I term this ideal "civic friendship," expand upon it, and illustrate how it might function in selected education policy contexts.

THE CASE FOR HUME'S NOTION OF REASONABLENESS

A typical contemporary claim of religious orthodoxy is correct at least this far: liberal freedom and equality no longer pose as bêtes noires of the status quo (however much it may be argued that these ideals are, really, still revolutionary when properly conceived and applied). All the while, the public image of liberalism—such as there is one—has grown staid and juridical, a constitutional proceduralism that wears black robes and attempts to speak from a vantage point beyond the fray, "the rule of law" itself. This unremitting juridical liberalism tends to rest on allegedly intuitive pronouncements about what seems to it "reasonable," and, indeed, in a true sign of its received grace, often thereby positions itself as the very voice of reason itself. "Reasonable" people do not support basing official policy on fairy tales and Bible stories; "reasonable" people do not distribute state benefits by blood and soil or according to the appropriateness of one's rectitude and salvific vision. As citizens, reasonable people are to remain steadfastly neutral about the "whys" of it all, politely mute if the conversation strays too far into symbolically risky territory. But it would be a mistake to view such reticence as a symptom of juridical liberalism's timidity. For it is actually a source of great power. This genius of forbearance, this "epistemic abstinence,"[2] actually increases the reach and confidence of the all-too reasonable liberal lawgiver. He or she becomes a modern-day Odysseus, whose self-deafening allows escape from the sirens, thereby enabling an efficient run through the wine dark sea. Liberal reasonableness in this way effects a portentous trade of meaning for movement.

But there is a cost to this prudent neutrality, this eminently reasonable quietude. It is borne by the sources of motivation and the conceptions of the Good that must, still, premise any actual person's adherence to all the reasonableness. And the highest cost is, strangely, to the very notion of reasonableness itself. If blind adherence to a cause is the very definition of unreason, then we may be suspicious of a conception of reasonableness that requires a self-imposed blindness regarding the deep sources of meaning and motivation. For such a conception would transform reasonableness into a kind of madness. It would also render the brand of liberalism arising from it illiberal, guaranteed to undercut its own motivational roots.

So is this allegedly liberal reasonableness really so reasonable? Can democratic education afford an excess of reason?

My answer is that democratic education should avoid an excess of reason that, in fact, turns out to be no reason at all. We need liberation from a bogus type of reasonableness. I draw my argument from Hume's account of moral psychology, still no worse for wear, which advances an "internalist" account of the relation between reason and the passions. I'll make an analogy between this internalism of Hume's and the above-introduced "excess of reason" problem that I see plaguing democratic education policy. The liberalism that informs the latter postures so frequently as the voice of "the reasonable" over and against putatively "unreasonable" voices and passions that it risks a severe and ultimately debilitating ignorance of itself and its own preconditions. As against an excessively rationalistic picture, Hume famously emphasizes reason's dependence on the passions. Whatever reason may be in the end, it emerges from Hume's account as no longer so simply "in control" as the unique bearer of our hopes for personal and collective moral improvement. Likewise unacknowledgedly dependent on passions, the juridical form of liberal reasonableness is similarly unable alone to premise education policy.

In order better to "see" justice, Plato famously suggests in the *Republic* that we first step back in order to consider it writ large in a community as a whole. Having thus gained this larger-scale understanding, it may be easier to identify it on the smaller scale, to find the just person. "It's not impossible, then, that justice might exist on a larger scale in the larger entity and be easier to discern. So, if you have no objection, why don't we start by trying to see what justice is like in communities? And then we can examine individuals too, to see if the larger entity is reflected in the features of the smaller entity."[3] For the present argument, I propose the same heuristic device, only in reverse. As a model for understanding the motivational requirements of democratic education, I want to explore elements of Hume's moral psychology, specifically his internalist doctrine of how the passions and reason are related. Humean internalism, I'll argue, provides a compelling model for how a universalizing force (such as reason) may shape, structure, and discipline particularizing forces (such as the various passions) without in any simple sense dominating or, certainly, extinguishing them. Hume's account of how reason is both a slave to the passions yet also an instrument for altering them shows how trans-spherical norms of universal rights can be both subservient to and also, in a sense that is crucial for liberals, boundary-keepers and interveners with regard to the various social spheres. Alongside other key democratic institutions, an education system of necessity sits astride this problematic. To maintain legitimacy, it must configure itself in ways that correspond to the larger social settlement in this regard; in doing so, a system of education always maintains a distinctive fingerprint of obligation.

For Hume, the received rationalist picture that morality involves a struggle between reason and the passions, one that should be resolved in favor of the former, is false. Humean moral psychology admits of no such struggle because reason is incapable of providing *by itself* a motivation for moral action. If reason is incapable of providing such a motivation, then a fortiori it cannot be party to such a motivational struggle. As John Rawls explains Hume's position, "Nothing can oppose a passion except a contrary passion; and no passion, or impulse, can arise from reason alone. Thus there is no struggle between reason and the passions."[4] Human beings are moved by passions to which, ultimately, reason is instrumental and hence subordinate. Thus Hume's famous line that "Reason is and ought only to be the slave of the passions, and can never pretend to any office than to serve and obey them."[5] Reason may generate well-formed and universally applicable propositions about moral principles, but what it can never do is by itself motivate an actual human being either to *care* about those principles or the other human beings toward whom those principles are directed. Bernard Williams vividly illustrates this point when he describes the task of talking a suicidal "amoralist" into caring about something. Williams speculates quite plausibly that rational argumentation in the "QED." sense will be of little assistance in such a situation. "We might indeed 'give him a reason' in the sense of finding something that he is prepared to care about, but that is not inducing him to care by reason, and it is very doubtful whether there could be any such thing. What he needs is help, or hope, not reasonings."[6] The best one might do is *point out* that-about-which and those-for-whom the suicidal person cares—hoping against hope that those bonds of care are still there, however obscured they may have become. If the bonds of care are altogether absent—by definition pathologically so—then all hope of persuasion would be gone. For good or ill, premising our moral choices is some thing (or set of things) that is irreducibly nonrational. Hume amplifies this point in another oftquoted passage, where he explains that "the understanding can neither justify nor condemn" a passion. "'Tis not contrary to reason to prefer the destruction of the whole world to the scratching of my finger."[7]

This is the sense in which Hume's psychologistic account of moral motivation may be labeled an "internalist" one: moral motivation arises not from generalizable laws of rationality (e.g., à la Kant, deontological principles that guide all rational creatures insofar as they are rational) but rather from the passions qua the set of already existing motivations that an individual has, from whatever ultimately naturalizable source.[8] Internalism is roughly the idea that if something is to count as a reason X for person Y, X has to "link up" with Y's already existing set of motivations. Given Hume's assumption that our passions are necessary conditions for our being moved, his account is an internalist one.[9] Hume would not say, for example, that Y *has reason* to do some action Z in any other sense than that Y has *her own reason* X for doing Z. (Alternatively, an "externalist" analysis might hold that there is some categorical sense in which Y does or does not *have reason* for doing Z, that is, in the normative sense of having a *good* reason.) If moral motivation is explained causally, this means that the passions are always at the end of any chain of reasoning meaning to explain moral action. And given that the relevant category (i.e., the passions) admits of variety, there are irreducibly plural sources for moral motivation. As Rawls puts it, "there are many possible stopping points given by the passions. The aims of the passions are many, and there is no single end, not even that of aiming at pleasure and avoiding pain."[10] In all of their monstrous and wonderful variety, the passions provide the "stopping points" for our furthest and deepest "whys?."

What is more, according to Hume, where rationalist philosophers and many ordinary people err is in confusing reason with what he calls the "calm" passions, as against those that are "violent." When, considered from my own point of view, someone reacts to a situation disproportionately, I might stress the importance of "being reasonable" to that person in order to calm him or her down. Despite the colloquial use of the term "reasonable" here, Hume thinks that what is most likely being appealed to in the situation is not reason but one of the calmer passions. Say I'm a police officer and I want to shoot a suspect who has just insulted me. My fellow officers implore me to be reasonable, perhaps expressing in whatever language sentiments like "It's not worth it," Y can't just kill someone like that," "You'll ruin your life," or "Think of your family." Let us say that I do "see reason" and calm down, avoiding the murder. One might be tempted to say that I stood down from the shooting because I was motivated by reason not to do it. But Hume would say that this kind of talk obscures what has really happened. A better explanation involves looking at the situation as one in which the calm passions have, happily in this case, triumphed over the more violent passions. The latter might include a sense of being disrespected, a "hot" desire for revenge, perhaps even sadism. The former, however, might include (corresponding to my colleagues' exhortations) calmer, more durable passions such as long-term self-preservation, a "natural" benevolence toward other human beings (e.g., as the fog of the violent passions dissipates I begin to "remember" the humanity of the prisoner) or, even more "naturally," a concern and love for my own family (e.g., my children will be fatherless if I am jailed for the crime). Hume does not see how an unadulterated reason could, by itself, enter into this picture; what we have here instead are certain passions jockeying for motivational status with others. Properly understood, the more "reasonable" course of action is the one motivated by the calmer passions which, although they may often seen nearly dormant in everyday situations, are capable when called on of overpowering their more effervescent violent counterparts.

Reason still has a central role for Hume, however. Despite the initial impression given by the "slave of the passions" remark, he is no simple irrationalist. Of critical importance to the present inquiry is how central a role reason still has. Hume presents a kind of moral-developmental account in which the acquisition of moral virtue requires not (crucially) the obliteration, shoving aside, or any other sort of demotion of the passions, but rather the *cultivation* of them, a "corrected sympathy," leading in the best case to a "progress of sentiments."[11] Although reason cannot itself provide motivational impetus (that is, it can neither snuff out the passions nor, given Hume's internalism, introduce ex nihilo any new ones), it can often perform crucial deliberative work on passions both calm and violent. This process of moral deliberation may happen in a number of different ways.[12] First, reason may *indirectly* augment, diminish or catalyze the replacement of our passions by supplying and helping us to organize relevant information concerning them. So, for example, my craving for the pasta primavera before me may vanish or turn into revulsion when I realize that it has been poisoned. This new information, placed by reason into a syllogism involving my getting sick or dying on eating the pasta, helps reconfigure my passions accordingly. My love of pasta primavera (perhaps playing the role of a violent passion) is not extinguished, but is instead temporarily displaced—through information and logic—by my greater, though usually calmer, passion to avoid dying.

Similarly, there may be passions that have been cultivated that are at bottom actually instrumental to greater and more durable passions, where new information and logic may be effective. For example, my wife has developed over many years a distaste for certain types of fattier meats, things she loved as a girl but later realized that she could not continue eating while also maintaining her health. One might call this a kind of asceticism but for the fact that she convincingly actually does—now—find the meats repugnant. In the Humean manner, she has over time corrected her passions owing to her rational understanding of the health effects of certain foods, even in the face of powerful countervailing forces around her, from less disciplined individuals and from the culture at large. By way of solidifying the point, one could imagine a future scenario where the correction goes in a different direction, maybe one akin to Woody Allen's zany 1970s movie *Sleeper,* in which future scientists discover that steak and chocolate pudding are actually the best things for you, where my wife reverses course and recalibrates those same sentiments. The acquired revulsion would still have to be unlearned though, presumably, a revulsion to chocolate would be easier unlearned than learned. The point, of course, is that a passion that is instrumental to another greater one is vulnerable to correction by reason if it is revealed in actuality to be ineffective or counterproductive.

Reason may also *specify* the passions.[13] My general hunger may find me looking about for fish and chips in particular, my desire to smoke for a pack of Marlborough reds, my impulse to take flight when I hear a noise may be specified into a specific desire to run up a tree to escape the menacing dogs I subsequently realize are making the noise, my love for children specified as a love for *this* child, and so on. Once again passions are corrected, this time by being brought into greater focus. Reason may also aid me in *scheduling* the attempted fulfillment of my passions: a smoke after dinner, a bottle of wine after work rather than before it, erotic involvements at appropriate times and places, and so on.[14] In such instances I am employing reason as an engine of comparison among my passions in the ensemble, where I widen and narrow the scope of my passions as the situation dictates, allowing for the range of what I value. Since I value drinking wine yet I also value the work I do during the day, I should schedule those activities so that I can accomplish both. Remember that it is not *reason* that is telling me not to drink before work, but the enacted acknowledgment of my sentiments regarding my work; it is because I want to enjoy two passions rather than one. The drunkard who loves his work but gets fired because of his drinking is actually *less* of a hedonist than the "rational" sequencer of work and drink.

Lastly, and most dramatically, I will from time to time need to *weight* my passions qua final ends.[15] Though Hume certainly does think that some passions are more basic than others, he seems always to speak of even the most basic passions in the plural. He writes, for example, of the calmer set of desires (the ones so often mistaken for reason itself) that they "are of two kinds; either certain instincts originally implanted in our natures, such as benevolence and resentment, the love of life, and kindness toward children; or the general appetite to good, and aversion to evil, consider'd merely as such."[16] If even our most basic set of passions admits of variety, then there is always the possibility of conflict among them. These are seen in the blessedly rare moments where we are confronted with a heart-rending choice between two courses of action either of which is "backed up" by an irreducibly powerful passion. Existentialists were always good at describing these. Sartre's example of the young man's agony over whether to stay and care for his aging mother or join the resistance against the Nazis comes to mind.[17] Hume would, I think, agree with the thesis Sartre means to support with the example, namely, that objective reason cannot provide some neutral set of rules, a decision procedure, through which we can solve such dilemmas. We must, in a way, make a certain leap of faith. Reason can be effective for Hume, though, where there is some disparity between the horns of the dilemma, that is, at least some way to differentiate them by their "felt" weightiness. Though Hume may be somewhat optimistic on this score (in the sense that for him such conflicts seem largely resolvable), reason may with the aid of such dilemmas help us establish for ourselves what one might call, after the economists, a personal "preference schedule," a "motivational set," or, perhaps more poetically, what Max Scheler calls an *ordo amoris,* an ordering of our love.[18]

To engage in these kinds of moral deliberation is precisely to embark on a progress of the sentiments, where reason facilitates the progress but never replaces the sentiments themselves. Ultimately, Hume has a much larger story to tell about how this progress leads us to embrace social conventions of justice (justice qua "artificial virtue," that is, au courant, a "socially constructed" one) on which all civilization depends and, ultimately, a shared sense of humanity where one's narrow sense of self yields to a larger intersubjective moral identity. "I esteem the man whose self-love, by whatever means, is so directed as to give him a concern for others, and to render him serviceable to society."[19] As Annette Baier elaborates,

> Hume has a famously fluid concept of the self, and the fluid ego boundaries that allows work interestingly in his moral psychology. One could say that, on a Humean version of moral development, the main task is to work to a version of oneself and one's own interests which both maximizes the richness of one's potential satisfactions and minimizes the likely opposition one will encounter between one's own and others' partially overlapping interests.[20]

So all of Hume's talk of the passions and reason emphatically does not entail any simple sort of egoism or moral solipsism, where I can never break out of the cage of my own narrowly defined interests. It might be said that in Humean moral psychology, my passions, my loves and fears, hopes and desires, are rather gateways or opportunities for me to grow toward my fellow human beings, the progress of such sentiments being motored by a fellow feeling, the basis for which is, fortunately, natural to the members of the species.[21] In this way, the latter day Humean might say, in the manner of contemporary evolutionary psychology, that the moral—the whole amalgamated reason-passion package—is continuous with the psychological. This is not to take a position in any nature versus nurture debate except to pay homage to the uncontroversial point that we are, all of us, some admixture of the two. Reason just *is* the arrangement and rearrangement of our passions, and its exercise does not place us somehow above or beyond them. Whatever it is, reason is no set of wings with which to escape ourselves.

Given this Humean picture, then, the dramatis personae of my analogy between Humean moral psychology and democratic education policy are as follows: reason plays the role of democratic reasonableness and the passions play the many roles assigned to them by perfectionistic individuals and groups who are motivated toward civic commitment by deep and comprehensive conceptions of the Good. These latter may certainly be altered by reason or reasonableness, but they do not in any clear sense *rest* on them. We may reject a perfectionist's comprehensive conception of the Good for its lack of reasonableness, as in the case of abandoning traditional religion because it posits metaphysical entities—God, angels, Hell, and so forth—for which there is no rational justification. But this is destructive work, the specialty of reason's acid corrosiveness. Something much closer to the passions is at work when it comes instead to constructing houses of belief to inhabit, realms of final meaning that give us at least provisional answers to the greatest "whys" of life, order and otherwise make sense of whatever virtues we take as such and, in politics and education, and decide what is worthwhile to pass on to future generations. Often these are of the calmer variety, and as such sometimes disguise themselves as reason. Reasons may be plentiful along the way, but at the end of the motivational line there is always a sentiment, not bare reasoning. The simplest and most childlike "why?" always forces any reason, even a chain of them, behind and beyond itself. We may indeed often "have our reasons." But whether or not we have the reasons we have the passions.

I think that a simple acknowledgment, à la Hume, of the dependency of our liberal democratic reasonableness on the many passionate ways in which we come to *care* about being democratically reasonable can go a long way. Reasonableness, as circularly defined by Rawls and other political liberals, is essentially a marker of agreement with certain basic liberal *grundnorms* of human equality and freedom.[22] A Taliban-like conception of the Good that involved the thoroughgoing disenfranchisement of females would ipso facto be considered to be unreasonable, as would be some other statist dystopia that massively suppressed civil liberties. These are to be regarded as unreasonable views because they are illiberal. They are illiberal because they egregiously enough violate liberal norms of equality and liberty. What this definitional fiat tends to conceal, however, is the extent to which this democratic reasonableness concerning the basic terms of political cooperation is parasitic upon some commitment—or, more likely, in a heterogeneous society, a set of them—deep and abiding enough to motivate political action on behalf of equality and freedom in the first place. However complementary with whatever may be our human nature and however much they may be nurtured, such democratic commitments are neither hardwired, bred, nor merely conditioned in us. They are *historically* developed, human platforms of facticity on which we build. But even though the basic democratic commitments are importantly "there" in the culture, it is internal to democracy's very meaning that our commitment to them must be to some appreciable degree conscious and reflective, not just aped. Learning democracy cannot be wholly like learning a mother tongue. It may have a "feel" to it, a "rhythm," even a "spirit" (e.g., the "Spirit of '76"). There may be reinforcing songs and slogans. But it must also be *cognitively* appropriated, to some extent consciously "fit in" and made deliberately to cohere with one's other motivating beliefs, and ultimately one's comprehensive conception of the Good, to the extent one has one. This is where we find the major premises for democracy's own moral arguments and justifications.

If it is to involve the *demos* actually ruling, democracy requires citizens who engage in, to use Gutmann's apt phrase, "conscious social reproduction," rather than mere reflexive social reproduction, however desirable may be that which is being reproduced.[23] It is necessary to embrace the democratic terms of cooperation mindfully rather than merely go through their motions. One can all too easily imagine what this "merely" means because we so often live it, perhaps of necessity in a large and complex society: proceduralist zombies, we often mindlessly follow "the rules" of allegedly fair procedures that we simply find "always already there," tacitly assuming they are there for good reason—*someone's* good reason. To a certain degree this everyday reflexive mindlessness is only practical (e.g., following traffic rules), but it is certainly not sufficient if it characterizes the whole of our embrace of the terms of cooperation. Democracy needs people—for its own stability and also for its very identity—who follow the important rules not merely out of habit but because in some important sense they have *decided* to follow them.[24] Any decent political education would concern itself centrally with this distinction. It is certainly good to develop participatory habits such as voting. But this surely isn't good enough. There also has to be a moment of reflective appropriation where one has some more or less justifiable understanding of exactly why voting is civically vital. In a democracy, there is a strong imperative for us to have some degree of self-knowledge, the "conscious" part of Gutmann's conscious social reproduction, such that we are doing what we do in a way that goes beyond simply being told to do so. A certain imaginative agility is needed, a dexterity at attaching—or at least *conceiving* the general outlines of the attachment—of one's democratic politics to one's most deeply held nonpolitical beliefs.

So democratic education centrally involves a vital moral-psychological linking operation. It must effect a rendezvous between the relatively thin and narrow political terms of cooperation (that are definitive of reasonableness) and the variously elaborated, thicker conceptions of the Good that provide meaning and direction to individuals and their collectivities in a more thoroughgoing manner. Like any competent pedagogue, democratic education must take people as it finds them and then transform them, hermeneutically appropriating the horizons provided by both the comprehensive commitments and also the relatively autonomous political commitments ("relatively autonomous" because they admit of multiple supports, precisely analogous to the institutional autonomy described in Chapter 3). When confronted with adherents of a comprehensive conception that seems ostensibly hostile to democratic reasonableness, the democratic educator will therefore avoid a neocolonialist strategy of "conversion." She will instead follow a more hermeneutic principle of charity that will assume until proven otherwise that the comprehensive conception in question is compatible with democracy. Now it may turn out that the charity was overextended. There are comprehensive conceptions that are not only nondemocratic but antidemocratic.[25] But, in all but the most extreme cases, one should probably always err on the side of continuing to extend the charity, the inherent illiberality of statist overreach being an independent worry.[26] Typically, in pursuing its linking strategy with anti-democratic-seeming groups, democratic education will seek alliance with the more liberal elements among the group's adherents and help them make the case to their fellows. With its well-documented catalog of abuses (some of them severe and chauvinistic) as well as successes (some of them glorious), American and other immigrant-absorbing democracies have long been engaging in this assimilative-educative dynamic. There are those who would see this assimilative linking process as worthy only of condemnation, emphasizing only the "trail of tears" abuses, those who would see democracy as hypocritical whenever it dares "touch" anyone else. To this point of view, it must be emphasized that democracy is not moral laissez-faire. Not everything goes. Though an abundance of caution must be used in making such a judgment, some things are indeed beyond democracy's pale. One does stand *somewhere* when one stands there.

Like Humean rationality, at its best democratic reasonableness is itself transformed even as it transforms. For as it forges the linkages between the terms of cooperation and the many comprehensive conceptions, it inevitably alters its own self-understandings and practices. When confronted by, say, the comprehensive conception of a Martin Luther King, Jr., it may expand its own working notion of the circumference of reasonableness qua inclusion—even as it "assimilates" a previously disenfranchised group into the political process. So it is not just a one-way street, a civilizing mission against irrational elements of the population. As with Humean internalism, it is not a matter of replacing passions with reason, but allowing reason its place alongside the passions so it can then transform and be transformed by them. These transformations, these linkages are themselves the work of reason, not a reason that stands alone, but a reason that is conjunctive and disjunctive, that links comprehensive commitments to democratic politics and that delinks, where necessary, items within those very same categories. When the democrat asks the partisan of a particular comprehensive conception to "be reasonable," she is not therefore asking him to *abandon* his comprehensive conception in favor of the nakedly reasonable. She is instead challenging him to explore ways to effect an acceptable linkage between the cherished comprehensive conception and the hoped-for democratic norms. It is in accepting this challenge that one begins to engage in democratic education. In the Deweyan vocabulary, one might call it "growth," where the process described by the linking operation is *itself* the "reasonableness." But democratic reasonableness does not itself provide motivation. Instead, it *brings motivation to bear* on the set of reasonable terms of political cooperation, anchoring them in the only way that such anchoring can work, by grounding them in something exterior, the deeper and less movable the better.

This linkage is itself the work of reason. Analytic and synthetic, it is parasitic upon that which it analyzes and that which it synthesizes. It does not stand alone. It is a making consistent, a catalyst for the hoped-far coherence in the lives of individuals of their democratic politics with their various comprehensive conceptions of the Good. This is really what democratic education writ large amounts to. From the point of view of intergenerational reproduction, it is a grand and hopefully virtuous circle of reasoning, a reflective equilibrium of sorts, with the emphasis on "reflective." But the democratic commitments that define "the reasonable" ought not be misrecognized as Hume thought reason itself so often is. The commitments that define the scope of the reasonable are themselves passions, albeit calmer, better-anchored ones. And they are calmer and better anchored not because they are above and apart from the passions, but precisely because they are ensconced so well within a healthily diverse range of them. It is almost like a cautious stock portfolio, where diversification and an eye toward the long range keeps one safe from the wilder ups and downs. But it is a matter of diversification, not divestment. The goal of democratic reasonableness is not to hunt down and eliminate the irrational. The goal is to stabilize democracy by making reasonableness a cherished part of peoples' lives, a necessary and durable component of their own self-understanding. I suspect that Hume, that passionate lover of moderation, has something like this in mind when he describes moral progress as a process of enlarging our sentiments such that we might come "to fix on some *steady* and *general* points of view."[27] Likewise, democratic education should "fix on some steady and general" conception of democratic reasonableness as a central goal. But we arrive at that reasonableness only through the passionate self-conceptions and ultimate purposes that we ourselves continue to forge.

REASONABLENESS AS CIVIC FRIENDSHIP: THE RAWLSIAN VIEW

So as autonomous human beings we do indeed need our own passionate self-conceptions and, however opaquely grasped, a conception of the ultimate purposes of our activity. Democracy in this way requires deeper moral roots for itself than it alone can provide. This requirement implies an urgent yet underemphasized educational imperative to shore up the reasonable comprehensively grounded moral anchorings that keep secure the political terms of cooperation that constitutional democracy needs in order to function. This idea is neither exotic nor alien to the American political tradition. As none other than George Washington emphasizes in his *Farewell Address*, "Of all the dispositions and habits which lead to political prosperity, religion and morality are indispensable supports . . . Whatever may be conceded to the influence of refined education on minds of peculiar structure, reason and experience both forbid us to expect that national morality can prevail in exclusion of religious principle."[28] Along with the cultivation of citizenship proper, this Washingtonian civic education concern with citizens' comprehensive groundings must therefore be recognized as a legitimate and even core aim of democratic education, one presenting a particular challenge to polities as heterodox as the United States and others. Analogous to capitalism's need for extracapitalistic virtues like loyalty and trust,[29] democracy requires extrademocratic virtues associated with the commitment to *some* reasonable comprehensive account of the Good, secular, or religious. For without the deeper groundings (and I emphasize "grounding*s*," in the plural), the political cooperation is placed at unacceptable risk.

A compelling way of framing this concern is in terms of what Rawls calls "civic friendship," an idea with a long pedigree in democratic thought, extending, at least, to the semi-antagonistic Platonic and Aristotelian conceptions.[30] Based on mutual respect and also a concern for democracy's stability, Rawlsian civic friendship enjoins us to have a certain kind of concern for one another's character, though not in the manner of the busybody who wants to scrutinize everyone's private lives. Civic friendship represents a public way of relating to one another *as citizens*, where we are not only civil in our discourse but we work positively to overcome mutual suspicion and hostility by bothering to try to understand something of our own and our fellow citizens' deepest moral motivations. I will argue that, although rightly constrained constitutionally by the Establishment Clause, the public school system can and should do a great deal more for civic friendship than it now does. My Washingtonian concern is how our public schools—presently enrolling some 90 percent of U.S. schoolchildren—might best advance civic friendship, both for the sake of our souls (so to speak) and also for our "national morality" and "political prosperity," that is, for democracy itself.

Civic friendship as an educational imperative encompasses two main goals: (1) securing a certain level of spiritual-moral-aesthetic depth in individual citizens' political commitments and (2) cultivating in citizens an ability to see and tolerate the divergent (within a reasonable range) depths possessed by their fellows. Civic friendship therefore involves a sort of "deep tolerance" beginning, so to speak, at home, that is, emanating from the very depths of the commitments themselves. There are many reasonable ways of being deeply supportive of democratic norms. What is unreasonable is to expect that these norms need no support outside themselves or that everyone must always support democratic norms in the same way. The drive toward uniformity of deep commitment will require a degree of overly intrusive and coercive state action that will become illiberal in its abridgement of individual liberty. To borrow a metaphor from evolutionary biology, with regard to the ways in which individual citizens support democratic politics, liberalism and its pedagogies must be satisfied with analogous rather than homologous commitments, that is, with those that look and function the same politically rather than with those that are identical "all the way down." But it would be equally mistaken to suppose that this required degree of moral-developmental laissez-faire means that the depthfulness of citizens' comprehensive conceptions of the Good (henceforward, "CCGs") is of no concern to liberalism. Again, the concern is rooted in stability. Since liberal contextualism cares about democratic politics, it must also care about what is necessary to preserve and perpetuate democratic politics. Complacency on this point is excessively risky as, following the building materials metaphor, history teaches that political norms that are unsupported in the sense that they are not really believed in, have a way of eventually collapsing. There is no reason to think this less true for democracies than for other political regimes.[31] Indeed, it may be more so.

With such concerns in mind, this section explores and defend civic friendship as a core aim of democratic education and what it might mean for U.S. school policy. In doing so, I'll pay particular attention to the First Amendment, most pertinently the "nonestablishment norm,"[32] a legal parameter that realistic education policy prescriptions must recognize. The embrace of civic friendship therefore involves a simultaneous acceptance of the legal constraints nonestablishment places on the actual teaching of CCGs. With both the imperative and constraints in mind, then, I'll describe and champion what I think are two good ideas: an extracurricular "school stamps" plan first proposed in the 1970s and a modified version of a "clergy in the schools" counseling program recently struck down by a federal circuit court.

Liberal contextualism, through schooling and other appropriate means, does what it can to respect and foster the depth of commitment that our many extant CCGs can supply. Following Rawls, the fact of plu-ralism—and not just that typically recognized by identity politics, but *all* kinds within wide boundaries of reasonableness—is not a matter for liber-als grudgingly to accept, a "compromise" with a less-than-perfect world. It is, rather, an expected and welcome product of liberty itself: insofar as they enjoy political freedom, rational individuals will diverge rather than converge as they attempt to find answers about the final ends of life. (I say this fully aware of the irony that liberal contextualism's Rawlsian assump-tion of heterogeneity, though protective of their autonomy at the political level, is also quite contrary to what many CCGs actually believe on their own terms.) This means "that the diversity of reasonable comprehensive religious, philosophical, and moral doctrines found in modern democratic societies is not a mere historical condition that may soon pass away; it is a permanent feature of the public culture of democracy."[33] From the point of view of liberal contextuaism, democracy must remain metaphysically humble. As Anthony Appiah elegantly expresses it, "as a political creed, [liberalism] does not claim to answer every ethical question, every shal-low puzzle or deep mystery about how one should live."[34] The lifeblood of such a system is the abiding conviction that no one has the final truth about the Good (and, a fortiori, how best to teach it), not even—perhaps especially not—those at the helm of government's police powers.

Consistent with this conviction, and like Rawlsian political liberal-ism, liberal contextualism differs in salient ways from a more staunchly comprehensive or Enlightenment liberalism, which I'll very roughly de-fine here as a liberalism confident that its core commitments (such as autonomy) matter "all the way down" and across all or most all spheres of life.[35] (For clarity's sake I should note here my implied contention that political liberalism and liberal contextualism are wholly consistent; for present purposes they are interchangeable doctrines.) Liberal contextual-ism lacks this confidence in its own comprehensiveness, however, and is therefore proportionately reluctant to impose itself as a CCG on other CCGs, particularly when this imposition involves the use of police pow-ers, as it often does and as it quite unambiguously does in U.S. school policy (e.g., truancy laws send parents to jail if their children do not at-tend a state-approved school). Sensitive to such considerations, following the Rawlsian conception, liberal contextualism holds those in positions of governmental power (legislative, executive, judicial) to an exacting "idea of public reason," where the appeal to any kind of orthodoxy, secular or reli-gious, is to be foresworn by the power-wielders *in their capacity as wielders of governmental power.* This applies to governmental actors involved with the basic structures of democracy; in constitutions, law courts, executive orders, legislative statutes, and the like, a certain justificatory abstinence is to be observed, in the same sense as in the enumerated constraints in the Bill of Rights ("Congress shall make no law . . ."). A judicial opinion should not cite Scripture as a basis for a ruling, a state governor should not appeal to a view about what she believes is "natural" or not (e.g., regarding homosexuality), an elected school board should refrain from most forms of ideologically motivated content-based viewpoint discrimination, and so on. The idea of public reason rules out certain ways of justifying governmental action, and as such it will be rejected by "those who believe that fundamental political questions should be decided by what they regard as the best reasons according to their own idea of the whole truth."[36] It is this insistence on the "whole" truth (a tendency of comprehensive belief) that is, from the perspective of political liberalism, "incompatible with democratic citizenship and the idea of legitimate law."[37] A "constitutional essential" depending upon *any* particular comprehensive conception—religious or secular—rather than upon, say, the political requirements of democratic citizenship, is therefore out of bounds.

If, *in my official administrative capacity* as a public school official, I create an Earth Day holiday on the grounds that the Gaia Hypothesis commands it or because I think consumerism is destroying our souls, then I have violated the idea of public reason, inasmuch as either rationale would seem to depend on some CCG. (The same would be true of having a day off for Good Friday rather than for spring break.) But if I explain Earth Day in terms not anchored to any comprehensive doctrine, perhaps appealing to the need to combat littering, promote recycling, or defeat a throwaway mentality that has deleterious environmental consequences, then I've abided by the idea of public reason. Rawls thinks individual citizens should also abide by the idea of public reason when debating matters of public policy, in effect, deciding such matters *as if* they were actual legislators. He calls this a "duty of civility": the idea that when we address one another as citizens, we should do so in ways that are not limited to the comprehensive doctrines we ourselves happen to hold. In the public square, then, there is indeed a duty either to bracket one's deepest beliefs in favor of more publicly accessible justifications or at least to follow what Rawls calls "the proviso" that one add such a publicly accessible justification where one has spoken of the proposal exclusively in terms of one's own favored comprehensive doctrine. It is important, though, to add that, as opposed to the idea of public reason as applied to governmental actors, this duty of civility applies to citizens and is a moral duty based on respect for persons rather than a legal one. A legal duty of civility would violate free speech.[38]

Despite these legal and moral duties, however, Rawls is at great pains to counter the common criticism of political liberalism that it excessively constrains public debate by ruling out comprehensive conceptions, gagging citizens by not letting them speak their full minds, disrespecting their deepest beliefs. This criticism misses that Rawlsian public reason and attendant considerations like the proviso apply to government actors in their official capacity and only in very special situations to private citizens (again: when they are debating essential matters of public policy, and even there only as moral not legal requirements). He emphasizes how the discursive restraints do not apply to what he calls the "background culture," which comprises just about everything outside the formal political structure, including, he says specifically, "institutions of learning at all levels."[39] "The idea of public reason does not apply to the background culture with its many forms of nonpublic reason nor to media of any kind. Sometimes those who appear to reject the idea of public reason actually mean to assert the need for full and open discussion in the background culture. With this political liberalism fully agrees."[40] In the background culture, then, the level of comprehensiveness with which we advance our views is to be unrestricted.

Yet the notion of the background culture upon which Rawls relies is overly vague when applied to the U.S. public school system. Because of their status as government actors who are exercising compulsion (starting with age-sensitive school attendance statutes), K–12 school personnel are subject to a host of Establishment Clause and other limitations on their basic freedoms, for example, the size of the religious trinkets they can wear, discussing their religious beliefs with students, the time off they are allowed for holidays, even the extent to which they are allowed to speak their minds (including on matters of public concern).[41] The nonestablishment norm separating church and state therefore *in practice* restricts schoolteachers and other school officials to something very much like the Rawlsian idea of public reason, more so than those in other areas of the background culture such as higher education (where attendance is formally voluntary), professional and community groups, the media, and also less compulsory areas of government itself (e.g., religious displays at certain government offices, prayers at the start of legislative sessions, etc.). Political liberalism must therefore accept restrictions on school officials such as those described in my Earth Day example, thereby repositioning public schooling as a constitutional essential or, at the least, qualifying its alleged status as merely part of the background culture. Either way, non-establishment must obtain in public schools.

Vital questions are therefore raised as to how liberal contextualism might guide education policy. For, through its Rawlsian conception of public reason, liberal contextualism effectively *expands* the principle of nonestablishment to cover the traditionally covered religious justifications as well as secular ones, including Enlightenment liberalism. Consistent with this insight, Rawls emphasizes how "[t]here is, or need be, no war between religion and democracy. In this respect, political liberalism is sharply different from and rejects Enlightenment liberalism, which historically attacked orthodox Christianity."[42] The question then arises as to how political liberalism can uphold what appears to be its own *expanded* principle of nonestablishment ("expanded" because it covers secular as well as religious doctrines) while also supervising a school system capable of sustaining the deep thinking and thoroughgoing (but diverse) commitments democracy needs in order to survive. In other words, how, given the ideological austerity imposed by expanded nonestablishment, can liberal contextualism integrate the CCG-inspired drive to connect pedagogy to final ends with the democratic-procedural impetus toward ensuring a fair and open educational system?

As if in implicit response to this question, too many "school wars" partisans have been tempted into a false choice between either orthodox Goodliness/Godliness against a soulless regulatory state or, perhaps, a litigious rights agenda posing as a heroic casting off of superstition. Liberal contextualism is different from either extreme because it takes seriously both liberal democracy's constitutional and also citizens' needs for a substantive moral grounding of their own choosing. Rawls provides an update of the Washingtonian sentiment quoted at the outset:

> The roots of democratic citizens' allegiance to their political conceptions lie in their respective comprehensive doctrines, both religious and nonreligious. In this way, citizens' allegiance to the democratic ideal of public reason is strengthened for the right reasons. We may think of the reasonable comprehensive doctrines that support society's reasonable political conceptions as those conceptions' vital social basis, giving them enduring strength and vigor.[43]

Understood as an expansion of nonestablishment *in the service of deepening citizens' chosen comprehensive allegiances*, liberal contextualism imagines a compromise that would orient school policy toward both the Right and the Good(s).

But any such compromise would be delicate and very difficult to pull off in practice in the U.S. public school system. For expanded nonestablishment means that state-run schools will *not* for the most part be in a position to accomplish what even a congruent CCG would require of them; school officials would be too restrictively gagged to fully provide the needed depth dimension (religious *or* secular) to a child's education.[44] Yet absent a comprehensive system of nonpublic schools accessible to all students, the state-run public schools will continue to be depended on by the vast majority—for very practical access reasons if for no other. These realities suggest that if there is to be a Washingtonian-cum-politically liberal effort at deepening the comprehensive moral groundings of young citizens through K–12 education, such an effort must: (1) work largely within the framework of the existing public school system, (2) not rely on public school personnel to provide the actual direct instruction about the particular comprehensive moral groundings and most important and challenging of all, (3) even if they create strange political bedfellows, undertake creative and large-scale experimentation involving collaboration between public schools and appropriate community groups—religious and nonreligious, "faith-based" and secular, "pervasively sectarian" and nonsectarian—that are oriented by some reasonable CCG.[45]

Such an agenda would doubtless cause a great deal of initial confusion and upheaval. But, I believe, the short-term turbulence would be more than made up by the long-term gains in legitimacy, creativity, and adaptability that would be won for the public education system as a whole. For all these reasons, the crucial goal of stability for that system would thereby also be aided, given that an educational system so reformed would be publicly recognized as generating its own support from a healthy number of parties with otherwise divergent interests[46] and, in the process, going some ways toward filling the vacuum of legitimacy left behind by the dissolution of yesteryear's broad public school coalition of business, labor, and others. For the many relevant CCGs, such an educational regime would be a door held wide open to their efforts to show young citizens how their everyday lives are (and ought to be) inextricable from their own and their fellows' yearning for proximity to the Good as they see it. Yet this reformed politically liberal educational regime would also respect an expanded nonestablishment principle that would not allow the state directly to support religious or other comprehensive instruction. By various means, the state would play a salutary *indirect* role, one consistent with nonestablishment and other relevant constitutional parameters.

CIVIC FRIENDSHIP APPLIED

How might all this work? By way of an answer, let me stress that any number of policies might be consistent with what I'm suggesting. It is neither possible nor desirable for a lone theorist to lay out a detailed menu of policies and procedures that will work for every locality within our still-kicking tradition of local control of schools, some 13,000 school districts in a daunting heterogeneity of settings. More, it would be implausible to suggest that any particular education policies follow deductively from the first principles—such as they exist—of liberal contextualism. From its metalevel perch, the prescriptive determinacy of this kind of political theory is limited. Full, detailed policy prescriptions do not spring from the head of liberal contextualism merely to be implemented by those "on the ground." On the contrary, one of the great strengths of liberal contextualism is that it provides a framework for innovation, where most of the creativity and excitement is properly relegated to the groups and individuals most directly involved, closest to the pulse of a particular practice or sphere of life.[47] It in no way implies that democracy's education policy must pursue the "one best system" of any description,[48] democratic process being best understood, in Joshua Cohen's terms, as "one kind of institutionalized process of reason giving."[49] Reason giving is quite different from dictating policy. There is a need for prescriptive modesty, then, the larger point being to defend the creation of the conditions for innovation rather than to issue directives detailing what those innovations must be.

Liberal contextualism aids democracy's durability by ensuring a salutary degree of moral capaciousness. It allows citizens to embrace democracy on their own terms, drawing support for democracy's requisite political conceptions from the perspectives of citizens' many different secular and/or religious comprehensive doctrines. Rawls himself is quite clear on this: "it is central to political liberalism that free and equal citizens affirm both a comprehensive doctrine and a political conception."[50] There will of course be those who do not arrive at conclusions that are in fact supportive of democracy. There can be no guarantee against this. As has long been noted, democracy stands or falls on the wager that the weight of enlightened opinion will fall on the side of the democratic political conclusions the system needs in order to survive. If things are so far gone that no sufficient overlapping consensus is sustainable, then the democracy in question is probably already dead, attention likely having turned in such a case from school policy and toward matters such as borders, treaties, and refugees.

Despite their centrifugal potential, however, as Washington emphasized, democracy also stands or falls according to the strength with which those many different comprehensive doctrines support the democratic political consensus—a point distinct from the mere existence of a consensus (e.g., there could be an anemic consensus, unsettled by the slightest disagreement). There is therefore a strong civic education imperative aimed both directly toward the political terms of cooperation themselves and also indirectly toward the multiple supports for that consensus. This in turn implies that democracy must foster in citizens a certain depth dimension in their own and their fellows' political commitments, though, as I've argued, this vital work must be done indirectly. This is the essence of Rawlsian civic friendship, through which those holding different comprehensive doctrines reassure one another (and, one might add, themselves) about their mutual commitment to democracy: each of us shows how, from our own doctrines, we can and do endorse a reasonable public political conception of justice with its principles and ideals. The aim of doing this is to declare to others who affirm different comprehensive doctrines that we also each endorse a reasonable political conception belonging to the family of reasonable such conceptions.[51] Pursuant to this stability-conducive "reassurance," democratic education must embrace civic friendship, even if it means exploring territory traditionally taboo for most liberals. This includes a willingness to creatively use public schools, in a manner consistent with nonestablishment, as a means for shaping citizens capable of real civic friendship. Civic friendship takes from traditional liberalism its guarantees for constitutional essentials (including nonestablishment). But it takes from extant CCGs the concern to anchor those guarantees in something beyond themselves. Though it thereby makes itself a more fertile field for certain kinds of principled dissent, a pluralistic democracy durably grounds itself nowhere else but in the groundedness of its individual citizens.

A balm for the wounds created by the "culture wars," a civic friendship reform agenda would embrace a wide range of school initiatives and reforms. Consistent with the foregoing discussion, I see the following categories of these as especially relevant:

First, educators must be much more willing than they have been to teach about citizens' many different religions—and a healthy portion of other actual and reasonable secular CCGs—in the public schools, and should embrace the many recent calls from thoughtful observers toward doing just that, including those of the U.S. Department of Education itself.[52] As the Supreme Court has repeatedly made clear,[53] teaching *about* religion per se raises no Establishment Clause worries, so long as it is done in a nondevotional manner, a requirement sufficiently clear for most pedagogical purposes.

The second area is more complex, as it involves rethinking aspects of the postwar Establishment Clause settlements as applied to public schooling and as such is little amenable to any summary generalization. In the broadest strokes, though, and consistent with what it seems to me a civic friendship mission would entail, states and local educational authorities should be allowed to make their schools more porous and penetrable by community groups with religious and nonreligious CCGs, including those one might call "pervasively comprehensive" groups.[54] Schools should continue to adhere to the nonestablishment norm guarding against children being coerced into religious activity by the state, for example, in the areas of school prayer within school and as part of major activities sponsored by the school,[55]creationism (rightly adjudged as having no secular purpose),[56] and in the extent to which schools and religious enterprises may consolidate their activities.[57] Yet the centrality of civic friendship to democratic education should direct policy makers and judges to adopt with regard to schools a looser "neutrality theory" (regarding public aid to private and religious groups performing functions coinciding with the public interest) rather than the stricter "no-aid" separationism that currently obtains in most areas of school policy.[58] In neutrality theory, which is the standard for public aid to competing community service providers (where the set of providers may include religious groups), public money is to be awarded according to religion-neutral criteria so that the religious or nonreligious character of the applicant is to be formally irrelevant.[59] This means, among other things, that a community service group that is religious is not to be ruled out (so long as they are not determined to be pervasively sectarian). Civic friendship would furnish a compelling justification for including religious and nonreligious groups operating according to comprehensive doctrines—even ones that are "pervasively" so—as potential recipients of public money for specified educational activities conducted by those groups. As I've argued, the compelling state interest supplied by civic friendship is the Washingtonian one of securing in individual citizens the deep religious groundings, secular groundings, or both necessary for anchoring their commitments to democracy.

Correlatively, it stands to reason that actual exposure to such groundings in the form of persons actually grounded by them will be the best means by which to induce these individual anchorings to occur. However, consistent with nonestablishment, and as reflected in current law, school personnel must be prohibited from providing these groundings themselves (particularly the religious ones). Given these constraints, the question arises as to what, constrained as they are by nonestablishment, schools might do for civic friendship, beyond what they already do (e.g., "celebrations" of the general idea of multiculturalism and freedom of conscience, neutralist dialogical and conflict resolution techniques, etc.)? My view is that, while the schools cannot and should not *themselves* teach the comprehensive doctrines, they can and should make greater room for the many responsible parties who are not so constrained, a kind of structural-programmatic accommodation, of which I'll give examples below. This is how schools should respond to mounting calls that religion and morality be taught more robustly than they currently are.

For starters, public schools should begin experimenting more urgently with ways they might responsibly delegate appropriate parts of their curriculum and/or extra-curriculum to community groups that adhere to comprehensive doctrines of various sorts. As have other democracies,[60] and consistent with some of the public debate surrounding policy initiatives such as school vouchers and charter schools in our own, U.S. democracy should begin to mature out of its persistent identification of public education exclusively with government-run education.[61] Gone are the days (if they ever actually existed) when one could confidently proclaim that CCGs are private matters in the sense that home and church alone will see to them. It is uncontroversial that the family, for one, is overextended and overburdened (witness, e.g., the decreasing amount of time parents spend with their children, the decreasing centrality of children in parents' lives and social policy generally, including the desperate need for proper daycare and after-school care[62]), so it would make very little practical sense at this historical moment to add yet another burden. It is much more likely that such matters will simply go unattended. As William Galston has pointedly remarked, "the greatest threat to children in modern liberal societies is not that they will believe in something too deeply, but that they will believe in nothing very deeply at all."[63] As it has at its proudest moments in the United States—the fifty state guarantees of schooling for all, the erection of the comprehensive high school,[64] the GI Bill, racial and disability-based desegregation, to name a few—democratic education must perpetually respond to contextual demands. Commitment-corroding large-scale forces of marketization and juridification comprise challenges just as formidable and action-necessitating as any that have come before. In the name of liberalism, some of the older and tidier traditional liberal assumptions may need to fall.

By way of clarification, I will conclude with two concrete recommen-
dations. One is a policy proposal that would help make public schools
more porous (in the above sense) vis-à-vis community groups with comprehensive orientations, while also maintaining nonestablishment and an
appropriate level of oversight. The other is drawn from a recent federal circuit court case outlawing a certain kind of collaboration between a public
school district and religious educators. I'll argue that the outlawed practice
could be easily modified to pass constitutional muster and that the resulting modified program would be consistent with nonestablishment and
conducive to civic friendship.

First, the policy proposal resurrects an idea first proposed in the 1970s
by longtime school voucher advocate and legal scholar Stephen Sugarman,
what he calls a "school stamps plan," in essence, a voucher plan for *extracurricular* activities that leaves in tact the compulsory part of the curriculum.[65] (Such a plan may also be viewed as potentially relevant within the
context of the current *No Child Left Behind Act,* which for schools "needing
improvement" mandates that at least curriculum-related tutorial services
be available at the cost of the school district and furthermore that those
services are not to be provided by the home districts themselves.) With
Sugarman's school stamps plan, families would be issued school stamps
redeemable for educational services of many different kinds, particularly
those most commonly found outside the regular school program. The possibilities for which the stamps could be used would be limited only by the
resources of the community and the suitability of the providers (which
could be certified in various ways—Sugarman suggests, for example, that
providers post a modest bond and file an affidavit with the local educational authority). Also, for feasibility and equity reasons, distribution of
the stamps might be means-tested. Building on Sugarman's idea, school
stamps might be used for foreign language instruction, supplementary
science courses, tutoring of all kinds, athletics, piano lessons, scouting,
acquiring educational material such as books and computer equipment,
certain types of before- and after-school programs for the youngest children, and also certain types of secular and/or religious moral education.[66]
With the Supeme Court's *Zelman v. Simmons-Harris* (2002) decision
clearing the way constitutionally for religiously neutrally intended whole-
school voucher programs involving religious schools, there would seem to
be little question regarding the constitutionality of carefully crafted school
stamps plans.[67] Indeed, such plans would seem if anything less likely to
raise less church-state separationist worries. School stamps plans would be
relevantly dissimilar because they are to a much greater extent outside the

ambit of state compulsory education laws (a factor typically augmenting nonestablishment protections). In addition to this, so long as the criteria for approval and oversight of potential providers were religion-neutral in terms of their intent, as prescribed by *Zelman*,[68] school stamps would constitute "indirect" rather than "direct" aid to provider organizations, in that individuals are doing the provider-choosing (as in the case, for example, of federal student loans to students attending religious colleges). Perhaps most significantly, school stamps would provide an impressive array of secular benefits not easily achievable in other ways. I would also add that such a program would be a natural site for the public service, or "service learning," proposals popular among many communitarians.[69] Sugarman provides some additional details:

> Many persons and groups could qualify as providers of goods and services for which the coupons could be used. The public schools themselves could offer after-school, evening, and weekend programs; but a pupil would not be restricted to the offerings of his own regular school. Other public institutions such as libraries and parks and recreation departments could also become providers. The state or district might even set up warehouses for the purpose of renting educational materials—telescopes, pocket calculators, and the like. Finally, private parties could offer programs in return for the coupons: dancing schools, photographic studios, financial institutions that could train in money management, reading clubs, and so on, as well as individual or small-group tutors of nearly every imaginable subject. Public schools have another role here: to lease space as their facilities for other offers to use. The school stamps plan could operate in the summer as well as during the school year . . . [70]

Administering a school stamps program would involve substantial resources, not only to fund the stamps themselves, but also to sort out the many logistical, clerical, governance, and liability complexities that would ensue. It would be a worthy challenge.

From the perspective of liberal contextualism and its civic friendship imperative, a well-run school stamps program would stand to offer a great deal. First and foremost, it would provide greater opportunities for helping children to discover and elaborate their own moral depths, particularly insofar as they were rendered more likely to come into contact with individuals, informal groups, and organizations who are actually expressing *and tangibly enacting* their various comprehensive commitments. Perhaps they might come to understand what really motivates some citizens to care for the planet, beyond just putting out the recycling every week. They might be more likely to see firsthand how strong religiously and/or secularly based moral views sustain many citizens in physically and emotionally demanding charitable work, such as Meals on Wheels, the foster care of disabled infants, organizing the town's annual parade, becoming a Big Brother or Sister, and working in a soup kitchen. Maybe school stamps will maximize their chances of experiencing directly how lively certain activities can become when animated by the deep and specific convictions rarely on display within public school walls: by participating in a church choir, working with those planning a Wiccan summer solstice festival, researching their own and others' genealogy and family history, interpreting their dreams with Freudians or Jungians, studying anti-Semitism and a trip to the Holocaust Museum in Washington, DC, learning an Asian martial art and its enveloping moral and spiritual code, and so on. This kind of thing would, I think, be very far from "cafeteria"-style multiculturalism and other superficial attempts at "celebrating" diversity currently afflicting many public schools. It would enable a much more authentic encounter with diversity of all kinds (including the moral and religious kinds of diversity systematically ignored by public schools) in an environment where those involved are infinitely freer than public school teachers to discuss and exhibit their comprehensive underpinnings. Young citizens would thereby be less cripplingly sheltered than they are now from people with strong, passionate commitments. For this exposure seems a sine qua non of civic friendship, where one develops an ability to perceive and, where appropriate, appreciate what lies beneath and behind the politics of those who agree and, most importantly, those who do not. Liberal contextualism aspires to forge a citizenry depthful enough to do this.

This leads to my second example. It involves a case from the U.S. Fifth Circuit Court of Appeals, *Doe v. Beaumont Independent School District* (5th Cir. 1999), striking down a school counseling program utilizing clergy as volunteers.[71] Beaumont Independent School District (BISD), a medium-size district in Texas, initiated in 1996 a "Clergy in the Schools" (CIS) program, where individual members of the local clergy were invited into the school to provide volunteer group counseling sessions to students at the school during school hours. CIS is part of a broader "School Volunteer Program" where BISD works with a range of community volunteer groups in order to take advantage of various types of expertise in the community so as to enhance students' education. CIS is open only to clergy, paralleling the composition of the other volunteer programs, which were also limited to individuals of the desired type (other programs utilized local attorneys, senior citizens, and businesspeople). "The Program's stated goals are to provide (1) meaningful dialogue between the clergy and the students regarding civic virtues and morality; (2) a safe school atmosphere; and (3) volunteer opportunities for an additional group of stakeholders in the public schools."[72] School administrators and the clergy volunteers meet to discuss central aspects of the program, including relevant First Amendment constraints on the counseling sessions (e.g., no praying with students, etc.), as the clergy members plan one or two visits to the schools annually (elementary schools are to be visited once, secondary schools twice). The majority of the clergy volunteers were Protestants, but there were others, including a rabbi. (The school explains this disproportion as reflecting the pattern of religious affiliation among the local population.) When they arrive on campus, school personnel escort the clergy volunteers inside, whereupon school officials (administrators and counselors) then select students for participation

> with an eye toward assembling a group diverse in ethnicity, academic ability, and school deportment. BISD officials then remove the selected students from class and assemble them in another schoolroom to participate in the group counseling, without parental notification or consent . . . students who are selected have the option of declining to participate. Each counseling session is attended by the school's principal and counselor. Under the Program's guidelines, the sessions are designed to comprise approximately thirty-five students and ten to twelve volunteer clergymen; the guidelines proscribe one-on-one meetings . . . [73]

The District had distributed a "Fact Sheet" further explicating the aims of CIS. These are detailed in Judge Emilio Garza's dissenting opinion:

> The Program sought to provide "a positive forum which contributes to open dialogue of students discussing concerns and problems of the 21st century," to create a meaningful dialogue between clergy and students, to make schools safer, and to give the clergy a volunteering opportunity. It included the following set of expectations for volunteers: be a positive role model for students; show concern for students' success; provide academic support for students; be aware of what is happening in the schools; provide a safe and secure atmosphere for students; provide a positive means for obtaining desired student behavior; and help students gain an understanding of the real world. It listed alcohol, peer pressure, racial issues, self-discipline, self-esteem, setting goals, stereotyping, respect, the reasons for rules, unity, and violence as possible discussion topics suggested by students.[74]

The District also stressed in the "Fact Sheet" that CIS did not concern religious issues and, in fact, explicitly prohibited discussion of them in the counseling sessions. It emphasized that clergy in particular were chosen, in the words of the "Fact Sheet," "to provide opportunities for students to dialogue with skilled resources in the community. Because the clergy has the natural skills of listening and communicating, BISD chose to tap this resource which has been previously not used to its fullest."[75]

The *Doe* parents filed for a temporary restraining order to halt the program on behalf of their minor children. This was denied, as was another motion to halt the program. The federal district court then granted a summary judgment in favor of BISD. Yet on appeal to the three-judge U.S. Fifth Circuit Court of Appeals, the Does won a reversal of the district court's ruling against them. The Fifth Circuit Court struck down the CIS program as an Establishment Clause violation, therefore "invalidating the Program and prohibiting its further implementation."[76]

After deciding the Does had standing to sue (none of the *Doe* children actually took part on the counseling sessions, though they were present in classrooms from which participant-students were drawn), the two-judge majority reasoned through the three main Establishment Clause violation tests and ruled that the CIS program flunked them all.

First is the tripartite *Lemon* test. The first prong of *Lemon* requires that the policy in question have a clear secular purpose that neither "advances nor inhibits religion." *Lemon*'s second prong requires that the challenged state action have a "primary purpose that neither advances nor inhibits religion." Finally, *Lemon* also prohibits the "excessive entanglement" of church and state officials in planning, administering, evaluating, and so forth. the activity.[77] The majority opinion finds that the secular purpose of the CIS, the main elements of which are stated above by BISD, is "merely pretextual," largely because of a public statement made by BISD Superintendent Carroll Thomas favoring prayer in the schools and also the fact that the CIS is an "exclusive counseling arrangement afforded to the clergy."[78] Because the *Lemon* test is disjunctive, this flunking of one prong would be enough to rule CIS an Establishment Clause violation. Yet the Court continued. Turning to the second part of *Lemon*, the majority points out that not only is aid to a particular religion prohibited, but also the favoring of religion over nonreligion.[79] Here the main problem also involves the exclusivity of the arrangement. Why did BISD think that only clergy were suitable for counseling on matters of civic virtue and morality? BISD, for example, failed to include lay professionals who might be equally qualified. "BISD does not select its volunteer counselors based on neutral criteria—such as listening or communication skills—but on the very fact that they are *religious* representatives."[80] In this way, BISD exhibits preference for religion over nonreligion, which violates *Lemon*'s second prong. CIS also fails the third "excessive entanglement" prong, owing to the extent of planning and oversight exercised over the program by its created ensemble of religious and government officials: the selection of clergy volunteers, the preliminary planning and "training sessions," program monitoring, the fact that school administrators and counselors attended and facilitated the sessions, and so on.

Second, the *Doe* majority also argues that CIS violates the coercion test laid out in *Lee v. Weisman* (1992) (school-sponsored prayers at graduation create "subtle coercive pressures" toward participation and so violate the Establishment Clause) and *Santa Fe v. Doe* (2000) (school-orchestrated but student-delivered prayers at high school football games violate the Establishment Clause), which prohibits government direction of a religious exercise where objectors are obliged to participate, even if the participation is formally noncompulsory and the obligation is generated merely by psychological or "peer" pressure.[81] Following *Lee,* the *Doe* majority argues that the student who is pulled from the classroom but "does not wish to participate is placed in the untenable position of having to choose either to attend a session he truly wants to avoid or to decline the 'invitation' and thereby risk actual or perceived opprobrium and ostracism from BISD administrators and faculty, not to mention from his peers. This affords the student no real choice, just a 'Hobson's Choice'—either to participate in the Program against his wishes or decline at the risk of becoming a pariah."[82] *Lee* establishes that such a "choice" does not count as voluntary. As for the question of whether the counseling sessions were religious exercises, the premise from which the coercion worry proceeds, the majority again relies on the exclusivity of the selection of clergy as volunteers, which causes "the exercise to lose its secular character entirely," though "in a vacuum student counseling is not an inherently religious undertaking . . ."[83]

Third and finally, the "endorsement test" seeks to determine whether government is endorsing religion by means of the action in question. Here, the government should never favor religion over nonreligion such that a reasonable observer might conclude that the government is taking a position on the matter, "or makes adherence to a religion relevant in any way to a person's standing in the political community."[84] "The government creates this appearance when it conveys a message that religion is 'favored,' 'preferred,' or 'promoted' over other beliefs."[85] There is a related idea of religious "neutrality" from the school vouchers case *Zelman,* which held that a government school voucher program does not violate the Establishment Clause even though most of the money ultimately went to parochial schools. Such indirect aid to religious institutions can be constitutional if the program under which the aid is distributed is explicitly neutral with regard to the religious or nonreligious nature of the aid recipients. Yet CIS does not seem quite neutral in this sense because of the selection and utilization of clergy to the exclusion of other qualified persons in the community capable of engaging in dialogue about morality with students. BISD thus officially "conveys the unmistakable message that religion is favored, preferred, and even promoted over other beliefs . . . Theirs is a message of endorsement that cannot possibly be lost on the young, impressionable, easily influenced schoolchildren whom the law entrusts to these very officials, *in loco parentis,* for the entire school day."[86] This would violate the endorsement test as well as the more recent post-*Doe, Zelman*-style neutrality.

From the perspective of the Establishment Clause, then, the *Doe* majority holds CIS in violation by every available standard. (And there is no reason to think that more recent decisions such as *Zelman*'s neutrality standard would alter that judgment.) Yet Judge Garza's spirited dissenting opinion disputes the majority opinion point by point. In his view, BISD exhibited an "unwavering commitment to a secular focus" sufficient to establish (not withstanding the stray comments of the Superintendent about prayer in schools) their sincerity. He also questions how CIS, in the context of the other volunteer programs that also have a particular focus (and so limit the selection of volunteers accordingly), could really be providing a benefit to religion when, in a situation such as this, it seems more accurate to say that the clergy-volunteers are the ones actually *providing* benefits to the students, not the other way around, and so any benefit the clergy-volunteers end up receiving is "no more than indirect or incidental."[87] More significantly, Garza questions the majority's argument that the exclusivity of BISD's reliance upon clergy for the counseling sessions is analogous to Bible-reading, prayer, or some other religious ceremony. Garza writes:

> Beneath this perception lies the assumption that the clergy are incapable of expounding on civic values from anything but a religious perspective.
>
> I reject the majority's position. That civic values bear a close relationship to certain religious beliefs proves neither that CIS lacks a secular purpose nor that its primary effect is the advancement of religion. BISD

may advocate civic values that "merely happen to coincide or harmonize with the tenets of some or all religions."[88]

For Garza, the exclusivity of the reliance upon clergy does not render CIS unconstitutional because the clergy are not here conducting anything resembling a religious observance and are, in fact, explicitly prohibited from doing so by BISD. Absent any performance of anything resembling distinctly religious duties, their mere *identity* as clergy should not prohibit a public school from inviting them to volunteer. Such a prohibition would risk a non-neutral discriminatory stance toward religion, a priori singling it out and excluding it from involvement in a government program in which groups of every other kind are eligible to participate. This would begin to look like a violation of Free Exercise. To underscore the point, Garza quotes approvingly from none other than Justice William Brennan, who writes, "The Establishment Clause does not license government to treat religion and those who teach or practice it, simply by virtue of their status as such, as subversive of American ideals and therefore subject to unique disabilities."[89]

However, Garza then proceeds to diminish the rhetorical force of his dissent with the intemperate accusation that the *Doe* majority would have to rule against a school speaker such as the Reverend Martin Luther King, Jr., or Archbishop Desmond Tutu.[90] That he would level this charge shows that Garza, despite his salutary caveats expressed above, does not recognize the full subtlety of the main issue. The majority rightly dismisses his mischievous inference, for, as indicated above, the salient issue is not the mere fact of the volunteers' religious identity, but the exclusivity of the selection of them according to that constitutionally singular identity. They respond by reinforcing just this point:

> BISD cannot design and implement a volunteer counseling program consisting *solely* of clergy members. The opinion in no way affects BISD's ability to create a broad-based program that truly integrates the clergy with nonreligious community representatives and certainly does not mandate that BISD discriminate against the clergy or bar a high-profile public figure from advising the student body simply because such [a] figure happens to be a cleric. Civil rights leaders like King and Tutu speaking as civil rights leaders do not lose their eligibility to speak publicly by virtue of their ordination.[91]

This clarification provides rather obvious instructions for how BISD or anyone else might revise such a program consistent with nonestablishment. As we have seen, CIS fails the Establishment Clause tests largely because of the element of exclusivity inherent in BISD's somewhat blind preference for mainstream, "respectable" religion as a teacher of civic virtues, morality, and the like.

If, however, following the majority's suggestion above, BISD had designed the program such that it was at least potentially inclusive of secular persons[92] with the relevant expertise or, to use the terminology of political liberalism, if it had constructed the program as an occasion whereby those adhering to CCG's, *secular or religious,* might participate, then such a program would plainly be in much better constitutional shape. This would also appear fit well with *Zelman*'s insistence on neutrality. The "religiousness" of the program thereby decreased, the other Establishment Clause concerns, such as coercion and endorsement, would proportionately decrease as well.

Such a reconstruction of the program would not only be more consistent with nonestablishment, it would also be more conducive to educating students toward civic friendship. For civic friendship requires citizens to be disposed and able to recognize and appreciate (in the sense at least of trying to understand) the CCGs underlying each of their fellow citizens' adherence to the overlapping democratic political consensus. So civic education is shortchanged when citizens are limited in the range of their fellow citizens' CCGs to which they are exposed. Civic friendship pedagogues would likely face tough pedagogical choices here, quasi-utilitarian dilemmas such as whether it would be better to know, say, three or four other comprehensive doctrines in depth or a dozen of them superficially. This would be an appropriate arena for the exercise of pedagogical expertise. In any event, it is the kind of problem with which educators *should* be wrestling: surely, even in a place like Beaumont, Texas, there is bound to be a wider range of comprehensive doctrines on which to draw than simply those represented by the town's mainstream religions. It is likely that the real reason not to reach beyond the mainstream—and for a school district like BISD to equate virtue and morality with religion—resides in the moral parochialism and consequent lack of ability for civic friendship found in many of the local government officials themselves, along with a large dose of prudent timidity regarding the preservation of school-community relations. As has been the case historically, school administrators are not typically known for their brazenness over and against their local communities.[93] This is largely because "we the people" have wanted it this way: the U.S.'s staunch commitment, relative to other democracies, to the local control of schools has in this respect reaped exactly what it's sown. Far from being a matter of fuzzy "niceness" or etiquette, then, civic friendship will often present something of a challenge to school administrators and local school boards, sometimes compelling them to confront elements of their local communities just often as they "partner" with those same communities. When fundamentalist parents complain about environmentalist volunteers, atheist parents about clergy, and the whole lot of them about who-knows-what, school officials should have something justifiable to say to them all. The teaching of civic friendship gives them a compelling *educational* reason to overcome curricular (and extracurricular) narrowness by both affirming and challenging their constituencies' comprehensive views, the latter accomplished by the school's pedagogical attention to multiple CCGs. The democratic educator's commitment to civic friendship therefore always gestures beyond itself, toward a wider world than is dreamed of in any single "philosophy." It is a social, interpersonal ideal that involves a salutary openness toward others along with a simultaneous willingness to challenge and be challenged by them.

Chapter Seven

The Educated Prejudices of
Liberal Contextualism

EDUCATIONAL, NOT METAPHYSICAL

Emphasizing intersubjective openness, the civic friendship imperative may leave an impression that liberal contextualism is a laissez-faire live-and-let-live sort of doctrine. While this is no doubt true relative to other theoretical alternatives, it is misleading. In this concluding chapter, I want to emphasize the nonneutrality of the idea by describing a couple of its key assumptions. This should correct any lingering impression that liberal contextualism, because it presupposes and in a way welcomes a robust pluralism with regard to comprehensive conceptions of the Good, is for that reason value-neutral. I also have another agenda. I shall illustrate how liberal contextualism's biases render it especially attractive to democratic educators. It is at bottom an *educational* outlook.

As argued previously, liberal contextualism is distinguishable from more comprehensive liberalisms in that its defining commitments are supportable extrapolitically in an indeterminate number of ways. Definitive of all forms of liberalism is the centrality of their commitment to individual liberty and equality. But liberal contextualism does not hold that liberty and equality necessarily possess any keys to larger questions of human existence, such as what sort of life one ought to lead, what we can expect after we die, what are our origins, and soon, in short, Kant's God-freedom-and-immortality sorts of questions. Liberal contextualism is from a moral point of view a large-scale conditional that says, "*If* we want a democratic form of political life, *then* we must embrace X, Y, and Z," where the variables are preconditions for democracy such as "one person, one vote," "state religious neutrality," "constitutional guarantees of basic rights," "universal education," and so on.

These preconditions are thus wholly contingent on the desirability of liberty, equality and the democratic from of political life to which the joint adherence to the two ideals gives rise. I care about "one person, one vote" because I care about equality, "constitutional rights" because of liberty, and "universal education" because of some fusion of the two. Yet the liberty-equality gestalt that animates liberal contextualism and morally premises any reasonable notion of democracy is itself not justifiable on its own terms. Whereas the Enlightenment liberal may find a reason for living and some cosmic satisfaction in a liberty-equality derivative, for example, a notion of autonomous individuals with inherent dignity (or some such thing), the liberal contextualist may or may not. Not necessarily inclined toward a liberalism that goes "all the way down," the contextualist wisely recognizes two important aspects of the liberty-equality gestalt and its moral psychology: first, it is typically not its own reward but is experienced as worthwhile by most people insofar as it can be made to fit into some more encompassing worldview; and second, there are many possible ways to commit, to plug liberty-equality into one of those encompassing worldviews. So, to put it in a way that consolidates several of the arguments of earlier chapters, liberal contextualism encourages both an *ideological coherence* for individual psyches (n.b.: *not* necessarily for the polity as a whole) and also, societally, a *justificatory capaciousness* regarding individuals' acquisition of that coherence.

But there is more. Liberal contextualism does not just acquiesce to societal pluralism, reluctantly acknowledging that one must "allow" for ideational diversity. Though neutral on some eudaimonistic matters, it is not a neutralist view. There are, for starters, the above-mentioned imperatives toward securing individual ideological coherence and justificatory capaciousness. But liberal contextualism also contains some deeply seated biases that are less noticed. I shall call these "prejudices," in the nonderogatory sense of Gadamerian hermeneutics.[1] These prejudices importantly distinguish liberal contextualism from neutralist rivals, such as a more purely contractarian modus vivendi accretion of interest maximization. These prejudices are prejudgments in the sense that they inform at an intuitive level liberal contextualism's characteristic concrete judgments and allegiances. But these prejudices are not typically explicitly acknowledged theoretically. They function more as Humean calmer passions that inform a longer-term sort of outlook; they endure through the shifting enthusiasms occasioned by particular policy disputes.[2] Just as an on-the-whole Stoic individual may have fits of passion over the course of a lifetime and still remain a Stoic, individual contextualists may throw themselves passionately into specific policy frays—even contesting one another in various disputes—while maintaining aspects of their overall outlook throughout. Liberal contextualism's capaciousness makes it very difficult for it to maintain any kind of party line regarding everyday politics. The kinds of prejudices with which I am concerned here reflect a deeper and more long-term outlook than will be displayed in everyday jostlings of normal politics. Though one might fashion a coherent justification for, say, a policy or candidate by deploying these prejudices (as distant major premises in a chain of reasoning or, perhaps, as more emotive rhetorical appeals), they are more likely to lie behind an argument than in front of it.

It should, I'd suggest, be intriguing for theory-minded educators to note how the very deepest of liberal contextualism's motivating prejudices seem to be *educational* in a more substantial way than is the case for other political ideologies. Admittedly, all political ideologies have an educational component. Fascists educate toward fascism, communists toward communism, monarchists toward monarchy, democrats toward democracy, and soon. Views of education informed by political commitments are for that reason "relativist" in Gutmann's sense that the education they envision is derivative from the politics.[3] But liberal contextualism differs on this point. Its animating prejudices imply a view of education as something more than an instrumental means for achieving predetermined political ends. There is some "predetermination," but it is very minimal relative to other views. My argument is that liberal contextualism allows for a richer and more wholehearted embrace of educational commitments because *it itself* is characterized by a profoundly educational orientation that is inseparable from it. It is an *educational* view. This is very clearly seen in what may be liberal contextualism's two most powerful orienting prejudices, preferences it has for certain kinds of arrangements, for the manifestation of certain qualities. The labels I'll give these are (1) *articulation* and (2) *complexity*, the former being a principle of individual justification, of reason-giving, and the latter a largely aesthetic preference for certain patterns of social life. Together, articulation and complexity bias liberal contextualism in a singularly educational manner.

ARTICULATION AND THE GIVING OF REASONS

As indicated in previous chapters, a distinctive feature of liberal contextualism is that it cannot justify on its own terms its basic moral-aesthetic precondition: what I've been calling the liberty-equality gestalt. The hope is that liberty-equality is already valued by citizens on the ground as they find themselves in their facticity, a collective valuation most likely arrived at in the form of an overlapping consensus forged through a series of historical hard knocks. As an agreement *in abstracto* on ideals of liberty and equality, the liberal value consensus must ultimately be defended extrapolitically in realms such as moral philosophy, religion, psychology, and/or aesthetics. From the political point of view, though, what really matters is less the particular direction from which one arrives at the consensus than it is whether or not one's participation in the consensus has a degree of durability. There is no predetermined best way to get there. When religious enthusiasts think of "equality" they will see behind it souls, divine sparks, Golden Rules, and the like. Others will think of "humanity," Kant, or rational bargaining. Still others will think of other things. In itself, the justificatory diversity is not worrisome. What matters is the availability of *some* justificatory pathway through which individuals exercise their practical reason and can embrace equality and liberty on those individuals' own terms. For this reason, despite well-publicized worries about dissensus and fragmentation, justificatory diversity probably aids social stability more than it hinders it. It makes it more likely that individuals will be able to "plug in" to the consensus on terms they actually take as their own; justificatory diversity allows more ways to say "yes."[4]

By emphasizing individuals' *own* terms, I mean to suggest that part of what individualism means—the individualism to which all liberals are by definition committed in some form—is that persons must in some key sense *voluntarily* embrace the basic terms of political cooperation that structure their political lives. This voluntariness is part of what it surely means to act as an individual; it is, existentially, what justifies the use of the first-person singular grammatically. As is recognized in law, it mitigates my personal responsibility if I "choose" to drive the burglar to the next town because he has a gun to my head. What I chose is not to get shot, and the assessment of whatever culpability I may have begins with this fact. This underscores that an important part of what it means *voluntarily* to embrace something is that one possesses conscious and individualized intent rather than, say, being forced or fooled into doing so (or, perhaps more complexly, being driven subconsciously, for example, going along with the crowd, where the latter is experienced as somehow psychologically irresistible). From all but the most exotic moral viewpoints, the forced and the fooled do another's bidding, not their own.

Admittedly, though, to decide the meaning of "true wanting" is to go down a philosophical path fraught with difficulties of the free will versus determinism variety. Maybe we are never perfectly compulsion-free or have complete enough information about anything in our lives to be sure we are not merely following another or being fooled, somehow, someway. The present inquiry may, I think, circumnavigate that set of problems. Happily, the plain and everyday meaning of "wanting" is enough for my comparatively simple present purposes. Under ordinary circumstances, for someone to want to do something means that one has some reason, some reason that, whatever its provenance, one can recognize *as one's own* reason. This implies, actually or hypothetically, that the wanter can give reasons for what one wants, bad ones, good ones, it does not matter. Take my being thirsty. Even if I can't speak for some reason, I *could* tell you about what I want and something about my reasons for wanting it, if only that thirst feels awful and I want that feeling to cease. When it comes to big abstract things we say we want, such as ideals like liberty and equality, the point is the same, even augmented. As for anything else, to want an ideal implies that one has some in principle articulable reason for so wanting. One can't just dumbly, mutely, directly want an ideal in an unmediated way *sans* some meaning-giving symbolic economy. Linguistic engines that we are, human beings constitutionally abhor a symbolic vacuum. This is especially obvious when it comes to desiring an abstraction, an abstraction that *needs* words in order to be understood, to have any sense made of it at all. For individuals properly to be considered to be wanting something, then, those individuals must have their in principle articulable reasons, however inchoate or disorganized or ultimately mistaken. In other words, for person X to be considered a bona fide wanter of ideal Y implies that X can in principle give one reasons for wanting Y. X can unfurl one symbolic banner Y-ward.

What liberal contextualism asks of citizens is consistent with this observation, namely that individuals must be allowed to have and indeed must in fact have their own reasons for desiring liberty and equality, that is, for desiring liberalism itself. Citizens' assent must therefore be minimally rational, "minimally" in the sense that they themselves must have *some* reason, whatever it may be, for supporting the liberal value consensus. The Kantian strain in liberalism prizes this thinking-for-oneself, this acting by one's own lights, as "autonomy," a characteristic of a "mature," that is to say, properly individuated, enlightened citizenry.[5]

This does not mean one cannot coherently reside outside the consensus, or even that it is necessarily irrational to oppose this sort of liberalism. Ayatollahs, commissars, monarchs, and chieftains each have their reasons for rejecting the centrality to politics of the liberty-equality gestalt. On present and past world stages, one finds abundant dissent from the liberal gestalt. It must be remembered that contextualists *assume* but do not argue independently for the very desirability of the liberal value consensus and its political priority. What they assume instead is the *presence* of such independent arguments—of whatever type—in the historically constituted hearts and minds of individual citizens. But as a convergence of those independent arguments, liberal contextualism does assume those arguments' conclusions; it cannot imagine a desirable society of any size and complexity that does not make individual liberty and equality central to its basic social structure along with whatever else it does. Normatively speaking, that's the ticket in. One may eloquently and justifiably emphasize philosophically (or theologically, spiritually, aesthetically, etc.) the moral and/or metaphysical limits of individualism. But if one wishes to inhabit a liberal democracy, then broadside *political* critiques that reject individualism as the locus of liberty and equality are without merit; while reasonable free speech guarantees (underwritten by the commitment to individual liberty) will always allow for the expression of such views, their rejection of the liberty-equality gestalt is sufficient reason to reject them out of hand as, literally, incredible. By definition, there is simply no such thing as a liberal democracy that does not value individual liberty and equality.

My argument about articulability is that within such a polity, there is an imperative internal to its own logic requiring individuals to have their own reasons for supporting it. Again, some may have reason to oppose the overlapping consensus (though within developed democracies, those who *really* oppose it, as opposed to those who might speculate about possible alternatives, remain relatively rare). Such persons are outside the consensus and thereby give rise to all sorts of interesting problems and predicaments for liberal theorists.[6] The key educational point, however, concerns those inside the consensus who must by definition not be driven like cattle toward it. In such a case, there would be no consensus, just a herd of unthinking nonindividuals. For liberals, individuals without reasons are no individuals at all. To the extent that an education system produces herd-animals who do not think their own thoughts, that system is an illiberal one. A great educational challenge for such a system is that the thoughts that people need to think in order to support the liberal value consensus must of necessity emanate from outside that value consensus. As the notion of civic friendship means to capture, this implies that liberal contextualism must guarantee citizens' extrapolitical education in order to guarantee their political education. But liberal contextualism cannot guarantee the extrapolitical education directly because it is just that: *extra*political. Consider, for example, the guardrails that have been set up to contain the impulse toward a lapse in this regard. Notable among these is the nonestablishment norm of the U.S. Constitution's First Amendment, which aims to prevent the state from directly championing sectarian religious agendas. Amid all this, liberal contextualism draws attention to a kind of paradox of dependent autonomy. The paradox is that individuals' *commitments* to autonomy are highly dependent on their antecedent extra-political belief systems. You are far more likely to be enamored of autonomy if you, nonautonomously, happen to have been educated to be so enamored by your family, school, community, political culture, and so forth. That's the "dependent" part of dependent autonomy. But still, despite the ministrations of all these detached and autonomy-generating institutions, you yourself—as an individual—have to choose it. That's the "autonomy" part which, as argued in the Descartes chapter, is inescapable for liberal contextualism.

This paradox presents great and important problems for the implementation of democratic education. To frame the question in Rousseauian terms, to what extent can children and adult citizens be *forced* to be free? Consideration of this problem aids my argument because its very persistence underscores the prior theoretical point that liberal contextualism generates its specifically educational commitments out of it's own internal logic. In requiring that people *choose* it, rather than merely follow or obey it, liberal contextualism requires that people have their own reasons, that they engage themselves and thereby one another in the justification of their political beliefs. This imperative toward articulation, toward practices, and competencies of reason-giving, makes its education system not just a priority for liberal contextualism (schooling was important to the Nazis and the Communists, too), but a definitive one. Liberal contextualism is in this way prejudiced specifically toward *universal* education. It seeks to shape individuals who are autonomous in the requisite sense that they are disposed and able to pass judgment on the world from *their own* point of view, which presupposes that they indeed have a point of view that is their own, one that is not merely another's. One must be oneself and not another. (It will come as good news to café dwellers everywhere that there is an existential imperative hidden within boring old liberalism.) One may accept another's view as one's own, and maybe that is all we ever do, but in that first-person singular moment of deliberate acceptance of the other's view resides liberal contextualism's civic rationale for championing an education system that extends to every individual. Every individual must have it, and to the extent that they do not the society in question is illiberal and undemocratic.

This educational prejudice toward articulation is not without potential problems. One might worry that defining full citizenship on the basis of the articulation of reasons, in other words, on deliberative capabilities, might disadvantage the traditionally disadvantaged, perversely exacerbating extant inequalities.[7] Perhaps in place of a poll tax or literacy test for voting, there would now be some kind of "deliberative capacity" qualification for political participation. Such an abuse of the articulation imperative would indeed be a problem. But there are at least three mitigating factors: First, unlike southern states' attempted disenfranchisement of black voters a generation ago, liberal contextualism's civic imperative toward articulation, as an ideological prejudice, would have merely moral and not legal force. Articulation is tied to the legitimacy of the democratic state as a whole, not to the legal status of individual citizens. This is analogous to how, even though there must be elections for certain offices, this does not mean that individuals are required either to vote or run as candidates in them. This leads to the second point. It would seem that the only thing worse than encouraging articulation would be *not* encouraging it. It would be to leap out of the frying pan and into the fire. Would it be better for the state to say to the powerless person, "Because of your oppressed status, we cannot expect too much of you. So you are less obliged than are the privileged to think your own thoughts, and so on"? I take it as obvious that this level of moral disrespect cannot make for a better response. What is better is to recognize the imperative of articulation as directed at least as much toward the *state* as toward individuals. This application of the imperative would actually *favor* the traditionally disempowered, at least as far as the distribution of educational resources, as the state would be obliged to do what it would take to secure articulation competencies in every sector of the population. The third point is that the worry about the erection of exclusionary civic participation criteria rests in part on a narrow understanding of "deliberation." This is one reason I favor the term "articulation," which seems to me to have broader, more inclusive connotations for individuals of different cultural traditions and how they might express themselves. The kind of deliberation characteristic of an academic seminar or the proverbial New England town hall meeting is not the only or necessarily best model for how individuals might articulate their political commitments. One can successfully articulate and "give reasons" via humor, visual arts, song, dance, and other forms of expression. In fact, the fuller the articulation for these purposes, the better. No one has a monopoly on the proper mode. Propaganda and manipulation via symbol is always a worry here, but this is true of all modes of political discourse, including the classically "rational" deliberative models. The big lie is often presented as a coolly rational matter of following the argument.

THE AESTHETIC PREFERENCE FOR COMPLEXITY

Intertwined with the liberty-equality gestalt is a second prejudice of liberal contextualism, one biased in favor of a certain *picture* of society, its overall "look." More than merely "tolerating" or "recognizing" pluralism, this prejudice leads liberal contextualism positively to encourage pluralism. I'll argue that this tendency is symptomatic of a very deep and little-noticed *aesthetic* preference for something very much like complexity over something very much like simplicity. Liberal contextualism as a social aesthetic favors richness, texture, polychromism. It wants surprises, the unexpected, the new way of seeing things. Though it wants stability and is "bourgeois" in its individualism and propensity for shallowness and consumerism (it does not realize that all that glitters is not gold), it is part of its nature to draw back from the monolith, the uniform, the tidy narrative in which everything has its ordered place.

This preference is not a narrow-minded obsession—almost by definition. There are many situations in which simplicity is to be preferred to complexity. But on the whole and in the long run, liberal contextualism rests on a picture of humanity that is not reducible to or alignable with any one quality or idea or set of either. The basic prejudice is a welcoming of the idea that, individually and collectively we are irreducible in our complexity. It is not that this accords with everyone's intuitions, if indeed everyone has intuitions about such matters. Some possess a predominant bent toward a hermeneutics of suspicion, the seeking of a unifying principle, the wish for an aerie of Truth from which to look down on the valley. While this kind of longing seems widespread (maybe we heirs of monotheism all long for it at some level), the complexity preference taps into a different longing. On a superficial level, it is one that wants merely to be entertained, to be dazzled by lights, colors, and sounds. Indeed, it wants to go shopping. But on a deeper level it can be seen as a delight in the endless varied richness of which human beings are capable. It looks forward to what's in store, expecting and desiring that we should continue to surprise, even amaze one another. It wants continually to be taught something more, to see with world-revealing new eyes that generate above all the desire for still further seeing. It is the "lifelong learner," not as a category of the education bureaucracy or ongoing job-skills inculcation, but as a species of lived hedonism.

On the model of scientific discovery, despite the keen satisfactions to be had in the dispelling of old mysteries, it is even more fun to replace them with newly compelling ones. Like the horror movie junkie, it is an aesthetic that loves to unsettle itself with the removal of old comforts and scare itself by opening doors to dark rooms.

Yet it may seem strange to see beauty in complexity as such. Surely simplicity can have just as great a claim: an austere landscape, a pure diamond, an elegant mathematical proof, a narrative unity, and so on. While the aesthetic case for complexity may proceed via unforeseen juxtapositions, richness of detail, combinations of media, harmonizations of varied elements, profusions of associations, images and sensations, and so forth, it seems clear that instances of beauty might be found under either abstract heading. It is the overall context, the relations among all the relevant elements, the hermeneutical situation, that determines the aesthetic quality of the experience, simple or complex. Like any other abstract binary pair—hot and cold, dark and light, natural and artificial, unity and difference—the quality of the experience is a function of its position within a semantic constellation. Radically isolating any one term from all others would literally sever it from the possibility of meaning. For this reason it would be very odd to express a wholly generic aesthetic preference for any abstract X over any Y, a metaphysically heroic all-or-nothing choice for, say, "difference" or "complexity," apart from what those terms might *mean* in some particular perceptual configuration.

Even so, human beings in wider contexts do seem capable collectively of expressing a kind of categorical aesthetic inclination, where for whatever reasons they have disposed themselves to appreciate things in *this* general way rather than *that*. There are human contexts, in other words, in which a collective aesthetic preference for some large-scale X over some large-scale Y may indeed be discernable. Not justifiable in any disembodied sense, but discernable. The great Jewish shift to monotheism is one of the grandest examples. In a parallel vein, consider a more focused example from the history of Christianity, one with analogues in other religions' histories. Christianity's past is characterized by protest movements that stress a purity of heart and simple faith over and against bureaucratic, clerical mediations and regulations, casuistical laxity regarding the circumscription of the basic monotheistic vision, and so on. Like their Abrahamic forbears, the aspirants toward Protestant reform might be said to have made central a certain kind of simplicity, not just cognitively recognizing that simplicity, but taking it, as it were, to heart and prizing it above other ways of seeing. It has an allure; it yields a multitude of satisfactions. Yet reformations of this type seem fated to be matched with counterreformations that prize the allure of the complex: an unfolding structure where all things have their place, an appreciation of the large range of everyday experience and its distinctive saints and guiding spirits, a distrust of the blinding flame of passionate single-mindedness, a crypto-pantheistic desire to see god(s) everywhere.

Abstracting oneself from its other aspects, including, of course, the horrendous human costs of it all, one might well see this recurring conflict in more or less aesthetic terms, as a clash between two different patterns of sense-making: the Protestant party of simplicity versus the Catholic party of complexity. It is not that Jan Hus and Martin Luther, or Ignatius Loyola and the Duke of Alba, were aesthetes in the sense that they self-consciously understood themselves to be engaged in warfare over what kind of human pattern looks best in some sort of world historical fashion show. Neither is it that the aesthetic pattern such a conflict seems to display reveals its *real* meaning vis-à-vis other analytic frames of reference (e.g., theological, economic, anthropological, or Darwinian analyses of religious conflict). The very weak claim worth defending is rather that it is productive to view the conflict through the complexity-simplicity lens. Ex hypothesi, there may be a point where it becomes counterproductive, too. Historical "theories," particularly reductionistic and simple ones, have a way of rather rapidly becoming obstructions rather than aids to human understanding. Still, pattern-seeking is one of the things human inquirers ineluctably do; to stop looking for patterns sounds a lot like stopping the looking altogether.

I am arguing from analogy that liberal contextualism prejudicially projects a social pattern that prioritizes complexity over prominently championed counteroptions associated with simplicity, where it is key that everyone be "on the same page," as they say: for example, social uniformity (communism) or harmony (Plato and other utopian schemes) or purity (fascism and ethnic nationalism). Liberal contextualism has little to do with the Duke of Alba, though. The unfolding of the dual allegiance to liberty and equality gives rise to a liberalism that sees itself instrumentally, as a regulatory structure that preserves and encourages an optimal amount of divergence and serendipity, that wants to be surprised, and delights in both building idols and knocking them down.[8] It feeds on innovation and novelty and grows with the conviction that the other person, culture, generation, gender, language, necessarily possesses experiences to at least some extent outside any other's scope. As such the other always represents a precious opportunity to learn. We make up intersubjectively a kaleidoscope and each one of us is, in turn, internally kaleidoscopic. I would note also that the intensity with which liberal contextualism welcomes this kaleidoscopic complexity helps distinguish it from other, more directive forms of liberalism and, certainly, from the many nonliberal visions of political life whose outlook is more, shall we say, "unified."

The politically liberal partisan of complexity sees the specter of the fanatic lurking in many visions of simplicity, in their purity of heart, their passion for the One True, their steadfastness and myopic bravery in the service of their Good, God or gods. Just as she must appear rudderless and wanton to them, they in turn frighten her with their focused intensity, the ingenious devices they build to direct human passion toward a goal about which they are so blazingly sure. She is mistrustful of a conception of the Good around which all else, including social and political life, is to be ordered. The frightening aesthetic here, at least in social life, is that of alignment and symmetry, whether the mono-vision is of God, authenticity, communism, the Volk, Mother Earth, or whatever else. In contrast, her conception of the Good is one in which the very *ensemble* provides the aesthetic, a passionate commitment not to some X, but a passionate commitment to the very existence of passionate commitments. She seeks comfort in qualitative differences. It may well be that this kind of multiplicity is not sustainable in the final analysis. It may be inconsistent in some deep logical or moral way. But as an aesthetic, its existence is concomitant with its appearance; like pain, that it appears as it appears is in a certain way enough to establish its reality. It is an *experience*.

It is easy to see an aesthetic of complexity as naturally allied with a robust and inclusive educational imperative. First of all, the blooming, buzzing diversity in which complexity takes such delight is a cultural product, a human achievement whose various elements need suitably acculturated individuals around to erect and maintain it. An enticingly broad and interesting menu of sociocultural options requires not just a few educated elites to maintain order but countlessly many educated individuals who will be able to participate in the continuance of the menu options, a sort of aesthetic Fordism, where producer and consumer are interlocked and interdependent. (Again: the metaphors of consumerism should be no surprise. This is part of what one gets with the complexity preference.) This need for others to do their part in maintaining a rich social fabric adds an important dimension to liberal contextualism's straightforwardly moral, liberty-equality-based, support for widespread, if not universal education. It adds a more holistic kind of support for universal education than liberty-equality by itself is capable of and, certainly, than is possible from the point of view of the narrower economic self-interest in schooling as value-addedness that dominates contemporary education policy discussion. In this light, the complexity aesthetic might therefore help us to see why, when the budget ax falls, we should be less quick to cut parts of the curriculum like art and music because they appear less directly relevant to the standardized tests measuring citizenship or job competencies. For what they lead to are cultural competencies that make our lives more interesting to ourselves and to each other. Under liberal contextualism's complexity aesthetic, for me successfully to seek my own good requires the thriving of an indeterminately large number of the others around me. Through their own, perhaps quite differently directed thriving, those others cultivate my own field of possibilities. This is a key to how one may derive an inclusion imperative from within the complexity aesthetic: if I want others continually to surprise me, by definition I cannot—without blowing whatever surprise may be in store—preselect which particular other ought to have the requisite capabilities to in fact generate surprise. To preselect surprises would be to eliminate them. Thus the best choice for surprise lovers is to maximize the efficacy of the potential sources of surprises, namely, everyone else, the geese who lay the golden eggs. To name it, this is, really, a hedonistic principle of educational inclusion. An educational concern even for the severely disabled makes a great deal of sense here, for example, much more so than attempting to derive that concern out of a common ratiocinative capacity or, even less, the likelihood of an "enlightened" egoistic long-run mutual enrichment via economic productivity. Hedonistic inclusion is also simply less austere, sanctimonious and potentially ressentiment-laden than the usual moralizing.[9] As anyone involved with raising children ought not to do, contextualists and their educator allies do not underestimate the serious significance of fun and games.[10] Life is to be *lived,* after all.

As in the case of articulation, the complexity preference is at the same time an educational prejudice. In both cases, the pedagogical concern for others successfully to acquire the requisite cultural competencies—and creative, higher-order ones that are expected to go beyond what is currently known and thought—is built right into liberal contextualism's basic outlook, powerfully reinforced by its prejudices. To critics who accuse allegedly neutralist contextualists of pursuing a value-laden hidden agenda, it is thus necessary to concede some argumentative ground.[11] Self-knowledge is always incomplete, but the discussion will be best-served if, as everyone should, contextualists do their best to acknowledge their own normative agenda, prejudices and all. For many, the prejudices of liberal contextualism will render it not less but more attractive as a political ideology. The educational aspects of these prejudices ought to make it especially attractive for educators. As forthrightly acknowledged prejudices, it is hard to justify them in any final sense. But articulation and complexity can provide normative ballast for much of the education policy agenda likely to be pursued by contextualists, including much of what has been argued in this book. They can also, I suspect, greatly enhance liberal contextualism's ability to make its case rhetorically, even emotionally. Both a mind *and* a heart are needed, after all. Complexity needs a liberalism with both.

Notes

CHAPTER ONE

1. I take the term "juridification" from Gunther Teubner, "Juridification: Concepts, Aspects, Limits, Solutions," in *A Reader on Regulation.* ed. Robert Baldwin, Colin Scott, and Christopher Hood (Oxford: Oxford University Press, 1998), 389–440.

2. For an argument "that Rawlsian political liberalism is really a kind of closet comprehensive liberalism," see Eamonn Callan, *Creating Citizens: Political Education and Liberal Democracy* (Oxford: Oxford University Press, 1997), 39–42.

3. John Rawls, *Collected Papers,* ed. Samuel Freedman (Cambridge, MA: Harvard University Press, 1999), 614. It would also include, as Rawls himself indicates, the early Rawls of *A Theory of Justice* (Cambridge, MA: Harvard University Press, 1971).

4. I am indebted to the sociologist James Davison Hunter's discussion of orthodoxy in *Culture Wars: The Struggle to Define America* (New York: Basic Books, 1991). Hunter juxtaposes orthodoxy against what he calls "progressivism," which would be analogous to what I am here calling "Enlightenment liberalism." My view differs from Hunter's in that I think orthodoxy's main antagonist is better described as proceduralism, which does not possess forthrightly the substantive core defining his progressives or my Enlightenment liberals. I do not think the anti-orthodox camp, as it actually exists, has any bona fide standalone conception of the Good, let alone one that is comprehensive. Hunter later appears to recognize this in his *The Death of Character: Moral Education in an Age Without Good or Evil* (New York: Basic Books, 2000).

5. Nathaniel B. Shurtleff, ed., *Records of the Governor and Company of Massachusetts Bay in New England* (Boston, MA: 1853–1854): II, 203, quoted in James W. Fraser, *Between Church and State: Religion and Public Education in a Multicultural Age* (New York: St. Martin's Press, 1999), 10–11.

6. Andrew Delbanco, *The Real American Dream: A Meditation on Hope* (Cambridge, MA: Harvard University Press, 1999), 27–28; John Cotton, *A Treatise of the Covenant of Grace* (London, 1671), 204, as quoted in Delbanco, 33; John Cotton, *Christ the Fountaine of Life* (London, 1651), 200, as quoted in Delbanco, 35.

7. Terminological homology notwithstanding, liberal education (as traditionally understood) actually belongs more on the orthodox side of the ledger because it represents a commitment to some substantive vision of the Good: a paideia, a Renaissance ideal, Arnoldian culture, the Western canon, and so on. The rise in higher education of so-called interdisciplinarity, the debates over political correctness and canonicity, combined with the rise of process goals such as "critical thinking," "information retrieval,"

and "multiculturalism," all represent, for better or worse, a severe dilution of the idea that an educated person *is* this or that kind of person. Rather, the educated person under liberal proceduralism is one who can fit in with certain sociopolitical processes. He or she possesses a set of harmonizing skills, dispositions, habits, and the like. The vestigial educated person of liberal education represents more of a eudaemonistic end in him- or herself, rather than a concatenation of skills which themselves lead to some larger and presumably desirable state of affairs.

8. *Pace* Peter Berkowitz's worthy intellectual history of liberal virtues, *Virtue and the Making of Modern Liberalism* (Princeton, NJ: Princeton University Press, 1999).

9. *"Croyez ceux qui cherchent la vérité, doutez de ceux qui la trouvent."* André Gide, *Journal, Vol. 2, 1926–1950* (Paris: Editions Gallimard, 1954), 1233.

10. Alasdair MacIntyre, *After Virtue: A Study in Moral Theory* (Notre Dame, IN: University of Notre Dame Press, 1981), 203.

11. Where orthodoxy begins tightly to control the means it begins to shade into what I would call "fanaticism," as I argue at length in David Blacker, "Fanaticism and Schooling in the Democratic State," *American Journal of Education* 106 (1998): 241–272.

12. Gaining much notoriety, the Kansas State Board of Education voted in 1999 to remove evolution from its state science standards. This decision was reversed in 2001 via the state's political process, where a newly installed Board reinstated the science standards' evolution component as a "cornerstone" of science education in the state. Kansas replayed essentially this same dynamic in the period 2004–2006. See Kate Beem, "About-face Came Relatively Quickly: Evolution Debate in Other States Took Much Longer," *Kansas City Star*, 17 February 2001, Metro, p. B1). The Dover case *Kitzmiller v. Dover Area School District* (M.D. Pa. 2005), held that "intelligent design" is equivalent to creationism for constitutional purposes. As such, as a mandatory part of the curriculum—even if the "mandate" is that it be included as an "option"—it is violative of the Establishment Clause. For an analysis, of the notion of intellectual design, see Jerry Coyne, "The Faith That Dare Not Speak Its Name: The Case Against Intelligent Design," *The New Republic*, 22 August 2005, pp. 21–33.

13. Robert Wright, "The Accidental Creationist," *The New Yorker* 13 December 1999, p. 62.

14. Michael Farris, "Study Indirectly Shows the Evils of Evolution," *Washington Times,* 1 February 2000, p. E5.

15. The single most common type of litigation in education involves negligence torts surrounding student injury. Michael Imber and Tyl van Geel, *A Teacher's Guide to Education Law* (New York: McGraw-Hill, 1995), 207.

16. Though in the 1940s there had been a smaller-scale student free speech victory regarding the compulsoriness of the Pledge of Allegiance. See *West Virginia State Board of Education v. Barnette* (1943) (allowing Jehovah's Witnesses to refuse to say the Pledge in public schools for reasons of conscience), reversing *Minersville School District v. Gobitis* (1940). *Barnette* famously asserts, "If there is any fixed star in our constellation, it is that no official, high or petty, can prescribe what shall be orthodox in politics, nationalism, religion, or other matters of opinion or force citizens to confess by word or act their faith therein. If there are any circumstances which permit an exception, they do not now occur to us" (642).

17. *Tinker v. Des Moines Independent Community School District* (1969), 503–505.

18. *Davis v. Monroe County Board of Education* (1999).

19. On the demise of contemporary school desegregation, see Gary Orfield's, *Dismantling Desegregation: The Quiet Reversal of Brown v. Board of Education* (New York: The Free Press, 1996) and "Conservative Activists and the Rush Toward Resegregation," in Jay Huebert, ed., *Law and School Reform: Six Strategies for Promoting Educational Equity* (New York: Yale University Press, 1999), 39–87; see also James Clotfelter, *After Brown: The Rise and Retreat of School Desegregation* (Princeton, NJ: Princeton University Press, 2004). On some of the disciplinary challenges this creates by the special education statues, see Abigail Thernstrom, "Courting Disorder in the Schools," *Public Interest* (Summer 1999): 18–34. Recent authorizations of the IDEA, in 1997 and 2004, have sought to answer these challenges by loosening somewhat some of the restrictions on schools' discretion in the area of discipline, for example, allowing schools more latitude when dealing with students guilty of more serious offenses.

20. *Tinker v. Des Moines Independent Community School District* (1969), 507.

21. *Hazelwood School District v. Kuhlmeier* (1988).

22. *Bethel School District No. 403 v. Fraser* (1986).

23. *Keyishian* v. *Board of Regents* (1967), 603, as quoted in *Tinker v. Des Moines* (1969), 507. Especially germane to the present discussion, the locus classicus of the "marketplace of ideas" metaphor is Justice Oliver Wendell Holmes's famous dissent in *Abrams v. United States* (1919), 630: "when men have realized that time has upset many fighting faiths, they may come to believe even more than they believe in the very foundations of their own conduct that the ultimate good desired is better reached by free trade in ideas—that the best test of truth is the power of the thought to get itself accepted in the competition of the market . . ."

24. *Board of Education v. Pico* (1982).

25. *Equal Access Act of 1984* (P.L. 98–377) and *Board of Education of the Westside Community Schools v. Mergens* (1990). .

26. *Lamb's Chapel v. Center Moriches Union Free School District* (1993) and *Good News Club v. Milford Central School* (2001).

27. Ellen Goodman, "The Downside of Open-Mindedness," *Boston Globe*, 16 March 2000, p. A25.

28. Gerald Grant, *The World We Created at Hamilton High* (Cambridge, MA: Harvard University Press, 1988), 187.

29. There may also be a liberty interest as well, given the extent to which one's education—and educational record—is relevant to one's ability to function freely. See *Goss v. Lopez* (1975).

30. See *San Antonio Independent School District v. Rodriguez* (1973).

31. Arthur G. Powell, Eleanor Farrar, and David K. Cohen, *The Shopping Mall High School: Winners and Losers in the Educational Marketplace* (Boston: Houghton Mifflin, 1985), 54.

32. Hunter, *The Death of Character*, 12.

33. *People v. Parker* (Ill. App. Ct. 1996).

34. Ibid., 816, quoting the earlier District Court ruling.

35. *Vernonia School District v. Acton* (1995); *Board of Education v. Earls* (2002).

36. It also helps create the sitting duck rhetorical targets of "big government," "unfunded mandates," and so forth.

37. Again: one could certainly imagine orthodoxies that prize the unfettered expression of children or some such thing, a sort of Summerhillian orthodoxy devoted to the free unfolding of individuality. There are people like this, of course, but I know of no politically significant example in contemporary U.S. education policy.

38. But one should take care not to overgeneralize about the religiosity of nineteenth-century public schools, many of which avoiding inevitably sectarian practices such as Bible reading. See Laurence R. Moore, "Bible Reading and Nonsectarian Schooling: The Failure of Religious Instruction in Nineteenth-Century Public Instruction," *Journal of American History* 86 (2000), 1581–1600.

39. *Pierce v. Society of Sisters* (1925).

40. Kent Greenawalt, *Private Consciences and Public Reasons* (New York: Oxford University Press, 1995), 16–18. It is important to note further that the de jure rules may not be followed de facto.

41. Powell, Farrar and Cohen, *The Shopping Mall High School,* 3.

42. I thank Kenneth Strike for emphasizing this important point to me.

43. See Francis Schrag, *Back to Basics: Fundamental Educational Questions Reexamined* (San Francisco: Jossey-Bass, 1995), 91.

44. James Dwyer, *Religious Schools v. Children's Rights* (Ithaca, NY: Cornell University Press, 1998), 133.

45. Thomas Jefferson, "Letter to Roger C. Weightman, 6/24/1826," in Adrienne Koch and William Peden, eds., *The Life and Selected Writings of Thomas* Jefferson (New York: The Modern Library, 1944), 729–730. I thank Jan Blits for bringing this quote to my attention.

46. Hannah Arendt, *Between Past and Future: Eight Exercises in Political Thought* (New York: Penguin Books, 1977), 173–196. An analogous point is also made in Harvey Siegel, "Radical Pedagogy Requires 'Conservative' Epistemology," *Journal of Philosophy of Education* 29 (1997), 33–46. A comparable position could also be identified along lines laid down in Martha Nussbaum, *Cultivating Humanity: A Classical Defense of Reform in Liberal Education* (Cambridge, MA: Harvard University Press, 1997), where Socratic self-examination is defended as fundamental to democratic education (a view I champion in chapter 6). This conviction does not automatically imply a *pedagogy* that is always "democratic" in an immediate, participatory sense.

47. See Anthony S. Bryk, Valerie Lee, and Peter Holland, *Catholic Schools and the Common Good* (Cambridge, MA: Harvard University Press, 1993).

48. Greenawalt, *Private Consciences and Public Reasons,* 22.

49. Stephen Gilles, "Hey, Christians, Leave Your Kids Alone!," *Constitutional Commentary* 16 (1999), 150. Dwyer writes, for example, that "millions of children in this country are presently attending schools whose pedagogical practices harm them in serious ways. The harm could be characterized in the most general terms as severe repression of their minds and bodies." James Dwyer, *Religious Schools v. Children's Rights,* 178.

50. Dwyer, *Religious Schools v. Children's Rights,* 151.

51. Ibid., 163.

52. Ibid.

53. Gilles, "Hey, Christians, Leave Your Kids Alone!," 149–211.

54. Ibid., 176.

55. A far superior justification on which Dwyer might have relied (and which he strangely ignores) is Amy Gutmann's well-known principle of "nonrepression," derived from democracy's morally built-in concern with "conscious social reproduction" (about which more in later chapters). Gutmann argues that whatever kinds of schooling are allowed, what must never be permitted is any practice that would inhibit a child's ability to use his or her own mind to reflect autonomously on his or her own life. See Amy Gutmann, *Democratic Education* (Princeton, NJ: Princeton University Press, 1987). One could still have parental rights, with nonrepression as a strong side-constraint, though this would short-circuit Dwyer's agenda of illegitimizing parental rights altogether. Dwyer's efforts would be more convincing if recast along these lines.

56. "We want character but without unyielding conviction; we want strong morality but without the emotional burden of guilt and shame; we want virtue but without particular moral justifications that invariably offend; we want good without having to name evil; we want decency without the authority to insist upon it; we want community without any limitations to personal freedom. In short, we want what we cannot possibly have on the terms that we want it." James Davison Hunter, *The Death of Character,* xv.

57. Gilles, "Hey, Christians, Leave Your Kids Alone!," 180.

CHAPTER TWO

1. Michael Walzer, "The Civil Society Argument," in Beiner, ed., *Theorizing Citizenship* (Albany, NY: SUNY Press, 1995), 153.

2. The key Dewey texts here are John Dewey, *Democracy and Education (1916)* in *The Middle* Works, vol. 9 (Carbondale: Southern Illinois University Press, 1980); and *Experience and Education (1938)* in *The Later Works,* vol. 13 (Carbondale: Southern Illinois University Press, 1991).

3. Howard Gardner, *Frames of Mind: The Theory of Multiple Intelligences* (New York: Basic Books, 1983) and *Multiple Intelligences: The Theory in Practice* (New York: Basic Books, 1993).

4. Arjun Appadurai, *Modernity at Large: Cultural Dimensions of Globalization* (Minneapolis: University of Minnesota Press, 1996).

5. Will Kymlicka, *Multicultural Citizenship: A Liberal Theory of Minority Rights* (Oxford: Clarendon Press, 1995).

6. A statement of this position is Michael Lind, *The Next American Nation: The New Nationalism and the Fourth American Revolution* (New York: The Free Press, 1995).

7. Nathan Glazer, *We Are All Multiculturalists Now* (Cambridge, MA: Harvard University Press, 1997).

8. One exception is T. Puolimatka, "Sphere Pluralism and Critical Individuality," *Studies in Philosophy and Education* 23 (2004): 21–39.

9. Plato, *Republic* 414b–415a.

10. "The Mending Wall," [1914] in *The Poetry of Robert Frost,* ed. Edward Lathem (New York: Holt Rinehart and Winston, 1969).

11. G. E. M. de Ste. Croix, *The Class Struggle in the Ancient World: From the Archaic Age to the Arab Conquests* (Ithaca, NY: Cornell University Press, 1981), 283–300.

12. Joel Spring, *The Sorting Machine Revisited: National Educational Policy Since 1945* (New York: Longman, 1988).

13. See Hans-Georg Gadamer, *Dialogue and Dialectic: Eight Hermeneutical Studies on Plato,* trans. Christopher P. Smith (New Haven, CT: Yale University Press, 1980), 73–92.

14. Michael Walzer, "Liberalism and the Art of Separation," *Political Theory* 12 (1984): 315–30.

15. Francis Oakley, *The Western Church in the Later Middle Ages* (Ithaca, NY: Cornell University Press, 1985).

16. Lauro Martines, *Power and Imagination: City-States in Renaissance Italy* (New York: Vintage Books, 1980).

17. In later formulations, this became: "no Man, of what Estate or condition that he be, shall be put out of Land or Tenement, nor taken, nor imprisoned, nor put to Death, without being brought in answer by due Process of Law (28 Edw. III, c. 3 [1354])," quoted in Kermit L. Hall, William Wiecek and Paul Finkelman, *American Legal History: Cases and Materials,* 2nd ed. (New York: Oxford University Press, 1996), 5.

18. *Griswold v. Connecticut* (1965).

19. Daniel Bell, *The Cultural Contradictions of Capitalism: Twentieth Anniversary Edition* (New York: Basic Books, 1996), 10.

20. See John Gray, *Isaiah Berlin* (Princeton, NJ: Princeton University Press, 1996), 44–50.

21. Charles Larmore, *The Morals of Modernity* (New York: Cambridge University Press, 1996), 141.

22. Michael Walzer, "Response," in David Miller and Michael Walzer, eds., *Pluralism, Justice, and Equality* (New York: Oxford University Press, 1993), 282.

23. For a compelling development of this theme, see Bent Flyvbjerg, *Making Social Science Matter: Why Social Inquiry Fails and How It Can Succeed Again* (New York: Cambridge University Press, 2001), 25–49.

24. John Rawls, *A Theory of Justice* (Cambridge, MA: Harvard University Press, 1971), 75–80

25. Michael Walzer, "Response," 297.

26. Among the best of these are Ronald Dworkin, *A Matter of Principle* (Cambridge, MA: Harvard University Press, 1985), Ch. 10; Joshua Cohen, "Review of *Spheres of Justice*," *Journal of Philosophy* 83 (1986): 457–468; Will Kymlicka, *Liberalism, Community*

and Culture (Oxford: Clarendon Press, 1989), 220–236; Georgia Warnke, *Justice and Interpretation* (Cambridge, MA: MIT Press, 1992), 13–37; and Shane O'Neil, *Impartiality in Context: Grounding Justice in a Pluralistic World* (Albany, NY: SUNY Press, 1997), 81–103.

27. David Miller, "Complex Equality," in David Miller and Michael Walzer, eds., *Pluralism, Justice, and Equality,* 208. As noted in chapter 4, Miller later systematizes his critique in *Principles of Social Justice* (Cambridge, MA: Harvard University Press, 2001).

28. Miller, "Complex Equality," 208.

29. For an in-depth exploration of this theme see my *Dying to Teach: The Educator's Search for Immortality* (New York: Teachers College Press, 1997).

30. The contemporary interest in the controversial German political theorist Carl Schmitt reminds us especially of this last point. Chantal Mouffe writes: "In the domain of collective identifications, where what is in question is the creation of a "we" by the delimitation of a "them," the possibility always exists that this we/them relation will turn into a relation of the friend/enemy type; in other words, it can always become political in Schmitt's understanding of the term. This can happen when the other, who was until then considered only under the mode of difference, begins to be perceived as negating our identity, as putting into question our very existence. From that moment onward, any type of we/them relation, be it religious, ethnic, national, economic or other, becomes the site of a political antagonism." (*The Return of the Political* (London: Verso, 1993), 2–3.

31. Patricia White, *Civic Virtues and Public Schooling: Educating Citizens for a Democratic Society* (New York: Teachers College Press, 1996), 26–37.

32. Ibid., 37.

33. Ibid., 36.

34. Miller, "Complex Equality," 223. Walzer clearly takes Miller's modification to heart when he writes, in a later statement of complex equality, "The more sites and settings, the more points of entry, the more associations where cultures are enacted and values sustained, the more opportunities for the collective defense of interests, the greater the number of engaged men and women—the more free and egalitarian society will be (Michael Walzer, "Pluralism and Social Democracy," *Dissent* [Winter 1998], 52).

35. Habermas describes the legitimation crisis in somewhat different but not incompatible terms: "A legitimation crisis then, must be based on a motivation crisis—that is, a discrepancy between the need for motives declared by the state, the educational system and the occupational system on the one hand, and the motivation supplied by the sociocultural system on the other." Jürgen Habermas, *Legitimation Crisis,* trans. Thomas McCarthy (Boston: Beacon Press, 1975), 74–75.

36. Richard Arneson, "Against 'Complex' Equality," in Miller and Walzer, eds., *Pluralism, Justice, and Equality,* 238.

37. Michael Walzer, *Spheres of Justice: A Defense of Pluralism and Equality* (New York: Basic Books, 1983), 318, 313.

38. Walzer, "Response," in David Miller and Michael Walzer, eds., *Pluralism, Justice, and Equality*, 286–287.

39. Ibid., 287.

40. Seyla Benhabib, "Liberal Dialogue Versus a Critical Theory of Discursive Legiti-mation," in *Liberalism and the Moral Life*, ed. Nancy L. Rosenblum (Cambridge, MA: Harvard UP, 1989), 155. She continues: "I do not want to be misunderstood: all human societies live with a boundary between the public and the private; there will always be a realm that we simply will not want to share with others and that we will wish to be pro-tected from the intrusion of others. Where I differ from the liberal political theorist is that, whereas he or she seems to be sure where these boundaries ought to lie, I am deeply suspi-cious of a politics of certainty attained without truly open debate" (ibid.).

41. Stephen Holmes, *Passions and Constraint: On the Theory of Liberal Democracy* (Chicago: University of Chicago Press, 1995), 162.

42. David Joravsky, *The Lysenko Affair* (Cambridge, MA: Harvard University Press, 1970).

43. For further uses of the "thick" and "thin" distinction, mostly in the realm of international relations, see Michael Walzer, *Thick and Thin: Moral Argument at Home and Abroad* (Notre Dame, IN: University of Notre Dame Press, 1994).

44. Raz, *Morality of Freedom* (Oxford: Clarendon Press, 1986), 398.

45. Ibid.

46. Joseph Raz, *Ethics in the Public Domain: Essays in the Morality of Law and Politics* (Oxford: Clarendon Press, 1994), 121.

47. For an elaboration of this point, see my "Teaching in Troubled Times: Democrat-ic Education and the Problem of 'Extra People'" *The Teacher Educator* 32 (1996): 62–72.

48. Walzer, "Pluralism and Social Democracy," 4.

49. William Julius Wilson, *When Work Disappears: The World of the New Urban Poor* (New York: Alfred A. Knopf, 1996).

50. See Joseph P. Shapiro, *No Pity: People with Disabilities Forging a New Civil Rights Movement* (New York: Times Books, 1993).

51. Ira Katznelson and Margaret Weir, *Schooling For All: Class, Race and the Decline of the Democratic Ideal* (Berkeley, CA: University of California Press, 1985), 10.

52. Amy Gutmann, *Democratic Education* (Princeton: Princeton University Press, 1987), 22–47.

53. Ibid., 46. Gutmann utilizes this form of argument on other occasions, includ-ing, more recently, in Amy Gutmann and Dennis Thompson, *Democracy and Disagree-ment* (Cambridge, MA: Harvard University Press, 1996), which outlines three procedural Grundnorms for political deliberation in a democracy: "reciprocity," "publicity," and "ac-countability." My own position strongly endorses this general form of justificatory argu-ment (though not necessarily all of the particulars of Gutmann and Thompson's presenta-tion) in that it stakes out universalistically grounded boundaries and then allows a wide degree of institutional latitude within those boundaries.

54. I read Gutmann and Walzer as essentially in accord here. Walzer writes in *Spheres of Justice*: "Autonomous schools are mediating institutions; they stand in a tension with

parents (but not only with them). Abolish compulsory education, and one loses the tension; children become the mere subjects of their families and of the social hierarchy in which their families are implanted. Abolish the family, and the tension is lost again; children become the mere subjects of the state (216); and further, "if schools are to have any inward strength at all, there must be limits on the state's activity—limits fixed by the integrity of academic subjects, by the professionalism of the teachers, by the principle of equal consideration—and by an associative pattern that anticipates democratic politics but is not dominated by the powers-that-be or the reigning ideologies" (226). Gutmann could have written this as well.

55. *Hendrick Hudson District Board of Education v. Rowley* (1982), 181.

56. Jane A. Van Galen and Mary A. Pitman. *Home Schooling: Political, Historical and Pedagogical Perspectives* (Norwood, NJ: Ablex Publishing, 1991); see also Gary J. Knowles et al. "Home Education as an Alternative to Institutionalized Education." *The Educational Forum* 58 (1994): 238–243.

57. Pierrette Hondagneu-Sotelo, *Gendered Transitions: Mexican Experiences of Immigration* (Berkeley, CA: University of California Press, 1994), 178. I thank Amee Adkins for suggesting this source to me.

58. See John Rawls, "The Idea of Public Reason," in James Bohman and William Rehg, eds., *Deliberative Democracy: Essays on Reason and Politics* (Cambridge, MA: MIT Press, 1997), 93–131.

59. See Theodore J. Lowi, *The End of Liberalism: Ideology, Policy, and the Crisis of Public Authority* (New York: Norton, 1969).

60. Gerald Gaus, *Justificatory Liberalism: An Essay on Epistemology and Political Theory* (New York: Oxford University Press, 1996), 247.

61. In making this distinction between a constitutional realm and one of a more everyday politics best discussed in terms of the clash of interests, I follow Bruce Ackerman, *We the People: Vol. 1, Foundations* (Cambridge, MA: Harvard University Press, 1991); and Alexander Bickel, *Least Dangerous Branch: The Supreme Court at the Bar of Politics* New Haven, CT: Yale University Press, 1986), 24–26, 30–31, 88ff. Rawls also seems to hold this view, see John Rawls, *Political Liberalism* (New York: Columbia University Press, 1995), 214. For a fuller discussion, see Gaus, *Justificatory Liberalism*, 232–233. Gaus resists this exact way of dividing things. For him, the realm of everyday politics is not simply the clash of (self) interest but is also a realm of moral argument, so there is no clean break between it and constitutional politics. Gaus's refinement "explains the difference between constitutional and normal politics without adopting a dualistic theory according to which they are about essentially different matters. Constitutional politics concerns what is conclusively justified, and so determines the agenda of normal politics. Widespread consensus is to be expected. Normal politics is about fundamental matters, but is not a search for consensus; it is the confrontation of undefeated, unvictorious judgments about the demands of basic principles" (232–233). Gaus's higher moral standard for normal politics has its merits but for my present purposes it is sufficient to note that all sides to this debate see the need to make *some form* of the distinction.

62. This is most famously articulated in Michael Sandel, *Liberalism and the Limits of Justice* (Cambridge: Cambridge University Press, 1982).

63. Christopher Hill, *Liberty Against the Law: Some Seventeenth-Century Controversies* (New York: Penguin, 1996).

64. Walzer, "Pluralism and Social Democracy," 53.

65. For a compelling discussion of what he calls "the ideal of equal effective social freedom," see James Bohman, "Deliberative Democracy and Effective Social Freedom: Capabilities, Resources, and Opportunities" in Bohman and Rehg, eds., *Deliberative Democracy,* 321–348.

66. See Anthony Giddens, *Central Problems in Social Theory: Action, Structure, and Contradiction in Social Analysis* (Berkeley, CA: University of California Press, 1979), 193.

67. Kenneth Strike, "Ethical Discourse and Pluralism," in Kenneth Strike and P. Lance Ternasky, eds., *Ethics for Professionals in Education: Perspectives for Preparation and Practice* (New York: Teachers College Press, 1993), 180–182.

68. See Tyche Hendricks, "Issue of Illegals Roiling Arizona: New Law Denies Public Services to Such Immigrants," *San Francisco Chronicle,* 28 February 2005, p. A1; and David Drucker, "Proposal Called 'Son of 187'; Backers Want Constitutional Amendment Limiting Immigrant Benefits," *The Daily News of Los Angeles,* 15 August 2004, p. N4. The proposed California amendment did not pass.

69. For a different sort of discourse analysis, an examination of email discussions among opponents of Proposition 187, see Kent Ono and John Sloop, *Shifting Borders: Rhetoric, Immigration, and California's Proposition 187* (Philadelphia: Temple University Press, 2003).

70. Editorial, "Proposition 187 and the Law of Unintended Consequences," *Los Angeles Times,* 2 October 1994. A parallel provision seemed to require health care professionals to deny basic health care to the undocumented—even in serious cases.

71. See *San Antonio Independent School District v. Rodriguez* (1973).

72. Walzer, *Spheres of Justice,* 201–202.

73. Ibid., 203.

74. *NBC Today Show,* 1 July 1997 (New York: NBC News Transcripts, National Broadcasting Co., Inc.).

75. Janice Bierley, "Teachers as INS Cops: An Ugly Lie," *Los Angeles Times,* 4 November 1994.

76. Gebe Martinez, "Kemp Draws Criticism for Voicing Opposition," *Los Angeles Times,* 20 October 1994.

77. Tupper Hill, "Prop. 187 Won't Target Educators," *San Francisco Examine,r* 1 November 1994.

78. Mary Ann Glendon, *Rights Talk: The Impoverishment of Political Discourse* (New York: Free Press, 1993).

Chapter Three

1. As must any liberal view, liberal contextualism must justify state intervention within particular spheres. The necessarily fuzzy U.S. judicial standard of a "compelling

state interest" is probably as good a start as any. It is easy to see how there is a clear compelling interest in some spheres such as law, education, policing, and even journalism (qua the fourth estate), whereas other spheres such as friendship, religion, and parenting are traditionally more removed to the private side of the leger. My present concern with liberal institutions most directly applies to spheres of the former type, that is, where most would agree there is a clear and compelling state interest. For more detailed discussion along these lines, see Charles Anderson, *Pragmatic Liberalism* (Chicago: University of Chicago Press, 1990).

2. The implied distinction between constitutional and non-constitutional law follows Bruce Ackerman, *We the People: Vol. 1: Foundations* (Cambridge, MA: Harvard University Press, 1991). John Rawls also seems to hold this view about "constitutional essentials," see *Political Liberalism* (New York: Columbia University Press, 1994), 214, as does Gerald Gaus in his *Justificatory Liberalism: An Essay on Epistemology and Political Theory* (New York: Oxford University Press, 1996), 232–233.

3. The phrase "moral capaciousness" is used in William Galston, "The Legal and Political Implications of Moral Pluralism," *University of Maryland Law Review* 57 (1998): 245.

4. Michael Oakeshott, "The Idea of a University," in Timothy Fuller, ed., *The Voice of Liberal Learning: Michael Oakeshott on Education* (New Haven: Yale University Press, 1989), 101–103; R. S. Peters, "The Justification of Education," in R. S. Peters, ed., *The Philosophy of Education* (London: Oxford University Press, 1973), 262–264.

5. "The Crisis in Education," in Hannah Arendt, *Between Past and Future: Eight Exercises in Political Thought* (New York: Penguin Books, 1977), 173–196. See also, in a work from which my own argument draws heavily, Richard E. Flathman, *Reflections of a Would-Be Anarchist: Ideals and Institutions of Liberalism* (Minneapolis, MN: University of Minnesota Press, 1998), 137–164.

6. Nel Noddings, *Caring: A Feminine Approach to Ethics and Moral Education* (Berkeley, CA: University of California Press, 1984) and *The Challenge to Care in Schools: An Alternative Approach to Education* (New York: Teachers College Press, 1992); Matthew Lipman, *Philosophy Goes to School* (Philadelphia: Temple University Press, 1988); Nicholas Burbules, *Dialogue and Teaching: Theory and Practice* (New York: Teachers College Press, 1993) and "Aporia: Webs, Passages, Getting Lost, and Learning to Go On," *Philosophy of Education 1997* (Urbana, IL: Philosophy of Education Society, 1997): 33–43.

7. Jane Roland Martin, "The Ideal of the Educated Person," *Educational Theory* 34 (1981): 97–110.

8. See Bill Readings, *The University in Ruins* (Cambridge, MA: Harvard University Press, 1996) and Alex Molnar, *Giving Kids the Business: Commercialization in America's Schools* (Boulder, CO: Westview Press, 1996).

9. David Miller, *On Nationality* (New York: Oxford University Press, 1995), 141–145.

10. See Michael B. Katz, *The Irony of Early School Reform: Educational Innovation in Nineteenth-Century Massachusetts* (Cambridge, MA: Harvard University Press, 1968); Ira Katznelson and Margaret Weir, *Schooling for All: Class, Race and the Decline of the Democratic Ideal* (Berkeley, CA: University of California Press, 1985); and Carl Kaestle, *Pillars of the Republic: Common Schools and American Society, 1780–1860* (New York: Hill and Wang, 1983).

11. Lloyd P. Jorgenson, *The State and the Non-Public School, 1825–1925* (Columbia, MO: University of Missouri Press, 1987).

12. On this vast topic, see Walter Feinberg, *Common Schools/Uncommon Identities: National Unity and Cultural Difference* (New Haven: Yale University Press, 1998) and Kevin McDonough, "Can the Liberal State Support Cultural Identity Schools?," *American Journal of Education* 106 (August 1998).

13. A rich presentation of this theme is found in Chaim Potok's novel *The Chosen* (New York: Fawcett Books, 1995).

14. Antonio Gramsci, "On Education," in Antonio Gramsci, *Selections From the Prison Notebooks* (New York: International Publishers, 1971), 26–43. See also Harold Entwistle, *Antonio Gramsci: Conservative Schooling for Radical Politics* (London: Routledge & Kegan Paul, 1979).

15. See the discussion in Flathman, *Reflections of a Would-Be Anarchist*, 153–164; and also Bonna Devora Haberman, "What is the Content of Education in a Democratic Society?" *Journal of Philosophy of Education*, 28 (1994): 184.

16. Amy Gutmann, *Democratic Education* (Princeton: Princeton University Press, 1987), 19–21.

17. David Miller, "Virtues, Practices and Justice," in John Horton and Susan Mendus, eds., *After MacIntyre: Critical Perspectives on the Work of Alasdair MacIntyre* (Notre Dame, IN: University of Notre Dame Press, 1994), 245–264.

18. Alasdair MacIntyre, "A Partial Response to My Critics," in Horton and Mendus, eds., *After MacIntyre*, 284–286

19. MacIntyre explains this as a process of "external goods" coming to dominate "internal goods," the former corresponding to what he calls "practices," the latter to "institutions." See Alasdair MacIntyre, *After Virtue: A Study in Moral Theory* (Notre Dame, IN: University of Notre Dame, 2nd ed., 1984), 190–194.

20. Ibid.

21. This usage has affinities with the well-known Marxist phrase, although in this case the autonomy is not simply relative to the economic substratum but, more comprehensively, to the entire panoply of spheres. The classic statement of the Marxist view as applied to U.S. schools is Samuel Bowles and Herbert Gintis, *Schooling in Capitalist America: Educational Reform and the Contradictions of Economic Life* (New York: Basic Books, 1976).

22. This exact point is capably developed in David Bromwich, *Politics by Other Means: Higher Education and Group Thinking* (New Haven: Yale University Press, 1992).

23. See Richard Schacht, *Nietzsche* (London: Routledge & Kegan Paul, 1983), 344–349.

24. Walzer himself emphasizes this indeterminacy: "I can't provide a diagram nor decide upon a definitive number (my own list was never meant to be exhaustive). There isn't one social good to each sphere, or one sphere for each good. Efforts to construct a systematic account along these lines quickly produce nonsense . . ." Michael Walzer, "Response," in Miller and Walzer, eds., *Pluralism, Justice and Equality*, 282.

25. John Rawls, *Political Liberalism,* 133–172.

26. Friedrich Nietzsche, *The Gay Science*, trans. Walter Kaufmann (New York: Vintage Books, 1974), 181.

27. I borrow and extend this metaphor from Carlos Forment's "liberalism as cartography," which he develops in the context of a critique of Walzer. Carlos Forment, "Peripheral Peoples and Narrative Identities: Arendtian Reflections on Later Modernity," in Seyla Benhabib, ed., *Democracy and Difference: Contesting the Boundaries of the Political* (Princeton: Princeton University Press, 1996), 317.

28. An influential example would be Allan Bloom, *The Closing of the American Mind* (New York: Simon & Schuster, 1987).

29. A classic study of this is Raymond Callahan, *Education and the Cult of Efficiency: A Study of the Forces that Have Shaped the Administration of the Public Schools* (Chicago: University of Chicago Press, 1962).

30. David Tyack and Larry Cuban, *Tinkering Toward Utopia: A Century of Public School Reform* (Cambridge, MA: Harvard University Press, 1995).

31. I thank the late Richard Venezky for suggesting this concern to me.

32. Immanuel Kant, "An Answer to the Question: What is Enlightenment?," in Hans Reiss, ed. and H. B. Nisbet, trans., *Kant: Political Writings* (New York: Cambridge University Press, 1991), 54–60.

33. See Flathman, *Reflections of a Would-Be Anarchist*, 153.

34. They call this the "principle of publicity." Amy Gutmann and Dennis Thompson, *Democracy and Disagreement: Why Moral Conflict Cannot Be Avoided in Politics, and What Should Be Done About It* (Cambridge, MA: Harvard University Press, 1996), 95–127.

35. One might note the augmented role not only for educators but for information specialists, librarians and the like, who help realize the implied democratic imperative toward openness, an imperative that must mean more than just formal openness but must also include citizens' actual and meaningful access.

CHAPTER FOUR

1. Since 2001, Michigan and Pennsylvania have contracted with the financial information services company Standard and Poor's for evaluating their schools. S&P's national "school evaluation service" is available at www.schoolmatters.com.

2. For another kind of defense of pluralism in systems of accountability not inconsistent with my own, see Kenneth A. Strike, "Centralized Goal Formation, Citizenship, and Educational Pluralism: Accountability in Liberal Democratic Societies," *Educational Policy* 12 (1998): 203–215.

3. Michael Walzer, *Spheres of Justice: A Defense of Pluralism and Equality* (New York: Basic Books, 1983).

4. Susan Moller Okin, *Justice, Gender and the Family* (New York: Basic Books, 1989).

5. Isaiah Berlin, *Four Essays on Liberty* (New York: Oxford University Press, 1990).

6. Amy Gutmann, *Democratic Education* (Princeton, NJ: Princeton University Press, 1987); Eamonn Callan, *Creating Citizens: Political Education and Liberal Democracy* (New York: Oxford University Press, 1997); and Stephen Macedo, *Diversity and Distrust: Civic Education in a Multicultural Democracy* (Cambridge, MA: Harvard University Press, 2000). Not that these texts are without their contextualist elements; for example, Gutmann's vision of democratic education involves a range of relevant social institutions, as does Macedo's "civic liberalism."

7. Immanuel Kant, *Critique of Pure Reason*, trans. Norman Kemp Smith (New York: St. Martin's Press, 1929), 93.

8. Though I take inspiration from David Miller's *Principles of Social Justice* (Cambridge, MA: Harvard University Press, 1999), these categories are my own. Miller's categories are "solidaristic community, instrumental association, and citizenship" (26f.).

9. Available at http://www.un.org/Overview/rights.html.

10. See Franz de Waal, *The Ape and the Sushi Master: Cultural Reflections of a Primatologist* (New York: Basic Books, 2001).

11. This is an allusion to the title of Rawls's famous essay, "Justice as Fairness: Political Not Metaphysical," *Philosophy and Public Affairs* 14 (1985): 223–251.

12. Stuart Hampshire, "Justice Is Conflict: The Soul and the City," in Grethe B. Peterson, *The Tanner Lectures on Human Values* (Salt Lake City, UT: University of Utah Press, 1998), 164.

13. Judith Shklar makes this point central in her *American Citizenship: The Quest for Inclusion* (Cambridge, MA: Harvard University Press, 1985).

14. See also Orlando Patterson, *Freedom: Vol. I: Freedom in the Making of Western Culture* (New York: Basic Books, 1991).

15. Gutmann, *Democratic Education*, 44–47.

16. Bruce Ackerman, *We the People: Vol.1: Foundations* (Cambridge, MA: Harvard University Press, 1991). As previously noted, my view of the realm of right accords with what Ackerman calls the "constitutional regime, the matrix of institutional relationships and fundamental values that are usually taken as the constitutional baseline in normal political life" (59).

17. The latter goals are more robustly embraced in democracies like the United Kingdom, which do not have church-state separation requirements that are as strict as the U.S.'s.

18. Again, analogous worries would apply if, say, religion or the Party were in control and were pushing exclusively for *its* own exclusive goods.

19. Educational institutions will have to make choices here. Are they hitched to some particular comprehensive conception, for example, are they to be "good Catholic schools"? Or are they to be public schools that have a wider locus of accountability—because they cannot be reduced to any particular set of demands from any one segment of society—and hence candidates for institutional autonomy?

20. Liberals may advocate cultural coherence, too, but ultimately because it is good for the individuals or, qua liberal contextualists, because individuals are served by societal

heterogeneity as such. I do not think any liberal can hold that a particular instance of cultural coherence is good as such, because it will always depend on the culture and the extent to which it is compatible with basic human rights.

21. Logically it is possible that the animating comprehensive conceptions have been replaced by others or are somehow no longer necessary (perhaps the weight of inertia keeps things going). The first possibility seems likely to be true here and there, but the second seems unlikely or, at best, a temporary phenomenon that may be gone through immediately prior to the collapse of a regime.

22. A countervailing force is where the patriarchal division of labor has dragooned its primary school teachers from a largely captive labor pool of females, as was the case for generations in the U.S.

23. See Kevin McDonough, "Can the Liberal State Support Cultural Identity Schools?," *American Journal of Education* 106 (1998): 463–480.

24. I thank Jeremy Waldron for the memorable phrase "liberal commissars."

25. There is no neat, mathematical model for this, however. Stalinism, for example, had its mythic aspects, drawing self-consciously on images and motifs of the Russian Orthodox Church, for example, and Nazism certainly had its own legal formalism. For the former, see Isaac Deutscher, "Marxism and Primitive Magic," in Tariq Ali, ed., *The Stalinist Legacy: Its Impact on 20th Century World Politics* (London: Penguin Books, 1984), 106–117.

26. As John Beck rightly emphasizes, this includes nonmoral motives that are often important for regime stability, such as "compliance" and "a certain taken-for-granted acceptance of the 'inevitability' of these unjust social arrangements." Beck continues: "Almost all theories of 'crisis' significantly underestimate the very considerable strength and durability of these non-normative bases of social integration." John Beck, *Morality and Citizenship in Education* (London: Cassell, 1998), 73–74.

27. David Hume, *Treatise on Human Nature*, in Henry D. Aiken, ed., *Hume: Moral and Political Philosophy* (New York: Hafner Press, 1948), 25.

28. A terror state that uses its terror to uphold a liberal conception of rights seems a logical impossibility.

29. An now-iconic example of this would be whether a private restaurant may maintain racial segregation, as dramatized in the famous 1960 Woolworth's lunch counter sit-in in Greensboro, NC.

30. See John Rawls, *Political Liberalism* (New York: Columbia University Press, 1993), 133–172.

31. This would give one the critical tools also to critique substandard instruction as an effective denial of educational resources to the children subjected to it. In this way, just like a lack of it, poor or miseducation can become a violation of rights.

32. Or at least a number of them. Liberal contextualism leaves plenty of room for apolitical individuals and eschews a proto-fanatical "participatory democracy" that would drag everyone into politics regardless of their comprehensive commitments (which might counsel them to avoid political engagement).

33. Aldous Huxley, *Brave New World* (New York: HarperPerennial, 1998).

34. Donna Shalala, at the time U.S. Secretary of Health and Human Services, testified before the U.S. Congress 14 September 1999 that "Youth suicide is an inseparable component of the problem of youth violence. Suicide is the third leading cause of death for young people, ages 15–24, in the United States. The rates have nearly tripled since 1950 but over the past decade have declined by about 10 percent. In 1997, according to the YRBS [the Center for Disease Control's Youth Risk Behavior Survey], about 21 percent of students in grades 9 through 12—more than one in five—reported that they seriously considered taking their own lives during the previous year. And almost 8 percent reported actually attempting suicide." The complete testimony is available at http://www.os.dhhs.gov/asl/testify/t990914a.html.

35. Hume, *Treatise on Human Nature,* L. A. Selby-Bigge, ed. (New York: Oxford University Press, 2nd ed., 1985), 581–582.

Chapter Five

1. For reasons of economy and scholarly convention, Descartes will be cited parenthetically in the main body of the text. All the citations are to "AT": C. Adam, and P. Tannery, eds., *Oeuvres de Descartes,* revised edition., 12 vols. (Paris: Vrin/CNRS, 1964–76). For example, the present citation (AT VI 10) means, "Adam and Tannery, Volume Six, page 10." Unless otherwise noted, I will use the English translations provided in the standard Anglophone collection: J. G. Cottingham, R. Stoothoff, and D. Murdoch, eds. and trans., *The Philosophical Writings of Descartes,* 2 vols. (New York: Cambridge University Press, 1985).

2. "*Sapere aude.*" See Immanuel Kant, "An Answer to the Question: What is Enlightenment?," in H. S. Reiss, ed., and H. B. Nisbet, trans., *Kant's Political Writings,* (Cambridge: Cambridge University Press, 1991), 54–60.

3. Reggae icon (and evident Kantian) Bob Marley expresses the sentiment better than most with this line from the anthemic "Redemption Song": "Free yourselves from mental slavery; none but ourselves can free our minds." (From Bob Marley & the Wailers, *Legend,* Polygram Records, 1984)

4. Amy Gutmann, *Democratic Education* (Princeton: Princeton University Press, 1987).

5. The literature on such conflicts involving autonomy and/or synonyms is too voluminous to cite here, let alone that of the related philosophical mainstay concerning free will and determinism. A lively recent discussion may be found in the opening chapters of Kwame Anthony Appiah, *The Ethics of Identity* (Princeton, NJ: Princeton University Press, 2005). Appiah attempts to split the difference between autonomy's staunchest defenders and antagonists by defending a Kant-inspired middle ground "compatibilist" position.

6. A helpful description of leading views is provided in Donald Kerr, "Devoid of Community: Examining Conceptions of Autonomy in Education," *Educational Theory* 52 (Winter 2002): 13–25. These views are: R. F. Dearden, "Autonomy and Education," in *Education and the Development of Reason,* R. F. Dearden, Paul H. Hirst, and R .S. Peters, eds. (London: Routledge and Kegan Paul, 1975); Eamonn Callan, *Autonomy and Schooling* (Montreal: McGill-Queen's University Press, 1988); and Kenneth Strike, *Liberty and Learning* (Oxford: Robertson, 1982).

7. Donald Kerr, "Devoid of Community": 13.

8. So see Christopher Winch's definition of autonomy as "the condition in which an individual is able to choose and act upon the choice of a certain way of living." Christopher Winch, "Strong Autonomy and Education," *Educational Theory* 52 (2002): 29.

9. John Rawls, *Political Liberalism* (New York: Columbia University Press, 1995), 30–33.

10. As any sensible account must, I therefore follow R. F. Dearden in emphasizing the matters of degree involved in autonomous choosing. See Dearden, "Autonomy and Education," 454, as discussed in Kerr, "Devoid of Community," 16.

11. Charles Taylor, *Sources of the Self* (Cambridge: Cambridge University Press, 1989), 32.

12. Eamonn Callan, "The Great Sphere: Education Against Servility," *Journal of Philosophy of Education* 31 (1997): 221.

13. Harry Brighouse, "Civic Education and Liberal Legitimacy," *Ethics* 108 (July 1998): 719.

14. Kenneth Strike, *Liberty and Learning*, 44. See also Christopher Winch, "Strong Autonomy and Education": 30: "the exercise of liberty requires something like the knowledge condition."

15. This elaborates why I suggested "true enough" parenthetically above. As "ought implies can," it is unreasonable ever to insist on *total* knowledge of anything—whatever that would mean. Exactly how much is enough? As precise quantification is obviously prohibitive, one might settle an appropriately vague and relatively open-ended "some reasonable amount suitable to one's purposes."

16. Cottingham continues, "Such genuine epistemic agency is precisely what Descartes offers us." John Cottingham, "Descartes and the Voluntariness of Belief," *The Monist* 85 (2002): 343.

17. Appiah, *The Ethics of Identity*, 48.

18. Plato, *Meno* 100b.

19. See also AT VI 17: "the large number of falsehoods that I had accepted as true in my childhood, and by the highly doubtful edifice that I had subsequently based on them."

20. See Stephen Graukroger, whose biography provides further evidence for Descartes's motivation to provide a foundation for his science or "natural philosophy." *Descartes: An Intellectual Biography* (New York: Oxford University Press, 1995).

21. Gail Fine, "Descartes and Ancient Skepticism," *The Philosophical Review* 109 (2000): 199.

22. See also AT VI 14: "But regarding the opinions to which I had hitherto given credence, I thought that I could not do better than undertake to get rid of them, all at one go, in order to replace them afterwards with better ones, or with the same ones once I had squared them with the standards of reason."

23. This is from *Rules for the Direction of Our Native Intelligence*, "Rule One."

24. The building metaphor is thoroughly Cartesian. See, for example, AT VII 18: "Once the foundations of a building are undermined, anything built upon them collapses of its own accord."

25. I'm alluding to the quote from the *Discourse* atop this chapter.

26. Janet Broughton, *Descartes's Method of Doubt* (Princeton: Princeton University Press, 2002), 2.

27. Neil Gascoigne, *Scepticism* (Montreal: McGill-Queens University Press, 2002), 32.

28. Diogenes Laertius, 9.63., as quoted in Martha Nussbaum, *Therapy of Desire* (Princeton: Princeton University Press, 1994), 314.

29. Nussbaum, *Therapy of Desire,* 313–314.

30. Louis E. Loeb, "Sextus, Hume and Peirce: On Securing Settled Doxastic States," *NOÛS* 32 (1998): 205–230.

31. Nussbaum, *Therapy of Desire,* 301–307.

32. See Miles Burnyeat, "Can the Skeptic Live his Skepticism?," in Miles Burnyeat, ed., *The Skeptical Tradition* (Berkeley, CA: University of California Press, 1983), 117–148.

33. David Hume, *Enquiry Concerning Human Understanding* (New York: Oxford University Press, 1999), 128. Burnyeat describes this as "Hume's Challenge," in Burnyeat, "Can the Skeptic Live His Skepticism?," 117–118.

34. The translation is that of the French publisher Henri Etienne (a. k .a. "Stephanus"). See Julia Annas and Jonathan Barnes, *The Modes of Skepticism: Ancient Texts and Modern Interpretations* (Cambridge: Cambridge University Press, 1985), 5–6. Annas and Barnes further conclude that "Sextus' hitherto obscure book rapidly rose to become the dominant philosophical text of the age. It was the rediscovery of Sextus and of Greek scepticism which shaped the course of philosophy for the next three hundred years" (ibid.).

35. Richard Popkin, *The History of Skepticism: From Savonarola to Boyle,* rev. and expanded edition (New York: Oxford University Press, 2003), 6–7. One contemporary report even had it that Savonarola "had been suggesting to his followers that they read Sextus Empiricus as an introduction to Christian faith." (ibid., 7).

36. As quoted in Popkin, *The History of Skepticism,* 144.

37. Burnyeat, "Can the Skeptic Live His Skepticism?," 118.

38. For a partly contrasting view, see Marjorie Grene, "Descartes and Skepticism," *Review of Metaphysics* 52 (1999), 553. While Grene agrees that the point of Descartes's skepticism was "the execution of his own major certainly non-skeptical program," she disagrees that Descartes was "a thinker troubled by skepticism who fought valiantly to overcome it" (ibid., 557). Why this disagreement over the interpretation of the same texts? While she agrees that Descartes distinguishes his own skepticism from the Pyrrhonian type, Grene takes the very ease and sharpness with which Descartes accomplishes the distinction as evidence that the skeptics did not much "trouble" him. On the very same evidence, I disagree. I think he wanted to emphasize how his prescribed hyperbolic doubt did not lead to the heretical outcome—or even serious danger—of a live option Pyrrhonist way of life.

39. Descartes may first have experienced it when he was in his twenties, ca. 1619, many years before both the *Discourse* (1637) and the *Meditations* (1641). See Geneviève Rodis-Lewis, "Descartes' Life and the Development of His Philosophy," in John Cottingham, ed., *The Cambridge Companion to Descartes* (New York: Cambridge University Press, 1992), 33.

40. Popkin, *The History of Skepticism*, 158.

41. Myles Burnyeat, "The Skeptic in His Place and Time," in Myles burnyeat and Michael Frede, eds., *The Original Sceptics: A Controversy* (Indianapolis: Hackett, 1997), 92. See also Gascoigne, *Skepticism*, who further describes Cartesian doubt as the mirror image of Sextus, where instead of trying to bring doubt into life, "the enquirer has to train his mind to *bracket out* any thoughts relating to the practical realm of common life" (78).

42. Broughton, *Descartes's Method of Doubt*, 88.

43. Hume, *Enquiry Concerning Human Understanding*, Section XII.

44. Pierre Hadot, *Philosophy as a Way of Life*, Arnold I. Davidson, ed. and Michael Chase, trans. (Oxford: Blackwell Publishers, 1995), 271.

45. Pierre Hadot, *What Is Ancient Philosophy?*, Michael Chase, trans. (Cambridge, MA: Harvard University Press, 2002), 264. See also Harry Frankfurt, *Demons, Dreamers and Madmen: The Defense of Reason in Descartes's Meditations* (Indianapolis: The Bobbs-Merrill Co., 1970), 4: "Religious meditations are characteristically accounts of a person seeking salvation, who begins in the darkness of sin and who is led through a conversion to spiritual illumination. While the purpose of such writing is to instruct and initiate others, the method is not essentially didactic. The author strives to teach more by example than by precept. In a broad way, the *Meditations* is a work of this sort: Descartes's aim is to guide the reader to intellectual salvation . . ."

46. Frankfurt, *Demons, Dreamers and Madmen*, 21.

47. See Benjamin Barber, "Liberal Democracy and the Costs of Consent," in Nancy Rosenblum, ed., *Liberalism and the Moral Life* (Cambridge, MA: Harvard University Press, 1989), 57–58. Barber defends a "participatory" model as a repudiation of consent models of political legitimacy.

48. Broughton, *Descartes's Method of Doubt*, 98.

49. This conception would have affinities with the therapeutic role for inquiry posited in ancient Stoicism, for example Lucretius in *On Nature*. From this perspective, Cartesian meditations might be considered neo-Stoic exercises of self-improvement via inquiry into the nature of things. This parallel is not idiosyncratic on my part. Hadot makes an explicit connection the Cartesian meditator and Stoical "spiritual" exercises in support of his claim that the "extent to which the ancient conception of philosophy is present in Descartes is not always adequately measured." In Pierre Hadot, *What is Ancient Philosophy?*, 265.

50. See Broughton, *Descartes's Method of Doubt*, 23.

51. Frankfurt, *Demons, Dreamers, and Madmen*, 4–5.

52. Broughton, *Descartes's Method of Doubt*, 27–28.

53. See Hadot, *What is Ancient Philosophy?*, 264.

54. Edmund Husserl, *Cartesian Meditations: An Introduction to Phenomenology,* Dorion Cairns, ed. (Boston: Martinus Nijhoff Publishers, 1960). There may be counterexamples of which I am unaware, but I have found this text strangely unacknowledged by contemporary Anglophone Descartes scholars.

55. Husserl, *Cartesian Meditations,* 7.

56. Ibid., 2.

57. Ibid., 2, n. 2, listed as *"Appended later."*

58. Ibid., 20.

59. Ibid., 27.

60. This is from the uncompleted dialogue, *Search for Truth,* as quoted in Broughton, *Descartes's Method of Doubt,* 113.

61. Membership in this *n* is of course a related monumentally important determination. Children? At what ages and in what respects? Noncitizens? The mentally disabled?

62. The most famous version of this image is the one popularized by W. V. O. Quine in *Word and Object* (Cambridge, MA: MIT Press, 1960): "Neurath has likened science to a boat which, if we are to rebuild it, we must rebuild plank by plank while staying afloat in it. The philosopher and the scientist are in the same boat. Our boat stays afloat because at each alteration we keep the bulk of it intact as a going concern" (3–4). The original quote from Neurath reads, "We are like sailors who must rebuild their ship on the open sea, never able to dismantle it in dry-dock and to reconstruct it there out of the best materials." From Otto Neurath, "Protocol Sentences," in *Logical Positivism,* by A. J. Ayer, ed. (Glencoe, IL: The Free Press,), 201. Both quotations are from Paul Thagard and Craig Beam, "Epistemological Metaphors and the Nature of Philosophy," *Metaphilosophy* 35 (2004): 508.

63. *Pace* Meira Levinson, who holds that "times of tension or conflict" are likely to occasion the questioning of "one's commitments," and so forth. For Levinson, this happens to "all adults and children . . . if we're being honest with ourselves." My view is that this latter is a bigger "if" than Levinson seems to appreciate; in fact, it renders her point somewhat circular in that "honesty" seems implicitly defined more or less as facing up to one's larger commitments. While Levinson is certainly right that tension or conflict may occasion the kind of deep self-questioning under examination here, there is no guarantee of this happening. It seems truer to human experience that it is not even especially likely. As history clearly shows, fanaticism, dogma, sentimentalism, and other antireflective phenomena prosper mightily in troubling circumstances. See Meira Levinson, "Is Autonomy Imposing Education Too Demanding?" *Studies in Philosophy and Education* 23 (2004): 226.

64. Desmond Clarke, *Descartes' Philosophy of Science* (University Park, PA: Penn State University Press, 1982), 39; see also the same author's "Descartes' Philosophy of Science," in *The Cambridge Companion to Descartes,* ed. John Cottingham (New York: Cambridge University Press, 1992), 279–281.

65. It would be an empirical question, but a massive shift of resources such that everyone has a tutor or at least very, very small schools staffed by the appropriate personnel could make some inroads. One could *imagine* this.

66. My notion of detached schools is from Meira Levinson, *The Demands of Liberal Education* (New York: Oxford University Press, 1999), 64–69.

67. A wonderful example of how philosophers could be made more interesting to the general public is that treasure trove of gossip, Diogenes Laertius's *Lives of Eminent Philosophers*, brimming with tales both tall and short about classical and Hellenistic-era Greek philosophers. Diogenes' *Lives*, though, is not noteworthy because of the philosophical explications it contains, but for the "good parts," the gossipy bits. It gives the impression of a sort of Wild West days of philosophy, where philosophers *lived* their considered views, no matter how odd or offensive. There is a certain romance in that—so long as it is accompanied by a measure of good humor. Diogenes Laertius, *Lives of Eminent Philosophers*, 2 vols., R. D. Hicks, trans. (Cambridge, MA: Harvard University Press, 1959).

68. For example, "Of all things the measure is man," Protagoras, Fragment DK80B1, in Kathleen Freeman, *Ancilla to the Pre-Socratic Philosophers* (Cambridge, MA: Harvard University Press, 1983).

69. Information about the IAPC can be found at http://cehs.montclair.edu/academic/iapc/. Exemplary texts in this genre include Matthew Lipman, *Philosophy Goes to School* (Philadelphia: Temple University Press, 1980) and Gareth Matthews, *The Philosophy of Childhood* (Cambridge, MA: Harvard University Press, 1996).

70. C. S. Lewis, *The Chronicles of Narnia* (New York: HarperCollins, 2004; Philip Pullman, *His Dark Materials Trilogy* (New York: Yearling Books, 2003); and the books comprising J. K. Rowling's *Harry Potter* series (New York: Scholastic, 1997–2005).

71. Created by the late Ken Knisely, *No Dogs or Philosophers Allowed* may be accessed at www.nodogs.org. Other examples would include the lively "college radio"–style *Guerilla Radio Show: The Cutting Edge Philosophy Talk Show,* broadcast on KCSB FM 91.9 (Santa Barbara, CA) and via webcast and archived at www.guerrillaradioshow.com. One might also note the earlier efforts of Bryan Magee's BBC radio and television series, revised transcripts available as Bryan Magee, *Talking Philosophy* (Oxford: Oxford University Press, 2001) and *The Great Philosophers*, 2nd ed. (Oxford: Oxford University Press, 2000).

72. See Christopher Phillips, *Socrates Café: A Fresh Taste of Philosophy* (New York: W. W. Norton & Co., 2002). Information on the various "Socrates Cafés" may be found at www.philosopher.org/.

73. See www.philosophynow.org and www.sas.ac.uk/philosophy/saptoday/.

Chapter Six

1. Famously, in Sartre's play *No Exit,* "hell" is conceived as other people. Jean-Paul Sartre, *No Exit and Three Other Plays* (New York: Vintage International, 1989), 47–123.

2. Joseph Raz, "Facing Diversity: The Case of Epistemic Abstinence," *Philosophy & Public Affairs* 19 (1990), 3.

3. Plato, *Republic, Robin* Waterfield, trans. (New York: Oxford University Press, 1997), 58 (368d–369a). Translation altered by the author, "justice" for "morality."

4. John Rawls, *Lectures on the History of Moral Philosophy* (Cambridge, MA: Harvard University Press, 2000), 29.

5. David Hume, *Treatise on Human Nature*, in Henry D. Aiken, ed., *Hume: Moral and Political Philosophy* (New York: Hafner Press, 1948), 25.

6. Bernard Williams, *Morality: An Introduction to Ethics* (Cambridge: Cambridge University Press, 1972), 3.

7. Hume, *Treatise on Human Nature*, L. A. Selby-Bigge, ed. (New York: Oxford University Press, 2nd ed., 1985), 416.

8. One should not take this label too far, though. As Dorothy Coleman rightly suggests, it would be anachronistic simply to ascribe to Hume a position in the contemporary internalism-externalism debate among philosophers. (Dorothy Coleman, "Hume's Internalism," *Hume Studies* 18 [1992]: 331–347.) In short, Hume is a naturalist who wants to give an account of how moral judgments are made. He does not undertake to justify morality as such, as he holds that certain end-of-the-line "sympathies" are definitive of humanity itself. He writes: "It is needless to push our researches so far as to ask, why we have humanity or fellow-feeling with others. It is sufficient, that this is experienced to be a principle of human nature." (David Hume, *Enquiry Concerning the Principles of Morals*, (Indianapolis, IN: Hackett Publishing Co., 1983), 219–220.

9. See Coleman, "Hume's Internalism": 331, and Rawls, *Lectures on the History of Moral Philosophy*, 28.

10. Rawls, *Lectures*, 32.

11. Annette Baier develops this point from a "care" perspective in *Moral Prejudices: Essays on Ethics* (Cambridge, MA: Harvard University Press, 1994), 64.

12. Here I follow Rawls's categorization, *Lectures on the History of Moral Philosophy*, 33.

13. Ibid.

14. Ibid.

15. Ibid.

16. Hume, *Treatise on Human Nature*, L. A. Selby-Bigge, ed., 417.

17. Jean-Paul Sartre, *Existentialism and Humanism* (London: Methuen, 1968), 35–37.

18. Max Scheler, *Selected Philosophical Essays*, David Lachterman, trans. (Evanston, IL: Northwestern University Press, 1973).

19. Hume, *Enquiry Concering the Principles of Morals*, 297; and Baier, *Moral Prejudices*, 71.

20. Baier, *Moral Prejudices*, 70.

21. Only the basis seems given, however, in the form of certain intimate attachments such as to one's own children. It is a shaky naturalistic proposition that there is any natural sympathy for humanity as a whole.

22. " . . . the reasonable is viewed as a basic intuitive moral idea; it may be applied to persons, their decisions and actions, as well as to principles and standards, to comprehensive doctrines and to much else . . . What constraints, though, are reasonable? We

say: those that arise from situating citizens' representatives symmetrically when they are represented solely as free and equal, and not as belonging to this or that social class, or as possessing these or those native endowments, or this or that (comprehensive) conception of the Good. While this conjecture may have an initial plausibility, only its detailed elaboration can show how far it is sound." John Rawls, *Justice as Fairness: A Restatement* (Cambridge, MA: Harvard University Press, 2001), 82.

23. Amy Gutmann, *Democratic Education* (Princeton, NJ: Princeton University Press, 1987).

24. As a perhaps apocryphal counterillustration, there is the story about Josef Stalin that he does not want his political decisions to be agreed with because "agreement" would imply some deliberative contingency on the part of the would-be agreer. Stalin had people who "agreed" with him shot.

25. Walter Feinberg, "Dewey and Democracy at the Dawn of the Twenty-first Century," *Educational Theory* 43 (1993): 2.

26. For an analysis of extreme cases, see my "Fanaticism and Schooling in the Democratic State," *American Journal of Education* 106 (1998): 2.

27. Hume, *Treatise on Human Nature,* L. A. Selby-Bigge, ed., 581–582.

28. George Washington, "The Farewell Address, September 17, 1796," in *The People Shall Judge: Readings in the Formation of American Policy, Volume I,* Staff, Social Sciences 1, The College of the University of Chicago, ed. (Chicago: University of Chicago Press, 1949), 492–493.

29. See Francis Fukuyama, *Trust: The Social Virtues and the Creation of Prosperity* (New York: The Free Press, 1995).

30. John Rawls, "The Idea of Public Reason Revisited," in Samuel Freeman, ed., *John Rawls: Collected Papers* (Cambridge, MA: Harvard University Press, 1999), 594. For some historical background, as well as an argument that civic friendship is inclusive of feminist concerns, see Sibyl A. Schwarzenbach, "On Civic Friendship," *Ethics* 107 (1996), 97. On the Greek conceptions, including a good overview of Plato and Aristotle (and later followers of both) on this point, see Horst Hutter, *Politics as Friendship: The Origins of Classical Notions of Politics in the Theory and Practice of Friendship* (Waterloo, Ontario: Wilfrid Laurier University Press, 1978), and also the relevant chapters in John Cooper, *Reason and Emotion: Essays on Ancient Moral Psychology and Ethical Theory* (Princeton: Princeton University Press, 1999).

31. Though we have disagreements about it, I thank Meira Levinson for pressing me on this point.

32. Michael Perry, *Religion in Politics: Constitutional and Moral Perspectives* (Oxford: Oxford University Press, 1997). It is, of course, a separate endeavor to examine the moral desirability of the nonestablishment norm.

33. Rawls, *Political Liberalism* (New York: Columbia University Press, 1993), 36.

34. K. Anthony Appiah, "Liberal Education: The United States Example," in Walter Feinberg and Kevin McDonough, eds., *Education and Citizenship in Liberal-Democratic Societies: Teaching for Cosmopolitan Values and Collective Identities* (Oxford: Oxford University Press, 2003), 58.

35. Important examples of strongly autonomy-centered views include Eamonn Callan, *Creating Citizens: Political education and Liberal Democracy* (Oxford: Oxford University Press, 1997), which also argues that "Rawlsian political liberalism is really a kind of closet comprehensive liberalism" (39–42); and Meira Levinson, *The Demands of Liberal Education* (Oxford: Oxford University Press, 1999), which, in the name of liberal autonomy, endorses a high degree of state regulation of private schools substantially higher than the current legal status quo. (161f.)

36. Rawls, "The Idea of Public Reason Revisited," 579.

37. Ibid.

38. Ibid., 577.

39. Ibid., 576, n. 13. Rawls does imply some distinction between K–12 and higher education when he adds that the notion of background culture applies "especially" to "universities and professional schools, scientific and other societies" (ibid.).

40. Rawls, "The Idea of Public Reason Revisited," 576.

41. Even when speaking out about a matter of public concern (e.g., a letter to the editor), the so-called *Pickering* balance weighs teachers' freedom of speech rights against other factors involving any potential serious disruption of the educational process. *Pickering v. Board of Education of Township High School District 205* (1968).

42. Rawls, "The Idea of Public Reason Revisited," 611.

43. Ibid., 592.

44. Some argue that all teaching is necessarily normative and hence nonneutral. This is true but trivial. For it is perfectly imaginable and even, arguably, an accurate description of many current practices, for a school to teach noncontroversial "moral" values such as politeness, honesty, and the like, without touching on anything deeper about why anyone should bother to be polite, honest, and so on, in the first place.

45. For greater specification as to what would count as "reasonable" in this context, see my "Fanaticism and Schooling in the Democratic State," *American Journal of Education* 106 (1998): 241–272.

46. "A conception of justice is stable if, given the laws of human psychology and moral learning, the institutions which satisfy it tend to generate their own support, at least when this fact is publicly recognized." John Rawls, "Distributive Justice: Some Addenda," in Samuel Freeman, ed., *John Rawls: Collected Papers* (Cambridge, MA: Harvard University Press, 1999), 71.

47. In this I follow the sense of earlier chapters. See Michael Walzer, *Spheres of Justice: A Defense of Pluralism and Equality* (New York: Basic Books, 1983).

48. David Tyack, *The One Best System: A History of American Urban Education* (Cambridge, MA: Harvard University Press, 1974).

49. John Rawls, "Pluralism and Proceduralism," *Chicago Kent Law Review* 589 (1994), 601.

50. Rawls, "The Idea of Public Reason Revisited," 608.

51. Ibid., 594.

52. See Warren Nord, *Religion and American Education: Rethinking a National Dilemma* (Chapel Hill, NC: University of North Carolina Press, 1995), and Robert Nash, *Faith, Hype and Clarity: Teaching About Religion in America's Schools* (New York: Teachers College Press, 1999). The widely disseminated "Joint Statement," reissued several times, has been available via the U.S. Department of Education since 1996, along with their several official publications advocating careful but greater collaboration between religious individuals and organizations and public schools. The "Joint Statement" is available at http://www.ed.gov/Speeches/04–1995/prayer.html.

53. " . . . it might well be said that one's education is not complete without a study of comparative religion or the history of religion and its relationship to the advancement of civilization. It certainly may be said that the Bible is worthy of study for its literary and historic qualities. Nothing we have said here indicates that such a study of the Bible or of religion, when presented objectively as part of a secular program of education, may not be effected consistently with the First Amendment." *School District of Abington Township v. Schempp* (1963), 203.

54. This echoes the "pervasive sectarian" notion used to distinguish between permissible and impermissible religious group recipients of public monies, as developed, *inter alia*, in *Hunt v. McNair* (1973), 743; and *Roemer v. Board of Public Works* (1976), 755–759. See Stephen V. Monsma, "The 'Pervasively Sectarian' Standard in Theory and Practice," *Notre Dame Journal of Law, Ethics and Public Policy* 13 (1999), 321.

55. *Engel v. Vitale* (1962); *School District of Abington Township, Pennsylvania v. Schempp* (1963); *Lemon v. Kurtzman* (1971); *Lee v. Weisman* (1992).

56. *Epperson v. Arkansas* (1968) and *Edwards v. Aguillard* (1987).

57. That is, the third "excessive entanglement" prong of the *Lemon* test (*Lemon v. Kutzman* (1971)). While there is ongoing controversy about the precise status of this third prong of *Lemon,* namely, concerning how decisive it might be in and of itself, the excessive entanglement idea is generally still acknowledged to provoke Establishment Clause concerns.

58. I am relying on the analysis of Carl Esbeck, "A Constitutional Case for Governmental Cooperation with Faith-Based Social Service Providers," *Emory Law Review* 46 (1997), 1–41.

59. See *Bowen v. Kendrick* (1988) (upholding federal grants under the Adolescent Family Life Act for teenage counseling, including faith-based centers for such counseling). See Esbeck, "A Constitutional Case for Government Cooperation with Faith-Based Social Service Providers," 7–15. Something like the neutrality principle as applied to school policy has been embraced by a plurality of the U.S. Supreme Court in *Mitchell v. Helms* (1999), which upholds certain forms of state aid, such as computer equipment, to private religious schools, and most importantly, by the majority in the long-awaited school vouchers case, *Zelman v. Simmons-Harris* (2002).

60. The United Kingdom and Holland are two examples. For a comparison among the United Kingdom, United States and France in this regard, see Meira Levinson, "Liberalism Versus Democracy? Schooling Private Citizens in the Public Square," *British Journal of Political Science* 27 (1997), 333–360.

61. I would suggest that the public debate over school choice and charter schools has on balance been salutary for civic friendship in that it has directed public attention to

some of the basic normative assumptions undergirding our educational system generally. An excellent example of how school choice might bring philosophical considerations to the fore is found in Harry Brighouse, *School Choice and Social Justice* (Oxford: Oxford University Press, 2000). Self-conscious of the irony of echoing the libertarian views of Milton Friedman, Brighouse presents a compelling and clear liberal critique of the identification of public education with state-run schools.

62. See Penelope Leach, *Children First: What Our Society Must Do—And Is Not Doing—For Our Children Today* (New York: Alfred A. Knopf, 1994).

63. William Galston, "Civic Education in the Liberal State," in Nancy L. Rosenblum, ed., *Liberalism and the Moral Life* (Cambridge, MA: Harvard University Press, 1989), 101.

64. This process was largely completed by the 1960s. See Robert L. Hampel, *The Last Little Citadel: American High Schools Since 1940* (Boston: Houghton Mifflin Company, 1986).

65. Stephen Sugarman, "Education Reform at the Margin: Two Ideals," *Phi Delta Kappan* (November 1977), 155–156.

66. Some of these examples are mentioned by Sugarman, some I am supplying myself.

67. *Zelman v. Simmons-Harris* (2002)

68. This would be to embrace a "neutrality theory" à la *Bowen v. Kendrick* (1988), where there are criteria that are neutral among religious providers and neutral between religious and nonreligious providers. *Zelman v. Simmons-Harris* (2002) also endorses this kind of neutrality: "where a government aid program is neutral with respect to religion, and provides assistance directly to a broad class of citizens who, in turn, direct government aid to religious schools wholly as a result of their own genuine and independent private choice, the program is not readily subject to challenge under the Establishment Clause" (652).

69. An example is found in Amitai Etzioni, *The Spirit of Community: The Reinvention of American Society* (New York: Touchstone Books, 1994). Service activities within the context of school stamps would also have the advantage of removing some of the more objectionable features of "forced" public service by making it voluntary. Public service in the context I'm recommending, however, is potentially more equitable than, say, a blanket high school graduation requirement, in the sense that the service requirements might not be as crucial for poorer kinds as wealthier ones. It probably makes a lot more sense for the rich kid to work in the soup kitchen, while the poor kid (who may be in the soup line!) gets ballet lessons he or she might otherwise not get. Both children benefit, but in different ways. One might even designate some of the components as "service learning experiences" and officially encourage students to take a certain proportion of those (though I would encourage the service experiences rather than require them: again, forced public spiritedness is a difficult pill to swallow).

70. Sugarman, "Education Reform at the Margin," 156.

71. *Doe v. Beaumont Independent School District* (5th Cir. 1999).

72. Ibid.

73. Ibid.

74. Ibid., 17.

75. Ibid.

76. Ibid.

77. *Lemon v. Kurtzman* (1971).

78. *Doe v. Beaumont Independent School District* (5th Cir. 1999), 8.

79. *Everson v. Board of Education of Education of Ewing* (1947).

80. *Doe v. Beaumont Independent School District* (5th Cir. 1999), 9.

81. *Lee v. Weisman* (1992) and *Santa Fe v. Doe* (2002).

82. Ibid., 10.

83. Ibid., 11.

84. *Doe v. Beaumont Independent School District* (5th Cir. 1999), quoting from *Ingebretson v. Jackson Public School District* (5th Cir. 1996), 280.

85. *Doe v. Beaumont Independent School District* (5th Cir. 1999), quoting from *Allegheny v. Greater Pittsburgh A.C.L.U.* 492 U.S. 573 (1989).

86. *Doe v. Beaumont Independent School District* (5th Cir. 1999), 12.

87. Ibid., 24.

88. Ibid., 25, quoting from *McGowan v. Maryland* (1961), 442.

89. *Doe v. Beaumont Independent School District* (5th Cir. 1999), 32–33, quoting from *McDaniel v. Paty* (1978), 641.

90. *Doe v. Beaumont Independent School District* (5th Cir. 1999), 25.

91. Ibid., 14.

92. I say "potentially inclusive" rather than de facto inclusion because it would seem permissible if it made eligible and treated equally both religious and nonreligious volunteers, but through no omission, misdeed or bias on the part of BISD. It might happen that no non-religious volunteer would apply, or those who did might happen to be ineligible for some requisite nonreligious reason, such as having a criminal record, insufficient experience working with children, or the like.

93. See Raymond Callahan, *Education and the Cult of Efficiency* (Chicago: University of Chicago Press, 1962).

Chapter Seven

1. Hans-Georg Gadamer, *Truth and Method*, 2nd rev. ed., Joel Weinsheimer and Donald G. Marshall, trans. (New York: Crossroad, 1989), 269–277.

2. Hume, *Treatise on Human Nature*, L.A. Selby-Bigge, ed. (New York: Oxford University Press, 2nd ed., 1985).

3. Amy Gutmann, *Democratic Education* (Princeton: Princeton University Press, 1987), 19–21.

4. Justificatory uniformity would conversely be cause for suspicion in a free and open society, particularly one that is culturally, theologically and ideologically diverse.

5. Immanuel Kant, "An Answer to the Question: What Is Enlightenment?" in Hans Reiss, ed., *Kant: Political Writings* (New York: Cambridge University Press, 1991), 54–60.

6. For example, the reams of analysis devoted to the *Mozert v. Hawkins County Board of Education* (6th Cir. 1987) and *Yoder v. Wisconsin* (1971) cases. See, for example, Rob Reich, "Opting Out of Education: *Yoder, Mozert* and the Autonomy of Children," *Educational Theory* 52 (2002): 445–462.

7. See Iris Marion Young, *Inclusion and Democracy* (New York: Oxford University Press, 2002).

8. On serendipity, see Jessica George, "Socratic Inquiry and the Pedagogy of Reference: Serendipity in Information Seeking," *Proceedings of the ACRL Twelfth National Congress* (Minneapolis, MN, 2005): 380–387.

9. Chris Higgins, "Teaching and the Good Life: A Critique of the Ascetic Ideal," *Educational Theory* 53 (2003): 131–154.

10. Martha Nussbaum wisely includes "Play. Being able to laugh, to play, to enjoy recreational activities" on her list of "central human functional capabilities." Martha Nussbaum, *Women and Human Development: The Capabilities Approach* (New York: Cambridge University Press, 2000), 78–80.

11. Not all of the ground, though: there are still key areas where liberal contextualism indeed counsels neutralism, for example, as argued in the previous chapter, state nonestablishment of religion (or, more precisely, a nonestablishment norm regarding *any* comprehensive conception of the good).

References

Ackerman, Bruce. *We the People: Vol. 1, Foundations.* Cambridge, MA: Harvard University Press, 1991.

Anderson, Charles. *Pragmatic Liberalism.* Chicago: University of Chicago Press, 1990.

Annas, Julia and Jonathan Barnes. *The Modes of Skepticism: Ancient Texts and Modern Interpretations.* Cambridge: Cambridge University Press, 1985.

Appiah, K. Anthony. *The Ethics of Identity.* Princeton, NJ: Princeton University Press, 2005.

————. "Liberal Education: The United States Example." In *Education and Citizenship in Liberal-Democratic Societies: Teaching for Cosmopolitan Values and Collective Identities,* edited by Walter Feinberg and Kevin McDonough. Oxford: Oxford University Press, 2003.

Appadurai, Arjun. *Modernity at Large: Cultural Dimensions of Globalization.* Minneapolis: University of Minnesota Press, 1996.

Arendt, Hannah. *Between Past and Future: Eight Exercises in Political Thought.* New York: Penguin Books, 1977.

Arneson, Richard. "Against 'Complex' Equality." In *Pluralism, Justice, and Equality,* edited by David Miller and Michael Walzer. New York: Oxford University Press, 1995.

Baier, Annette. *Moral Prejudices: Essays on Ethics.* Cambridge, MA: Harvard University Press, 1994.

Barber, Benjamin. "Liberal Democracy and the Costs of Consent." In *Liberalism and the Moral Life,* edited by Nancy Rosenblum. Cambridge, MA: Harvard University Press, 1989.

Beck, John. *Morality and Citizenship in Education.* London: Cassell, 1998.

Beem, Kate. "About-face Came Relatively Quickly: Evolution Debate in Other States Took Much Longer." *Kansas City Star,* 17 February 2001, Metro, B1.

Bell, Daniel. *The Cultural Contradictions of Capitalism: Twentieth Anniversary Edition.* New York: Basic Books, 1996.

Benhabib, Seyla. "Liberal Dialogue Versus a Critical Theory of Discursive Legitimation." In *Liberalism and the Moral Life,* edited by Nancy L. Rosenblum. Cambridge, MA: Harvard University Press, 1989.

Berkowitz, Peter. *Virtue and the Making of Modern Liberalism.* Princeton, NJ: Princeton University Press, 1999.

Berlin, Isaiah. *Four Essays on Liberty*. New York: Oxford University Press, 1990.

Bickel, Alexander. *Least Dangerous Branch: The Supreme Court at the Bar of Politics*, 2nd edition. New Haven, CT: Yale University Press, 1986.

Bierley, Janice. "Teachers as INS Cops: An Ugly Lie." *Los Angeles Times*, 4 November 1994.

Blacker, David. "Fanaticism and Schooling in the Democratic State." *American Journal of Education* 106 (1998).

———. *Dying to Teach: The Educator's Search for Immortality*. New York: Teachers College Press, 1997.

———. "Teaching in Troubled Times: Democratic Education and the Problem of 'Extra People.'" *The Teacher Educator 32* (1996).

Bloom, Allan. *The Closing of the American Mind*. New York: Simon & Schuster, 1987.

Bohman, James. "Deliberative Democracy and Effective Social Freedom: Capabilities, Resources and Opportunities." In *Deliberative Democracy: Essays on Reason and Politics*, edited by James Bohman and William Rehg. Cambridge, MA: MIT Press, 1997.

Bowles, Samuel and Herbert Gintis. *Schooling in Capitalist America: Educational Reform and the Contradictions of Economic Life*. New York: Basic Books, 1976.

Brighouse, Harry. "Civic Education and Liberal Legitimacy." *Ethics* 108 (1998).

———. *School Choice and Social Justice*. Oxford: Oxford University Press, 2000.

Bromwich, David. *Politics By Other Means: Higher Education and Group Thinking*. New Haven, CT: Yale University Press, 1992.

Broughton, Janet. *Descartes's Method of Doubt*. Princeton, NJ: Princeton University Press, 2002.

Bryk, Anthony S., Valerie Lee, and Peter Holland. *Catholic Schools and the Common Good*. Cambridge, MA: Harvard University Press, 1993.

Burbules, Nicholas. *Dialogue and Teaching: Theory and Practice*. New York: Teachers College Press, 1993.

———. "Aporia: Webs, Passages, Getting Lost, and Learning to Go On." *Philosophy of Education 1997*, edited by Susan Laird. (Urbana, IL: Philosophy of Education Society, 1997.

Burnyeat, Myles. "The Skeptic in His Place and Time." In *The Original Sceptics: A Controversy*, edited by Myles Burnyeat and Michael Frede. Indianapolis: Hackett, 1997.

———. "Can the Skeptic Live His Skepticism?" In *The Skeptical Tradition*, edited by Miles Burnyeat. Berkeley, CA: University of California Press, 1983.

Callahan, Raymond, *Education and the Cult of Efficiency: A Study of the Forces that Have Shaped the Administration of the Public Schools*. Chicago: University of Chicago Press, 1962.

Callan, Eamonn. *Creating Citizens: Political Education and Liberal Democracy*. Oxford: Oxford University Press, 1997.

———. "The Great Sphere: Education Against Servility." *Journal of Philosophy of Education* 31 (1997).

————. *Autonomy and Schooling*. Montreal: McGill-Queen's University Press, 1988.

Clarke, Desmond. "Descartes' Philosophy of Science." In *The Cambridge Companion to Descartes*, edited by John Cottingham. New York: Cambridge University Press, 1992.

————. *Descartes' Philosophy of Science*. University Park, PA: Penn State University Press, 1982.

Clotfelter, James. *After Brown: The Rise and Retreat of School Desegregation*. Princeton, NJ: Princeton University Press, 2004.

Cohen, Joshua. "Review of *Spheres of Justice*." *Journal of Philosophy* 83 (1986).

Coleman, Dorothy. "Hume's Internalism." *Hume Studies* 18 (1992).

Cooper, John. *Reason and Emotion: Essays on Ancient Moral Psychology and Ethical Theory*. Princeton, NJ: Princeton University, 1999.

Cottingham, John. "Descartes and the Voluntariness of Belief." *The Monist* 85 (2002).

Cox, Harvey. *Fire from Heaven: The Rise of Pentecostal Spirituality and the Reshaping of Religion in the Twenty-First Century*. New York: Perseus Books, 1996.

Coyne, Jerry. "The Faith That Dare Not Speak Its Name: The Case Against Intelligent Design." *The New Republic* 22 (29 August 2005).

Dearden, R. F. "Autonomy and Education." In *Education and the Development of Reason*, edited by R. F. Dearden, Paul H. Hirst, and R. S. Peters. London: Routledge and Kegan Pauo, 1975.

Delbanco, Andrew. *The Real American Dream: A Meditation on Hope*. Cambridge, MA: Harvard University Press, 1999.

Descartes, René. *The Philosophical Writings of Descartes*. 2 vol. Edited and Translated by J. G. Cottingham, R. Stoothoff, and D. Murdoch. Cambridge: Cambridge University Press, 1985.

Dewey, John. *Democracy and Education (1916)*. In *The Middle Works*, Volume 9, edited by Jo Ann Boydston. Carbondale, IL Southern Illinois University Press, 1980.

————. *Experience and Education (1938)*. In *The Later Works*, Vol. 13, edited by Jo Ann Boydston. Carbondale, IL: Southern Illinois University Press, 1991.

Deutscher, Isaac. "Marxism and Primitive Magic." In *The Stalinist Legacy: Its Impact on 20th Century World Politics*, edited by Tariq Ali. London: Penguin Books, 1984.

Diogenes Laertius. *Lives of Eminent Philosophers*. 2 Vol. Translated by R. D. Hicks. Cambridge, MA: Harvard University Press, 1959.

Drucker, David. "Proposal Called 'Son of 187'; Backers Want Constitutional Amendment Limiting Immigrant Benefits." *The Daily News of Los Angeles*, 15 August 2004, p. N4.

Dworkin, Ronald. *A Matter of Principle*. Cambridge, MA: Harvard University Press, 1985.

Dwyer, James. *Religious Schools v. Children's Rights*. Ithaca, NY: Cornell University Press, 1998.

Entwistle, Harold. *Antonio Gramsci: Conservative Schooling for Radical Politics*. London: Routledge & Kegan Paul, 1979.

Esbeck, Carl. "A Constitutional Case for Governmental Cooperation with Faith-Based Social Service Providers." *Emory Law Review* 46 (1997).

Etzioni, Amitai. *The Spirit of Community: The Reinvention of American Society*. New York: Touchstone Books, 1994.

Farris, Michael. "Study Indirectly Shows the Evils of Evolution." *Washington Times,* 1 February 2000, E5.

Feinberg, Walter. *Common Schools/Uncommon Identities: National Unity and Cultural Differences*. New Haven, CT: Yale University Press, 1998.

————. "Dewey and Democracy at the Dawn of the Twenty-First Century." *Educational Theory* 43 (1993).

Fine, Gail. "Descartes and Ancient Skepticism." *The Philosophical Review* 109 (2000)

Flathman, Richard E. *Reflections of a Would-Be Anarchist: Ideals and Institutions of Liberalism*. Minneapolis, MN: University of Minnesota Press, 1998.

Flyvbjerg, Bent. *Making Social Science Matter: Why Social Inquiry Fails and How It Can Succeed Again*. New York: Cambridge University Press, 2001.

Forment, Carols. "Peripheral Peoples and Narrative Identities: Arendtian Reflections on Later Modernity." In *Democracy and Difference: Contesting the Boundaries of the Political*, edited by Seyla Benhabib. Princeton, NJ: Princeton University Press, 1996.

Frankfurt, Harry. *Demons, Dreamers and Madmen: The Defense of Reason in Descartes's Meditations*. Indianapolis: The Bobbs-Merrill Co., 1970.

Fraser, James W. *Between Church and State: Religion and Public Education in a Multicultural Age*. New York: St. Martin's Press, 1999.

Freeman, Kathleen. *Ancilla to the Pre-Socratic Philosophers*. Cambridge, MA: Harvard University Press, 1983.

Frost, Robert. "The Mending Wall [1914]." In *The Poetry of Robert Frost,* edited by Edward Lathem. New York: Holt, Rinehart and Winston, 1969.

Fukuyana, Francis. *Trust: The Social Virtues and the Creation of Prosperity*. New York: The Free Press, 1995.

Gadamer, Hans-Georg. *Dialogue and Dialectic: Eight Hermeneutical Studies on Plato,* translated by Chrstopher P. Smith. New Haven, CT: Yale University Press, 1980.

————. *Truth and Method*. 2nd edition. Translated by Joel Weinsheimer and Donald G. Marshall. New York: Crossroad, 1989.

Galston, William. "The Legal and Political Implications of Moral Pluralism." *University of Maryland Law Review* 57 (1998).

————. "Civic Education in the Liberal State." In *Liberalism and the Moral Life*, edited by Nancy L. Rosenblum. Cambridge, MA: Harvard University Press, 1989.

Gardner, Howard. *Frames of Mind: The Theory of Multiple Intelligences*. New York: Basic Books, 1983.

————. *Multiple Intelligences: The Theory in Practice*. New York: Basic Books, 1993.

Gascoigne, Neil. *Scepticism*. Montreal: McGill-Queens University Press, 2002.

Gaukroger, Stephen. *Descartes: An Intellectual Biography*. New York: Oxford University Press, 1995.

Gaus, Gerald. *Justificatory Liberalism: An Essay on Epistemology and Political Theory*. New York: Oxford University Press, 1996.

George, Jessica. "Socratic Inquiry and the Pedagogy of Reference: Serendipity in Information Seeking." *Proceedings of the ACRL Twelfth National Conference*. Minneapolis, MN (2005).

Giddens, Anthony. *Central Problems in Social Theory: Action, Structure and Contradiction in Social Analysis*. Berkeley, CA: University of California Press, 1979.

Gide, André. *Journals, Vol. 2: 1926–1950*. Paris: Editions Gallimard, 1954.

Gilles, Stephen. "Hey, Christians, Leave Your Kids Alone!" Review of *Religious Schools v. Children's Rights,* by James G. Dwyer. *Constitutional Commentary* 16 (1999).

Glazer, Nathan. *We Are All Multiculturalists Now*. Cambridge, MA: Harvard University Press, 1997.

Glendon, Mary Ann. *Rights Talk: The Impoverishment of Political Discourse*. New York: The Free Press, 1993.

Goodman, Ellen. "The Downside of Open-Mindedness," *Boston Globe,* March 16, 2000, A25.

Gramsci, Antonio. *Selections from the Prison Notebooks*. New York: International Publishers, 1971.

Grant, Gerald. *The World We Created at Hamilton High*. Cambridge, MA: Harvard University Press, 1988.

Gray, John. *Isaiah Berlin*. Princeton, NJ: Princeton University Press, 1996.

Greenawalt, Kent. *Private Consciences and Public Reasons*. New York: Oxford University Press, 1995.

Grene, Marjorie. "Descartes and Skepticism." *Review of Metaphysics* 52 (1999).

Gutmann, Amy. *Democratic Education*. Princeton, NJ: Princeton University Press, 1987.

Gutmann, Amy and Dennis Thompson. *Democracy and Disagreement: Why Moral Conflict Cannot Be Avoided in Politics, and What Should Be Done About It*. Cambridge, MA: Harvard University Press, 1996.

Haberman, Bonna Devora. "What Is the Content of Education in a Democratic Society?" *Journal of Philosophy of Education* 28 (1994).

Habermas, Jürgen. *Legitimation Crisis*, translated by Thomas McCarthy. Boston: Beacon Press, 1975.

Hadot, Pierre. *Philosophy as a Way of Life*. Edited by Arnold I. Davidson and translated by Michael Chase. Oxford: Blackwell Publishers, 1995.

———. *What Is Ancient Philosophy?* Translated by Michael Chase. Cambridge, MA: Harvard University Press, 2002.

Hampshire, Stuart. "Justice Is Conflict: The Soul and the City." In *The Tanner Lectures on Human Values*, edited by Grethe B. Peterson. Salt Lake City, UT: University of Utah Press, 1998.

Hendricks, Tyche. "Issue of Illegals Roiling Arizona: New Law Denies Public Services to Such Immigrants." *San Francisco Chronicle*, 28 February 2005, p. A1.

Hall, Kermit L. and William Wiecek and Paul Finkelman, *American Legal History: Cases and Materials*, 2nd edition. New York: Oxford University Press, 1996.

Hampel, Robert L. *The Last Little Citadel: American High Schools Since 1940*. Boston: Houghton Mifflin, 1986.

Higgins, Chris. "Teaching and the Good Life: A Critique of the Ascetic Ideal." *Educational Theory* 53 (2003).

Hill, Christopher. *Liberty Against the Law: Some Seventeenth-Century Controversies*. New York: Penguin Books, 1996.

Hill, Tupper. "Prop. 187 Won't Target Educators." *San Francisco Examiner*. 1 November 1994.

Holmes, Stephen. *Passions and Constraint: On the Theory of Liberal Democracy*. Chicago: University of Chicago Press, 1995.

Hondagneu-Sotelo, Pierrette. *Gendered Transitions: Mexican Experiences of Immigration*. Berkeley, CA: University of California Press, 1994.

Hume, David. *An Enquiry Concerning the Principles of Morals*. Indianapolis, IN: Hackett Publishing Co., 1983.

———. *Treatise on Human Nature*. 2nd edition. Edited by L. A. Selby-Bigge. New York: Oxford University Press, 1985.

———. *An Enquiry Concerning Human Understanding*. New York: Oxford University Press, 1999.

Hunter, James Davison. *The Death of Character: Moral Education in an Age Without Good or Evil*. New York: Basic Books, 2000.

———. *Culture Wars: The Struggle to Define America*. New York: Basic Books, 1991.

Husserl, Edmund. *Cartesian Meditations: An Introduction to Phenomenology*. Edited by Dorion Cairns. Boston: Martinus Nijhoff Publishers, 1960.

Hutter, Horst. *Politics as Friendship: The Origins of Classical Notions of Politics in the Theory and Practice of Friendship*. Waterloo, Ontario: Wilfrid Laurier University Press, 1978.

Huxley, Aldous. *Brave New World*. New York: HarperPerennial, 1998.

Imber, Michael and Tyll van Geel. *A Teacher's Guide to Education Law*. New York: McGraw-Hill, 1995.

Jefferson, Thomas. *The Life and Selected Writings of Thomas Jefferson*, Adrienne Koch and William Peden, eds. New York: The Modern Library, 1944.

Jorgenson, Lloyd P. *The State and the Non-Public School, 1825–1925*. Columbia, MO: University of Missouri Press, 1987.

Joravsky, David. *The Lysenko Affair*. Cambridge, MA: Harvard University Press, 1970.

Kaestle, *Pillars of the Republic: Common Schools and American Society, 1780–1860*. New York: Hill and Wang, 1983.

Kant, Immanuel. "An Answer to the Question: What Is Enlightenment?" In *Kant: Political Writings*, edited by Hans Reiss and translated by H. B. Nisbet. New York: Cambridge University Press, 1991.

———. *Critique of Pure Reason*. Translated by Norman Kemp Smith. New York: St. Martin's Press, 1929.

Katz, Michael B. *The Irony of Early School Reform: Educational Innovation in Nineteenth-Century Massachusetts*. Cambridge, MA: Harvard University Press, 1968.

Katznelson, Ira and Margaret Weir. *Schooling for All: Class, Race and the Decline of the Democratic Ideal*. Berkeley, CA: University of California Press, 1985.

Kerr, Donald. "Devoid of Community: Examining Conceptions of Autonomy in Education." *Educational Theory* 52 (2002).

Knowles, Gary J., et al. "Home Education as an Alternative to Institutionalized Education." *The Educational Forum* 58 (1994).

Kymlicka, Will. *Multicultural Citizenship: A Liberal Theory of Minority Rights*. Oxford: Clarendon Press, 1995.

———. *Liberalism, Community and Culture*. Oxford: Clarendon Press, 1989.

Larmore, Charles. *The Morals of Modernity*. New York: Cambridge University Press, 1996.

Leach, Penelope. *Children First: What Our Society Must Do—And Is Not Doing—For Our Children Today*. New York: Alfred A. Knopf, 1994.

Levinson, Meira. "Is Autonomy Imposing Education Too Demanding?" *Studies in Philosophy and Education* 23 (2004).

———. *The Demands of Liberal Education*. New York: Oxford University Press, 1999.

———. "Liberalism Versus Democracy? Schooling Private Citizens in the Public Square." *British Journal of Political Science* 27 (1997).

Lewis, C. S. *The Chronicles of Narnia*. New York: HarperCollins, 2004.

Lind, Michael. *The Next American Nation: The New Nationalism and the Fourth American Revolution*. New York: The Free Press, 1995.

Lipman, Matthew. *Philosophy Goes to School*. Philadelphia: Temple University Press, 1988.

Loeb, Louis E. "Sextus, Hume and Peirce: On Securing Settled Doxastic States." *NOÛS* 32 (1998).

Lowi, Theodore J. *The End of Liberalism: Ideology, Policy, and the Crisis of Public Authority*. New York: Norton, 1969.

Macedo, Stephen. *Diversity and Distrust: Civic Education in a Multicultural Democracy*. Cambridge, MA: Harvard University Press, 2000.

MacIntyre, Alasdair. *After Virtue: A Study in Moral Theory*. Notre Dame, IN: University of Notre Dame Press, 1981.

Magee, Bryan. *Talking Philosophy*. Oxford: Oxford University Press, 2001.

———. *The Great Philosophers*, 2nd ed. Oxford: Oxford University Press, 2000.

Marley, Bob and the Wailers. "Redemption Song." Polygram Records, 1984.

Martin, Jane Roland. "The Ideal of the Educated Person." *Educational Theory* 34 (1981).

Martines, Lauro. *Power and Imagination: City-States in Renaissance Italy*. New York: Vintage Books, 1980.

Martinez, Gebe. "Kemp Draws Criticism for Voicing Opposition." *Los Angeles Times,* 20 October 1994.

Matthews, Gareth. *The Philosophy of Childhood*. Cambridge, MA: Harvard University Press, 1996.

McDonough, Kevin. "Can the Liberal State Support Cultural Identity Schools?" *American Journal of Education* 106 (1998).

Miller, David. "Virtues, Practices and Justice." In *After MacIntyre: Critical Perspectives on the Work of Alasdair MacIntyre*, edited by John Horton and Susan Mendus. Notre Dame, IN: University of Notre Dame Press, 1994.

———. "Complex Equality." In *Pluralism, Justice and Equality*, edited by David Miller and Michael Walzer. New York: Oxford University Press, 1995.

———. *Principles of Social Justice*. Cambridge, MA: Harvard University Press, 2001.

Molnar, Alex. *Giving Kids the Business: Commercialization in America's Schools*. Boulder, CO: Westview Press, 1996.

Monsma, Stephen V. "The 'Pervasively Sectarian' Standard in Theory and Practice." *Notre Dame Journal of Law, Ethics and Public Policy* 13 (1999).

Moore, R. Laurence. "Bible Reading and Nonsectarian Schooling: The Failure of Religious Instruction in Nineteenth-Century Public Instruction." *Journal of American History* 86 (2000).

Mouffe, Chantal. *The Return of the Political*. London: Verso, 1993.

Nash, Robert. *Faith, Hype and Clarity: Teaching About Religion in America's Schools*. New York: Teachers College Press, 1999.

Neurath, Otto. "Protocol Sentences." In *Logical Positivism*, edited by A. J. Ayer. Glencoe, IL: The Free Press, 1966.

Nietzsche, Friedrich. *The Gay Science,* translated by Walter Kaufmann. New York: Vintage Books, 1974.

Noddings, Nel. *Caring: A Feminine Approach to Ethics and Moral Education*. Berkeley, CA: University of California Press, 1984.

———. *The Challenge to Care in Schools: An Alternative Approach to Education*. New York: Teachers College Press, 1992.

Nord, Warren. *Religion and American Education: Rethinking a National Dilemma*. Chapel Hill, NC: University of North Carolina Press, 1995.

Nussbaum, Martha. *Women and Human Development: The Capabilities Approach*. New York: Cambridge University Press, 2000.

———. *Cultivating Humanity: A Classical Defense of Reform in Liberal Education*. Cambridge, MA: Harvard University Press, 1997.

————. *Therapy of Desire: Theory and Practice in Hellenistic Ethics*. Princeton, NJ: Princeton University Press, 1994.

Oakeshott, Michael. "The Idea of a University." In *The Voice of Liberal Learning: Michael Oakeshott on Education*, edited by Timothy Fuller. New Haven, CT: Yale University Press, 1989.

Oakley, Francis. *The Western Church in the Later Middle Ages*. Ithaca, NY: Cornell University Press, 1985.

Okin, Susan Moller. *Justice, Gender and the Family*. New York: Basic Books, 1989.

O'Neil, Shane. *Impartiality in Context: Grounding Justice in a Pluralistic World*. Albany, NY: SUNY Press, 1997.

Ono, Kent and John Sloop. *Shifting Borders: Rhetoric, Immigration, and California's Proposition 187*. Philadelphia, PA: Temple University Press, 2003.

Orfield, Gary. *Dismantling Desegregation: The Quiet Reversal of Brown v. Board of Education*. New York: The Free Press, 1996.

————. "Conservative Activists and the Rush Toward Resegregation." In *Law and School Reform: Six Strategies for Promoting Educational Equity*, edited by Jay Huebert. New Haven: Yale University Press, 1999.

Patterson, Orlando. *Freedom: Vol. I: Freedom in the Making of the Western Culture*. New York: Basic Books, 1991.

Perry, Michael. *Religion in Politics: Constitutional and Moral Perspectives*. Oxford: Oxford University Press, 1977.

Peters, R. S. "The Justification of Education." In *The Philosophy of Education*, edited by R. S. Peters. London: Oxford University Press, 1973.

Phillips, Christopher. *Socrates Café: A Fresh Taste of Philosophy*. New York: W. W. Norton & Co., 2002.

Plato. *Republic*. Translated by Robin Waterfield. New York: Oxford University Press, 1998.

————. *Meno*. Translated by G. M. A. Grube. Indianapolis: Hackett Publishing Company, 1976.

Popkin, Richard. *The History of Skepticism: From Savonarola to Boyle*, rev. and expanded ed. New York: Oxford University Press, 2003.

Potok, Chaim. *The Chosen*. New York: Fawcett Books, 1995.

Puolimatka, T. "Sphere Pluralism and Critical Individuality." *Studies in Philosophy and Education* 23 (2004).

Powell, Arthur G., Eleanor Farrar, and David K. Cohen. *The Shopping Mall High School: Winners and Losers in the Educational Marketplace*. Boston: Houghton Mifflin, 1985.

Pullman, Philip. *His Dark Materials Trilogy*. New York: Yearling Books, 2003.

Quine, W. V. O. *Word and Object*. Cambridge, MA: MIT Press, 1960.

Rawls, John. *A Theory of Justice*. Cambridge, MA: Harvard University Press, 1971.

————. "Justice as Fairness: Political Not Metaphysical." *Philosophy and Public Affairs* 14 (1985).

————. "Pluralism and Proceduralism." *Chicago Kent Law Review* 589 (1994).

————. *Political Liberalism.* New York: Columbia University Press, 1995.

————. "The Idea of Public Reason." In *Deliberative Democracy: Essays on Reason and Politics,* edited by James Bohman and William Rehg. Cambridge, MA: MIT Press, 1997.

————. *Law of Peoples.* Cambridge, MA: Harvard University Press, 1999.

————. *Collected Papers,* edited by Samuel Freedman. Cambridge, MA: Harvard University Press, 1999.

————. *Lectures on the History of Moral Philosophy.* Cambridge, MA: Harvard University Press, 2000.

————. *Justice as Fairness: A Restatement.* Cambridge, MA: Harvard University Press, 2001.

Raz, Joseph. *Ethics in the Public Domain: Essays in the Morality of Law and Politics.* Oxford: Clarendon Press, 1994.

————. "Facing Diversity: The Case of Epistemic Abstinence." *Philosophy & Public Affairs* 19 (1990).

Readings, Bill. *The University in Ruins.* Cambridge, MA: Harvard University Press, 1996.

Reich, Rob. "Opting Out of Education: *Yoder, Mozert* and the Autonomy of Children." *Educational Theory* 52 (2002).

Rodis-Lewis, Geneviève. "Descartes' Life and the Development of His Philosophy. In *The Cambridge Companion to Descartes,* edited by John Cottingham. New York: Cambridge University Press, 1992.

Rowling, J. K. *Harry Potter.* 5 Volumes. New York: Scholastic, 2004.

de Ste. Croix, G. E. M. *The Class Struggle in the Ancient World: From the Archaic Age to the Arab Conquests.* Ithaca, NY: Cornell University Press, 1981.

Sandel, Michael. *Liberalism and the Limits of Justice.* Cambridge: Cambridge University Press, 1982.

Sartre, Jean-Paul. *No Exit and Three Other Plays.* New York: Vintage International, 1989.

————. *Existentialism Is a Humanism.* London: Methuen, 1968.

Schacht, Richard. *Nietzsche.* London: Routledge & Kegan Paul, 1983.

Scheler, Max. *Selected Philosophical Essays.* Translated by David Lachterman. Evanston, IL: Northwestern University Press, 1973.

Schrag, Francis. *Back to Basics: Fundamental Educational Questions Reexamined.* San Francisco: Jossey Bass, 1995.

Schwarzenbach, Sibyl A. "On Civic Friendship." *Ethics* 107 (1996).

Shapiro, Joseph. *No Pity: People with Disabilities Forging a New Civil Rights Movement.* New York: Times Books, 1993.

Siegel, Harvey. "'Radical' Pedagogy Requires 'Conservative' Epistemology." *Journal of Philosophy of Education* 29 (1997).

Spring, Joel. *The Sorting Machine Revisited: National Educational Policy Since 1945*. New York: Longman, 1988.

Strike, Kenneth. *Liberty and Learning*. Oxford: Robertson, 1982.

———. "Ethical Discourse and Pluralism." In *Ethics for Professionals in Education: Perspectives for Preparation and Practice*, edited by Kenneth Strike and P. Lance Ternasky. New York: Teachers College Press, 1993.

———. "Centralized Goal Formation, Citizenship, and Educational Pluralism: Accountability in Liberal Democratic Societies." *Educational Policy* 12 (1998).

———. "Schools as Communities: Four Metaphors, Three Models, and a Dilemma or Two." *Proceedings of the Philosophy of Education Society of Great Britain* (2000).

Sugarman, Stephen. "Education Reform at the Margin: Two Ideals." *Phi Delta Kappan*, November 1977, p. 154.

Taylor, Charles. *Sources of the Self*. Cambridge: Cambridge University Press, 1989.

Teubner, Gunther. "Juridification: Concepts, Aspects, Limits, Solutions." In *A Reader on Regulation*. Edited by Robert Baldwin, Colin Scott, and Christopher Hood. Oxford: Oxford University Press, 1998.

Thagard, Paul and Craig Beam. "Epistemological Metaphors and the Nature of Philosophy." *Metaphilosophy* 35 (2004).

Thernstrom, Abigail. "Courting Disorder in the Schools," *Public Interest* (Summer 1999).

Tyack, David. *The One Best System: A History of Urban Education*. Cambridge, MA: Harvard University Press, 1974.

Tyack, David and Larry Cuban. *Tinkering Toward Utopia: A Century of Public School Reform*. Cambridge, MA: Harvard University Press, 1995.

Van Galen, Jane A. and Mary A. Pitman. *Home Schooling: Political, Historical and Pedagogical Perspectives*. Norwood, NJ: Ablex Publishing, 1991.

de Waal, Franz. *The Ape and the Sushi Master: Cultural Reflections of a Primatologist*. New York: Basic Books, 2001.

Walzer, Michael. *Politics and Passion: Toward a More Egalitarian Liberalism*. New Haven, CT: Yale University Press, 2005.

———. "Pluralism and Social Democracy." *Dissent* (Winter 1998).

———. "The Civil Society Argument." In *Theorizing Citizenship*, edited by Ronald Beiner. Albany, NY: SUNY Press, 1995.

———. *Thick and Thin: Moral Argument at Home and Abroad*. Notre Dame, IN: University of Notre Dame Press, 1994.

———. "Response." In *Pluralism, Justice and Equality*, edited by David Miller and Michael Walzer. New York: Oxford University Press, 1993.

———. "Liberalism and the Art of Separation." *Political Theory* 12 (1984).

———. *Spheres of Justice: A Defense of Pluralism and Equality*. New York: Basic Books, 1983.

Warnke, Georgia. *Justice and Interpretation*. Cambridge, MA: MIT Press, 1992.

Washington, George. "The Farewell Address, September 17, 1796." In *The People Shall Judge: Readings in the Formation of American Policy, Volume I,* edited by the Staff, Social Sciences, University of Chicago. Chicago: University of Chicago Press, 1949.

White, Patricia. *Civic Virtues and Public Schooling: Educating Citizens for a Democratic Society.* New York: Teachers College Press, 1996.

Williams, Bernard. *Morality: An Introduction to Ethics.* Cambridge: Cambridge University Press, 1972.

Wilson, William Julius. *When Work Disappears: The World of the New Urban Poor.* New York: Alfred A. Knopf, 1996.

Winch, Cristopher. "Strong Autonomy and Education." *Educational Theory* 52 (2002).

Wright, Robert. "The Accidental Creationist," *The New Yorker* (December 13, 1999).

Young, Iris Marion. *Inclusion and Democracy.* New York: Oxford University Press, 2002.

Court Cases Cited

Abrams v. United States, 250 U.S. 616 (1919).

Allegheny v. Greater Pittsburgh A.C.L.U., 492 U.S. 573 (1989).

Bethel School District No. 403 v. Fraser, 478 U.S. 675 (1986).

Board of Education v. Earls, 536 U.S. 822 (2002).

Board of Education v. Pico, 457 U.S. 853 (1982).

Board of Education of the Westside Community Schools v. Mergens, 496 U.S. 226 (1990).

Bowen v. Kendrick, 487 U.S. 593 (1988).

Davis v. Monroe County Board of Education, 526 U.S. 629 (1999).

Doe v. Beaumont Independent School District, 173 F.3d 274 (5th Cir. 1999).

Edwards v. Aguillard, 482 U.S. 578 (1987).

Epperson v. Arkansas, 393 U.S. 97 (1968).

Engel v. Vitale, 370 U.S. 421 (1962).

Everson v. Board of Education of Education of Ewing, 330 U.S. 1(1947).

Good News Club v. Milford Central School, 533 U.S. 98 (2001)

Goss v. Lopez, 419 U.S. 565 (1975).

Grisswold v. Connecticut, 381 U.S. 479 (1965).

Hazelwood School District v. Kuhlmeier, 484 U.S. 260 (1988).

Hendrick Hudson District Board of Education v. Rowley, 458 U.S. 176 (1982).

Hunt v. McNair, 413 U.S. 743 (1973).

Ingebretson v. Jackson Public School District, 88 F.3d 274 (5th Cir. 1996).

Keyishian v. *Board of Regents*, 385 U.S. 589, 603 (1967).

Kitzmiller v. Dover Area School District (M.D. Pa. 2005)

Lamb's Chapel v. Center Moriches Union Free School District, 508 U.S. 384 (1993).

Lee v. Weisman, 505 U.S. 577 (1992).

Lemon v. Kurtzman, 403 U.S. 602 (1971).

McDaniel v. Paty, 435 U.S. 618 (1978).

McGowan v. Maryland, 366 U.S. 420 (1961).

Minersville School District v. Gobitis, 310 U.S. 586 (1940).

Mitchell v. Helms, 530 U.S. 793 (2000).

Mozert v. Hawkins County Board of Education, 827 F.2d 1058 (6th Cir.).

New Jersey v. T.L.O., 469 U.S. 325 (1985).

People v. Parker, People v. Parker, 672 N.E.2d 813 (Ill. App. Ct. 1996).

Pickering v. Board of Education of Township High School District, 391 U.S. 563 (1968).

Pierce v. Society of Sisters, 268 U.S. 510 (1925).

Roemer v. Board of Public Works, 426 U.S. 755 (1976).

San Antonio Independent School District v. Rodriguez, 411 U.S. 1 (1973).

Santa Fe Independent School District v. Doe, 530 U.S. 290 (2000)

School District of Abington Township v. Schempp, 374 U.S. 203 (1963).

Tinker v. Des Moines Independent Community School District, 393 U.S. 503 (1969).

Vernonia School District v. Acton, 515 U.S. 646 (1995).

West Virginia State Board of Education v. Barnette, 319 U.S. 624 (1943).

Wisconsin v. Yoder, 406 U.S. 205 (1972).

Zelman v. Simmons-Harris, 536 U.S. 639 (2002).

Index

accountability (educational), 3, 4, 34, 89, 98–120, 206n53; democratic, 112; realms of, 105–115; selective preference satisfaction and, 101–102; social justice and, 119

Ackermann, Bruce, 207n61, 212n16

aesthetics, 3, 15, 43–44, 52, 63, 76, 84, 87, 89, 92, 107, 112, 116, 164, 187–188, 190, 193–198. *See also* beauty.

African-Americans, 55, 84, 151

Alba, Duke of, 195

Althusser, Louis, 92

Appiah, Anthony, 128, 166, 214n5

anarchism, 56, 85, 89, 112

animals, 107

Annas, Julia, 216n34

arête, 53

Aristotle, 48–49, 53, 96, 144, 164

Arendt, Hannah, 33, 57, 82

Arneson, Richard, 55

articulation, 187–193

asceticism, 157

association (realm of), 106, 109–112

ataraxia, 132–133

athletics (and sports), 3, 43, 82, 111, 113, 143, 175.

Augustine, Saint, 135

authenticity, 13, 112–113, 130, 196

authority, 22, 46, 48–49, 96, 108, 203n56; educational, 32, 64–67, 86; illegitimate, 58, 114; moral, 26. *See also* parents (and parenting), parental authority and

autonomy, 123, 150, 189, 191, 215n8; as self-direction, 140; as overarching "good," 105; democracy and,

79, 151; democratic education and, 123; educational institutions and, 64, 86; educational, 94, 97; Husserl's conception of, 139; institutional, 95, 97, 111, 161, 212n19; professional, 4; relative, 75, 88, 91–93, 97, 161, 210n21; spherical, 91; thinking and, 147; traditional liberalism and, 50, 60–62

Baier, Annette, 158

Barber, Benjamin, 217n47

Barnes, Jonathan, 216n34

beauty, 97, 126, 193–4

Beck, John, 213n26

Bell, Daniel, 47

Benhabib, Seyla, 57–58, 206n40

Berlin, Isaiah, 103

Bill of Rights (U.S. Constitution), 46, 58, 106, 108, 167

Bolshevism, 10, 113

Bowles, Samuel, 210n21

Brennan, William (Justice), 24, 73, 182

Brighouse, Harry, 127, 224n61

Broughton, Janet, 131, 135–136, 138

Bryan, William Jennings, 17

Buddhism, 44

Burbules, Nicholas, 83

Burnyeat, Miles, 217n41

business, 1, 3–4, 40, 45, 58, 63–64, 69–70, 82–83, 88, 93–94, 96, 103–104, 110–111, 118, 170, 177. *See also* capitalism

Callan, Eamonn, 104, 126, 222n35

capaciousness, 97, 187; justificatory, 186; moral, 82, 171, 209n3